AS I SEE IT: THE NATURE OF REALITY

by
GOD

Rev. Joseph Adam Pearson, Ph.D.

Copyright

Foreword

Dear Readers,

This is the first in a three-book series on Christian metaphysics: (1) *As I See It: The Nature of Reality by God;* (2) *God, Our Universal Self: A Primer for Future Christian Metaphysics;* and (3) *Divine Metaphysics of Human Anatomy.* Although these three books are not fiction, they constitute a trilogy because they are all interconnected by the common theme of Christian metaphysics. And, although I have listed them in a specific sequence, readers may read each book on a stand-alone basis — or read all three books in any order — without feeling a sense of disconnect. For people especially interested in the theme of Christian metaphysics in relation to cosmology and apocalyptic events, I have also written a fourth book, entitled *Hello from 3050 AD!* This fourth book provides an overview of the Pre-Millennium, the Millennium, and the Post-Millennium. Although *Hello from 3050 AD!* is complementary to the three-book series, it does not need to be read at any specific juncture in relation to the series. (Information for all of my books is given in the section entitled Books by the Author at the end of this book.)

Although I have written *As I See It: The Nature of Reality by God* in the first person singular as if God were writing, it is not my intent to mislead the reader into thinking that I think that I am God or that I think that I am the possessor of all truth. To be sure, I do not think that I am God, and I do not subscribe to any philosophic or religious position that I can ever be God or equal to God. And, although I would like to think that everything that I have written within this book is true as well as written with the consent of the Holy Spirit, please know that I do not think that I am "channeling" God or that I have written Holy Scripture. The Creator alone is the Lord God Almighty (which is to say, "Supreme Being"). I am simply part of God's huge creation.

Although I know that God loves me, I also know that God does not love me any more than He loves any one of you. Like you, I have substantial imperfections, vulnerabilities, weaknesses, and infirmities. I am someone special to God only to the same degree that each one of you is special to God. So, if this book does what I am hoping that it will do, then please praise God for it and thank God's Holy Spirit, the only teacher of all truth. If I have missed the mark in any area within this book, it certainly is not God's fault.

It is my hope that, either *while* reading or *after* reading this book, readers will: (1) come to some epiphanies concerning how Scripture *might* be viewed as they develop their own personal theologies based on, and consistent with, the Holy Bible; and (2) learn more about what Scripture has to say by seeking to refute the perspectives presented in this book through comparing what I have presented to what is actually stated in the Holy Bible. If this book does nothing more than stimulate you to read and reread the Holy Bible, then I will be satisfied that this book has done what I wanted it to do. If I have misstated something in relationship to the Holy Bible, then God's Holy Spirit will show you (either immediately or eventually) where I am wrong as you become more familiar with the one true and only real Scripture, the Holy Bible.

As I See It: The Nature of Reality by God expresses the personal theology that I developed over a lifetime of studying the Holy Bible. By using the first person singular, as if God were writing this book, I have tried to express my own personal theology in a conversational manner that, I believe, will most easily engage its readers. I think that fewer people would be as easily engaged if I wrote in the third person singular (*for example,* "God said"). And, although I believe that there is a triadic plurality to God's unity (see the postscript to this letter for definitions of "triadic plurality"), I think that for me to have written in the first person plural ("WE") would have confused more than a few readers into concluding that I was trying to turn my book into some sort of bogus religious encyclical as God's "chosen prophet for this hour," or that I was trying to force one particular Christian perspective, doctrine, or denominational position upon the reader. I realize that I still run that risk by having God speak in the first person singular ("I") rather than the first person plural ("WE"), but I think there is less risk and that this calculated risk is more understandable to a greater number of people.

Please know that I have no interest in promoting any Christian denomination over another because I believe that, in most instances, creating and/or perpetuating division within the Body of Christ is dishonoring to our Lord and that the time for such division is over. And I have no interest in beginning my own Christian denomination or cult because, although I may think that I have *some* charisma, I do not believe that I am charismatic enough to found a popular denomination or cult. And, although it might be easier for me to found an unpopular one, that is not appealing to me either.

In the final analysis, it is my heart's desire to bring more honor, glory, and praise to the Lord God Almighty through this work at the same time that the Body of Christ is edified and uplifted. Time will tell whether that desire is achieved. And, of course, my heavenly Dad ("our Father in Heaven") will let me know when I see Him face-to-face.

I have only reported in this book what I can see. And, like you, I can only see to the extent that God has granted me a glimpse of the truth, and only to the degree that I am not indulging self-pride and self-will. My job has involved a lifetime of learning to try and best articulate my view.

To be sure, I am most grateful that our heavenly Father has granted me the education, life experiences, and time to do this.

God be with all of you always and in all ways.

Much love in Jesus Christ,

[signature: Joseph Adam Pearson]

Rev. Joseph Adam Pearson, Ph.D.
(One of Many Friends of God)

P.S. In this book, the phrase "triadic plurality" (as opposed to, *for example,* "dyadic plurality" or "quadratic plurality") refers to: (1) the *troika,* or triumvirate of "persons," that comprises the Godhead; (2) the tripartite Creator-God who sovereignly rules the Universe, or *All-that-is;* (3) the one Supreme Being who is partitioned into three consubstantial, coexistent, and united parts.

Notes

As used in this book, *KJV* is an abbreviation for the public domain *King James Version* of the Holy Bible. To ensure their accuracy throughout this book, all paraphrases of the public domain *King James Version* of the Holy Bible were finalized only after first checking: (1) the Masoretic Hebrew text of the Tanakh (the Jewish Bible) for accuracy of passages from the *KJV Old Testament;* and (2) the earliest Greek text extant for accuracy of passages from the *KJV New Testament.* Additionally, to enhance readability of the public domain *KJV* text, the present author has changed words like *hath, thou,* and *ye* to their modern equivalents.

Although God the Father *(the Lord God Almighty)* and God the Son *(the Lord Jesus Christ)* are consubstantially united in the Godhead along with God the Holy Spirit, in order to distinguish *God the Father* from *God the Son*, an upper case "H" is used for personal pronouns specifically referring to *God the Father (He, His,* and *Him)* and a lower case "h" is used for personal pronouns specifically referring to *God the Son (he, his,* and *him).*

Some transliterated Hebrew and Greek words referenced within the text of this book are noted by their respective numbers [in brackets with a preceding "H" for Hebrew or "G" for Greek] from the *Dictionary of the Hebrew Bible* and the *Dictionary of the Greek Bible* found in *Strong's Exhaustive Concordance of the Bible* by James Strong (Copyright 1890), Crusade Bible Publishers, Inc., Nashville.

Finally, whenever the title *God* is used in this book, the reader should assume that it is referring solely to: (1) the God of the Holy Bible — who is the *Lord God Almighty* or *Yahweh* (YHWH); (2) the one true and only real Creator-God; (3) *His* tripartite nature; (4) *His* sevenfold Spirit; and (5) *His* various facets.

Although the Creator-God does not possess a human gender, there are no apologies for the use of the male pronouns *He, His, and Him* when referring to the Lord God Almighty in this book for the following reasons: (1) In general, certain words in theology and philosophy are capitalized to show that they represent qualities and characteristics that transcend human understanding and experience. This includes the pronouns *He, His,* and *Him* and even the word *God* itself. (2) *She* and *Her* are not used in this book when referring to the Creator-God because many people, if not most, tend to confuse the use of female pronouns with advocating Wicca and other pagan cults that worship the Mother-Goddess — such as those devoted to Aphrodite (Venus), Artemis (Diana), Astarte, Cybele, Hecate, Maat, Morrigan, etc.

For the sake of clarity, when the author of this book uses the phrase *the present author* in this book, he is referring to himself.

Table of Contents

Chapter One

It's ME, God!

On Prayer

When I created you, I basically committed to a "hands-off" approach unless you personally invite ME into your life. I resolved to not intervene in your daily life unless you first ask ME. Most of you have wondered: if I know what ails you, if I know what you need, and if I know what you desire (and I do know all these things), then why don't I simply heal you, deliver you, instantly provide for your every need, and grant your every heart's desire without being asked? Here are two major reasons:

First, that I require you to ask ME is actually an integral part of the wonderful gift of free will that I gave to you. If you do not ask, then MY presumption is that you want to live and experience your own individual lives without interference from ME. Although I never intended for created beings to be self-sufficient and independent from their Creator, I honor any and all of your requests to be separate from ME. You might say that you don't recall ever asking for self-sufficiency and independence, but I would reply that the request does not need to be in words. Instead, the request can be reflected in actions, attitudes, and behaviors. Until you change your mind that MY "interference" is actually "intercession" on your behalf, and until you ask ME for help, I will respect your boundaries and withhold MY help. How can MY answers and solutions be forthcoming to your questions that are never asked and for your problems that are never acknowledged to yourself let alone to ME?

MY "hands-off" approach is easily seen in what I offer to you in MY Grace and Mercy. I do not force you to accept the gift of salvation, the gifts of the Holy Spirit and their operations, deliverance from difficult situations, healing of physical disorders, daily provisions, earthly rewards, and even spiritual blessings. I do not force created beings to accept anything from ME, even if it would be good for them to do so.

Although I provided MY Plan of Salvation for you, I will never force acceptance of it upon you. You are free to accept or reject MY Plan. Similarly, if you do not call upon ME to release your spiritual gifts and for ME to be in charge of their operations, they will lie dormant, under-used, or misused. You must call upon ME to release your spiritual gifts and ensure their correct operations in accordance with MY Will, which is always pure, and with MY Timing, which is always perfect. (Spiritual gifts are supposed to be used by saved human beings for developing their interdependence on each other as they grow increasingly dependent on ME.) Similarly, you need to ask ME for deliverance and healing if you want ME to intercede. Otherwise, I will respect your boundaries, which are simply the lines that you have drawn to separate yourselves from ME (and not the other way around).

Didn't you think it strange that I asked you to pray for your daily bread[1] at the same time that I cautioned you not to worry or be anxious?[2] How do these two lines of thinking intersect? As long as you are making your requests known to ME daily, there is no need for you to be anxious or worry. This relates to a second reason for requiring you to ask ME to intercede. I want you not only to know but also to acknowledge openly that I AM the Lord God Almighty and that I AM your Creator and the only Creator-God (I deserve that acknowledgement); and I want you to trust ME (I also deserve your trust). Requiring you to ask ME helps

1   Matthew 6:11 & Luke 11:3: King James Version
2   Matthew 6:25-31; Luke 12:22-31

you to demonstrate your trust in ME at the same time that you grow increasingly dependent on ME as your Creator, Provider, Healer, Savior, Teacher, Counselor, Encourager, Indweller, Rewarder, and Blesser. As your Creator, I never intended for you to function independently of ME (that is, act outside of MY Will) — although you may do so if you choose.

"To pray" means "to ask." Praying without ceasing includes solidly fixing your gaze upon ME at the same time that you are eternally aware of MY Presence and MY availability to you ("eternal" awareness transcends space-time as you know it). As you become eternally aware of MY Presence, you eventually become conscious of ME every waking and sleeping moment. Even when your mind wanders, you cannot help but return right back to ME in thought, in feeling, and even in deed. This is what the Apostle Paul meant when he directed you to "pray without ceasing."[3]

What keeps you from asking ME for anything is a result of the arrogance of your false ego. So, why not ask ME? Why not ask ME to participate in your lives? Why not ask ME to forgive you? Why not ask ME to heal you of a physical condition or deliver you from a difficult situation? To be sure, asking ME does not mean that I will grant every prayer request as you perceive that each prayer should be answered. It may mean that you will not be healed or delivered in accordance with your timeline if I know that the difficult condition or experience: (1) will increase your capacity to understand ME, (2) will increase your overall stamina in ME (that is, your ability to stand fast in ME), or (3) will benefit the greater good. Here, "greater good" refers to that which is for the good of an "us all" and not just for the good of an individual. Remember, I created the whole of which you are a part. You alone are not the whole.

What are the elements of an effective prayer?

---

3 1 Thessalonians 5:17, King James Version

You must have some faith. You must believe that I AM and that I AM a rewarder of those who diligently seek ME.[4] You must be honest, humble, and sincere. It does not matter if you pray in a loud voice or quiet voice or if you pray silently. However, because of the way that your brain functions, it is probably better not to pray silently. (When you pray silently, most of you lose focus because you allow your mind's eye to wander in directions where it ought not to go and to remain in places where it ought not to be.) Praying aloud with your voice, or silently with your hands in the language of the hearing impaired, enables you to deliver your prayer request more effectively, efficiently, and cogently to ME. You are then able to be a bit more objective about whether your prayer is reasonable as well as articulated accurately.

To pray effectively, you must also know who I AM, even if you only know that I AM the God of Abraham, Isaac, and Jacob or the God of Moses. You must not confuse ME with a false god. It is not required that you know all about ME because that would be unreasonable, and impossible. Nevertheless, you must know something about ME. *For example,* you could know that I AM the only one full of grace and mercy, or that I AM "the Father." (By the way, I AM not repulsed by the appellation "Mother," but that title gets most of you who use it into trouble because your limited comprehension causes you to confuse ME with a mother goddess, a force of nature, an impersonal power, or a social agenda. Besides, if it was good enough for Christ Jesus to call ME "Father," then it should be good enough for you.) Also, it would be good for you to know that I AM not *the Father* because I have many children (and I do), but because I have an only-begotten Son, whom you know, and should know, as Jesus the Christ, Y'shua H'Moshiach.[5] (Later, I will answer this riddle for

---

4 Hebrews 11:6, King James Version

5 Often transliterated from Hebrew as *Messiah* and translated into Greek as *Christos.*

you: "Which father is his own son, and which son is his own father?" and explain MY answer. But not now.)

When you pray, you really should *not* expect ME to answer your prayers: (1) because you are a "good person;" (2) because you "have lived a good life;" or (3) for the sake of your own name, faith legacy, or posterity. Rather, you should expect ME to hear your prayers and to answer them: (1) because I AM WHO I SAID I AM; (2) because I AM the ONLY giver of good gifts; and (3) for the sake of MY own Name's reputation, marketing, and advertising. Although "marketing and advertising" might seem worldly to you, both witnessing of ME and giving testimony about ME go a long way to help others understand that I AM and that I AM a rewarder of those who diligently seek ME so that these others might want to seek ME, find ME, and eventually acknowledge ME through praise, too.

Sincere and honest praise should be a part of prayer. Praise catches MY attention and invokes MY Presence. Using MY Son's Name in a respectful way also invokes MY Presence and, therefore, MY Power. As a postage stamp ensures that a letter is delivered to an addressee, so, too, does using MY Son's Name ensure that your prayer request is delivered to ME.

Praying for yourselves individually is as important as praying for those who might not have the necessary strength, wherewithal, faith, or knowledge to pray for themselves. *For example,* when MY prophetess Miriam became arrogant, I struck her with a horrible flesh-rotting disease that I healed only in response to a prayer request from MY servant Moses.[6]

Praying for others aggressively is important. Aggressive prayer includes:

---

6 Numbers 12:1-15

1. Believing that **I AM**, and believing that **I AM** a rewarder of those who diligently seek **ME**.[7]

2. Praying regularly *(for example*, every day at a specific time).

3. Praying for a specific purpose.

4. Making a commitment to pray until something changes *(for example,* praying for a person until the person either receives healing or comes to accept that a specific condition is God-ordained for a specified time).

5. Building (that is, perfecting) a prayer in writing and/or in speaking.

6. Expressing your understanding of a situation to **ME** and asking **ME** to clarify and/or correct your understanding. (Do not assume that you completely understand a situation or the reasons for its conditions.)

7. Asking for **MY** Mercy in addition to **MY** Grace (grace is receiving what you do not deserve and mercy is not receiving what you do deserve). *Examples* of grace include salvation, gifts of the Spirit and their operations, peace, joy, the redemption of your bodies, and entrance into the Kingdom of Heaven. *Examples* of mercy include healing of a disease that you have brought upon yourself, not going to Hell, and not being limited by your own understanding or misunderstanding.

8. Praying for **MY** "Name's sake" (as opposed to praying for a person because that person is deserving or a "good guy" or a "nice person" or "has been through enough").

---

7   Hebrews 11:6, King James Version

9. Praying in the belief that MY Will is always pure and that MY Timing is always perfect.

10. Trusting ME in patience for MY Will to be done concerning the situation at a time that I choose to act in response to your prayer.

11. Extolling MY Virtues (praising ME) not for the purpose of manipulating ME but because I deserve your praise even if I choose not to do anything else for you other than to grant you salvation.

12. Praying that a person is granted repentance[8] for sins committed as well as forgiveness for the sins he or she confesses.

13. Accepting that I forgive you of confessed sins the precise moment that you confess them in repentance to ME.

14. Proclaiming MY Goodness for forgiving your sins.

15. Praying that an underlying condition is understood and healed rather than just an effect of the cause. *For example,* some substance abusers are substance abusers because they have an anxiety disorder. Praying just for recovery from substance abuse is not good enough. You need to pray for the healing of the person's anxiety disorder.

There are some people with faith in ME who become judgmental about others who have unyielding physical conditions or unchanging earthly circumstances — which is to say, situations that are seemingly unresponsive to prayer. Such judgmental people misinterpret the conditions and circumstances as the

---

8 Acts 11:18 & 2 Timothy 2:25: King James Version

result of a lack of faith on the part of the afflicted. MY advice for those afflicted is to remind these judgmental people that the affliction might be unyielding or unchanging because of a lack of faith on their part rather than a lack of faith on the part of the afflicted. In what way? Because I also heal and deliver the afflicted based on the prayers of others who have strong faith, perhaps those who are being judgmental lack the necessary faith to "pray through" for the healing and deliverance of the afflicted. In response to this fair turnabout, those who are being judgmental might claim that their own faith is strong enough to "pray through" for others but that their prayers are being thwarted by the negative thinking of the afflicted. Here, I need to remind all that when I choose to do something, including healing and deliverance, nothing keeps it from happening because I AM WHO I AM and I AM WHO I SAID I AM.

Similarly, I can heal despite the medications that the afflicted may be taking. When I heal people who are on medications, they eventually learn from their physicians and/or improving physical conditions that they no longer need the medications. If you feel moved to throw your own medications away because you are believing ME for a miracle and as a sign of your faith in ME, that is your own prerogative (which is to say, a result of your own free will). To tell someone else to throw their medications away is irresponsible. And to believe that your faith is sufficient to heal a child entrusted to your care is presumptive, arrogant, and should be unthinkable. For children, you should always use all legitimate resources available to you. If I choose to heal you or your loved ones, including children, I can heal despite the continuing medical treatments they receive. People who have faith in ME concerning MY healing a physical condition sometimes forget that the primary healing is the healing of a soul that has been separated from its Creator.

When the Apostle Paul asked ME (praying *is* asking) three times to remove the figurative thorn in his flesh (which is to say, take away a physical condition from him), I replied that I would not because "MY Grace is sufficient" for him — or anyone else, for that matter — to endure any difficulty because "MY Strength is made perfect in weakness."[9] If I had removed the thorn, the Apostle Paul would have become prideful and arrogant because of the revelations that I gave to him and because of the leadership position into which he was placed by ME. Then, he would have lost sight of MY Purpose for him and become ineffective. By the way, if you have a genuine thorn in your flesh and not a trumped-up sign of your own feigned martyrdom, I might permit the thorn to remain for a short time, a long time, or a lifetime.

To summarize why I sometimes permit physical, mental, and emotional disorders:

1. To encourage you to call out to ME, and cry out to ME, for MY healing touch.

2. To help you know what suffering really means so you are better able to minister to those who truly suffer, including the brokenhearted.

3. To lay claim to the truth that I AM Sovereign Ruler and that I AM the source of all healing virtue (which is to say, divine power) that heals and restores.

4. To bring more glory to ME through your sustained praise of ME. (Do you praise ME through bad times as well as good times?)

5. To test, add to, and strengthen your individual and collective resolve to exercise your faith.

6. To help you yield your individual and collective will to MY Will.

7. To help you develop a more mature prayer life and

---

9 2 Corinthians 12:9, King James Version

more intimate relationship with ME.

8. To discipline and chasten you as well as teach others of MY Sovereignty through your condition.

You should never be presumptive or arrogant enough to believe that you know all the reasons for a physical, mental, or emotional disorder before I reveal the reasons to you, if and when I do. Such presumption or arrogance would also be a sign of great ignorance. (Simply speaking, ignorance is the lack of an inquiring mind.)

Disequilibrium

As one enters into successively higher states of grace, the conscious functioning self is able to step aside to allow one's higher self, or supraself, to take over. The supraself is herewith defined as "that part of each human being that communes directly with the Creator on a higher (and, sometimes, the highest) plane of consciousness." On which plane you are communing with ME depends on which state of grace you have entered. Creative "flow" occurs within MY Spiritual Universe *to* and *from* that part of yourselves known as the supraself. The supraself, however, cannot take over in the throes of your succumbing to any form of disequilibrium, or instability. Spiritual, mental, emotional, physical, and social distractions can create various forms of disequilibrium; the distractions cause you to shift your focus away from ME toward whatever distraction that causes the disequilibrium. (For the sake of clarification, *MY Spiritual Universe* is used interchangeably in this book with "MY Heavenly Consciousness," "Heaven," "the Kingdom of Heaven," "the Kingdom of God," "Paradise," and "Eden.")

Factors that are correlated with disequilibrium include, but are not limited to: physical illness, mental illness, unresolved emotional issues (hurt, embarrassment, and/or anger), active addiction (daily, you are either in recovery *from* sin or in active addiction *to* it), egotism, fear, bitterness, and hatred. I use the word "correlated" here because, although disequilibrium is the primary cause of any one of, or any combination of, the various factors indicated previously, each factor itself compounds, or adds to, the causes of disequilibrium when that factor is indulged.

The relationship between an epileptic seizure and the brain condition that permits the seizure is analogous to the relationship between disequilibrium and the spiritual condition of the soul that permits the disequilibrium. Iniquity (that is, unrighteousness) is the culprit here. However, because the shed blood of the Lord Jesus Christ cleanses you of all iniquity, you are capable of having your consciousness elevated by believing on that shed blood.

Although a number of human beings have discovered certain spiritual, or metaphysical, truths and have elucidated those truths in various literary works, you need to know that, unless the shed blood of Jesus Christ enters into the picture of those truths (that is, the way you envision them), those truths cannot be applied with any measure of success. Without the shed blood of Jesus Christ, all spiritual truths are of null effect within your personal lives. To be sure, the truths are not untrue and are not of null effect within MY Spiritual Universe; they are just "untrue" in your personal lives (that is, there is no efficacy to them within your day-to-day experience). Without employing a solid understanding of the shed blood of Jesus Christ, declarations of truth will get you nowhere.

It is recognizing and understanding the efficacy of the shed blood of Jesus Christ that brings heart to the superior intellect. The truth be told, the superior intellect is superior to nothing without heart (that is, without application of the shed blood of Jesus Christ to the truths that the intellect discerns). It is the shed blood of Jesus Christ that permits the intersection of the supernal, eternal, and *absolutely* real with the earthly, temporal, and transitory.

Even though indulging sinful behaviors adds to one's disequilibrium, all addictive behaviors (that is, sinful behaviors) are symptomatic of disequilibrium. And, whenever you make your equilibrium (or stability) dependent on anything other than your Creator, such dependence causes disequilibrium.

Healing as it Relates to Disequilibrium

Healing is the same and different for all human beings. It is the same in that all healing is dependent on the shed blood of the only-begotten Son of God, Jesus Christ. It is different depending on where each person is in his or her own spiritual development and journey. Often, immature authentic Christians (spiritual "infants" and spiritual "adolescents") need only pray, or be prayed for, to have their various healing needs met. However, mature authentic Christians (spiritual "adults" and spiritual "elders") need to declare, affirm, and "lay claim to" spiritual truths in order to have their various healing needs met.

"Various healing needs met" does not mean that all people will be healed physically before they die (depending on circumstance, death of the mortal body itself can be the ultimate form of physical healing). For immature and mature authentic Christians, physical healing does or does not take place depending on what a person's individual needs are as well as the needs of those who are close to the person and/or whose lives may be impacted by that person. This is why authentic Christians should not be disappointed if they do not receive a physical healing when they think they should receive a physical healing.

The Body of Christ (the "Church Universal") is an "us all." The Body of Christ is composed of those already in Heaven as well as those on Earth who are already saved. To be sure, there are those who will be saved at some point in the future and, then, at that time be added to the Body of Christ. Because the Body of Christ is an "us all," MY Spiritual Universe functions in multivariate ways regarding physical healing (which is to say, there are many factors that come into play). Although physical healing may not always occur, I always give you sufficient strength to meet your daily challenges. Such strength is actually part of your "daily bread."

The Godhead

I know what your theology books state about who I AM and what I AM supposed to be. Through your interpretations of who I AM, I find that there is "oneness," "twoness," and "threeness" or, if you like, "unitarian" (not the religious denomination), "binitarian," and "trinitarian" paradigms to explain ME. If I wasn't God, it would all be quite confusing. Since I AM God, I see that each of these perspectives has some truth to it. When asked by MY people to explain MYSELF — that is, reveal who I AM — I try to keep it simple, but that in itself poses at least some difficulty. Nevertheless, I will try to explain MYSELF to help you come to better understand and know who I AM.

I WAS always ONE before the creation, but before the creation I decided to partition MYSELF at the precise moment of the creation in order to place into motion MY Plan of Salvation that I devised for immortal beings who would enter a fallen state (mortal state) soon after their creation. (More about this later in the section entitled "MY Plan of Salvation.")

At the time of creation, I partitioned MYSELF into YHWH (the Fiery Part of MY Being, or "the Father"), the Logos (MY Spoken

Word, or "the Son"), and the Spirit (the invisible ME, or "the Holy Spirit").

In the first three verses of Genesis, you see immediately the three partitions about which I now write:

1. In the beginning God *[the Father]* created the heaven and the earth.

2. And the earth was without form, and void; and darkness was upon the face of the deep. And the Spirit of God *[the Holy Spirit]* moved upon the face of the waters.

3. And God said: "Let there be light!" *[the Logos or Spoken Word]* And there was light.[10]

Implicit in Genesis 1:1-3 (along with John 1:1-3) is that I created — and still create (and even re-create) — through MY Spoken Word, which is MY Logos (i.e., MY only-begotten Son, Jesus Christ).

I partitioned MYSELF into YHWH in order to remove the Fiery Part of MY Being far from you because it would annihilate you if you were to see ME in this way. The Fiery Part of MY Being is like a wheel of fire infolding itself inside another infolding wheel of fire.[11] (I AM the Wheel of all wheels and the Vortex of all vortices.) Partitioning the Fiery Part of MY Being compartmentalized MY Fierceness and MY Wrath (MY Justifiable Anger), but that is not all that it compartmentalized. Ironically, the Fiery Part of MY Being also contains the Fullness of MY Grace and MY Mercy (flip sides of the same coin, so to speak). One can also say that the "Fiery Part of MY Being" represents the Fullness of MY Glory.

---

10 Genesis 1:1-3, King James Version [Brackets mine]
11 Ezekiel 1:4 & 16, King James Version

No human being can see the Fiery Part of MY Being without being annihilated. Human beings, even saved human beings, cannot see ME in this way without being burned up (that is, without being consumed). Moses was the only one in the flesh that I permitted to view a portion of the Fiery Part of ME, but, even then, I had to shield him from becoming *undone,* so to speak.[12] The Prophet Isaiah,[13] the Apostle Paul,[14] and the Apostle John[15] also caught a glimpse of the Fiery Part of MY Being, but only when their souls were caught up into a spiritual state of being and not while their souls were still abiding in their flesh.

Although I withdrew the Fiery Part of MY Being into a dimensionless reality that is far beyond your physical reach, mental grasp, and mortal comprehension, I did not withdraw MY Logos (MY Spoken Word) nor MY Spirit from you. Given the right set of heavenly-determined conditions, MY Logos and MY Spirit have had, and still have, direct access to you and vice versa (but never on your terms, only on MINE).

I partitioned MYSELF into the Logos to visit you from time to time, which visits are recorded in MY Holy Bible and often interpreted by theologians as "theophanies" (that is, MY personal appearances in a physical state of being). The Logos is actually the creative part of ME that would eventually walk among you as "God-in-the-flesh" (God Incarnate) in the person of Jesus the Christ, Y'shua H'Moshiach, who, through his atoning sacrifice, re-creates you from your fallen state back to the original state of spiritual being you had when I first created you. (In other words, you are rebirthed by MY Spirit the moment that you believe on MY Son and in his mission.) The Logos can trigger MY Wrath, as well as MY Grace and MY Mercy, to fall upon you. Unfortunately, many of you have misconcluded that

---

12 Exodus 33:20

13 Isaiah 6:1-7

14 2 Corinthians 12:1-4

15 Revelation 1:9-10

you can trigger MY Wrath, Grace, and Mercy by entertaining a supposed requisite magical thinking through your own imagery or by mentally unlocking a mystical combination by coming to know certain "secret stuff," which is absolutely ridiculous.

Finally ("finally" here is not referring to a sequential act), I partitioned MYSELF into the Holy Spirit in order to freely communicate MY thoughts and emotions to human beings and, eventually, in order to indwell them without annihilating them. To reiterate, MY Spirit is the invisible part of ME that is available to touch you intimately and to communicate with you personally without destroying you. MY Spirit is imparted to you at the precise moment that you believe on MY Son and in his mission, which is clearly articulated in MY Holy Bible. Once you realize that MY Holy Spirit is living in you, you must be careful not to offend, insult, or ridicule MY Holy Spirit in thought, in word, or in deed.

At the time of the end, after all things have been placed under the feet of Jesus the Christ, Y'shua H'Moshiach, and all saved souls are indwelt by MY Spirit, and MY Wrath has been fully appeased, then I will release the Fiery Part of ME to fill all creation and, once again, be *All-in-all*.[16] Remember, I partitioned MYSELF to keep you from being annihilated by the Totality of MY Being. Despite this partitioning, MY entire Being has always remained whole, united, and complete within the framework of a space-time that you cannot fully know or fully comprehend in your present condition of being (which is to say, in corporeality).

If you have been using addition to represent MY tripartite Nature ($1 + 1 + 1 = 3$), then you have been using the wrong metaphor. It will make more sense if you use a base of one raised to the third power (1^3) since that equation more accurately represents the essence of MY tripartite Nature ($1 \times 1 \times 1 = 1$).

---

16 1 Corinthians 15:28, King James Version

Although you call MY Spirit "Holy" (and it is), so is the Fiery Part of ME "Holy" and so is the Logos "Holy." I ALONE AM HOLY. In order to approach ME, you must be Holy as I AM Holy. (However, you cannot be as holy as I AM.) In order to approach ME, you must be wearing the crown of salvation, which in the world of Spirit reads in Hebrew as "Kodesh L'Shem," or in English as "Holiness to the LORD." That crown is only received by you once you accept MY Plan of Salvation and never turn back by rejecting it (i.e., throwing your salvation away).

The Tri-Unity of the Godhead

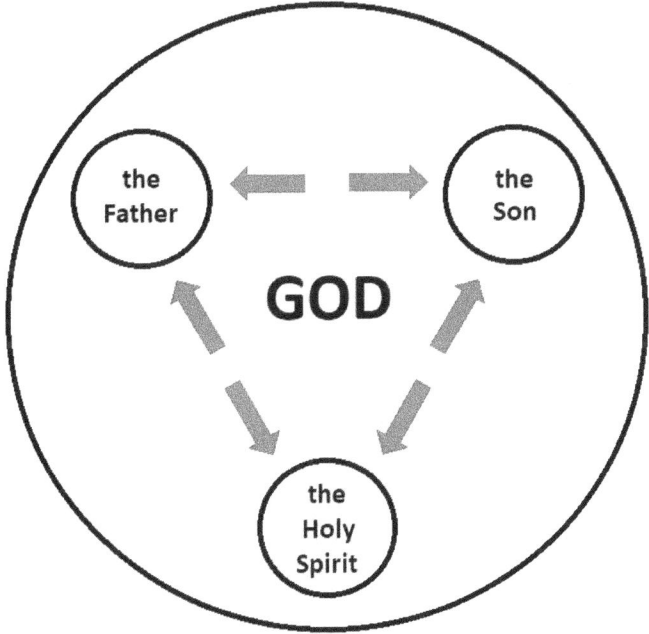

← ⟶ represents "is one with"

From "The Threeness of God" (page 76)

©2021 by Rev. Joseph Adam Pearson, Ph.D.

www.christevangelicalbibleinstitute.com/English3.pdf

My Plan of Salvation

In order to wear the crown mentioned in the previous section, you must accept MY Only Plan of Salvation at the same time that you reject everything contrary to that Plan. Rejecting everything contrary to MY Plan goes hand-in-hand with accepting MY Plan as the Only Plan.

Before the beginning of creation, I knew that once I created beings with free will, they would test their individual free wills and go against MY Guidelines to live in accordance with MY Will. (Don't your own children do that, too?) For immortal beings who would fall from doing MY Will and, thereby, bring condemnation upon themselves and their progeny, I devised MY Plan of Salvation to enable them to avoid eternal separation from ME.

Why did I provide for the salvation of fallen beings?

The answer is because:

1. I AM gracious and merciful;[17]

2. I did not want to lose those who, given the opportunity, would return to ME after they realized, confessed, and repented of their errant ways;[18] and

3. I did not want to give MY Inheritance and MY Glory to another (that is, Satan).[19]

Thus did I provide for the salvation of fallen beings.

---

17 Exodus 33:19, King James Version
18 1 Kings 8:47-52; Ezekiel 18:30-32; Matthew 9:13; Mark 1:15, 2:17; Luke 13:5, 24:47; Acts 17:30-31; Revelation 3:3, 3:19
19 Isaiah 42:8, King James Version

In contrast, I did not provide a plan of salvation for Lucifer, who was once MY "Light-bearer," because he fell as a result of his own arrogance and narcissism, which he developed consciously on his own and not by succumbing to some external temptation. And I did not provide a plan of salvation for angels who chose to go against MY Will by following Lucifer's lead because these spiritual beings (that is, incorporeal beings) who rebelled against ME did so in full view of the magnificence of MY Being. However, I AM lenient with those beings who fell from doing MY Will (honoring MY command) because their disobedience was a result of yielding to external temptation.

Who can understand the Fullness of MY Compassion? In your current state of being, MY Compassion is too good for you to fully comprehend just as MY Will is too good for you to fully know. You can comprehend ME and know ME only through MY Holy Spirit, who begins residing within you at the precise moment that you accept the earthly mission of MY Logos as "the only-begotten Son of God."

Because I knew that human beings, who had turned from ME by going against MY Will, would require an acceptable offering to ME to propitiate (that is, appease) MY Wrath (or MY Justifiable Anger) against them, I devised a Plan that included the shedding of innocent blood to atone for (that is, "cover") and remit (that is, "cancel completely") all debts for their transgressions against ME. To execute MY Plan of Salvation, I partitioned MYSELF at the time of the creation into YHWH (to be known later to you as "LORD" and "the Father"), the Logos (to be known later to you as "the Word," "Lord," and "the Son of God"), and the Spirit (to be known later to you as "the Holy Ghost" and "the Holy Spirit").

When Jesus the Christ, Y'shua H'Moshiach, bore all of the transgressions of human beings upon the cross of his crucifixion, that was the only instant in eternity that the Fiery portion of ME had to look away from the Logos portion of ME and the only instant in eternity that the Logos would be unaware of MY Fiery Presence. If the Fiery Part of MY Being were to look upon sin in your space-time, the bearer of that sin would be forever annihilated. The instant that Jesus Christ bore all of mankind's transgressions (past, present, and future) upon the cross, it was the only moment in eternity that he was unaware of MY Fiery Presence, which — until that moment — burned effortlessly within his soul because of his sinlessness. It was this brief separation that caused the Logos, as MY only-begotten Son, to cry out upon the cross: "Eli, Eli, lama sabachthani! My God, My God, why have you forsaken me?"[20]

Regardless of the Fiery Part of MY Being "looking away" from the Logos for that one brief instant, and regardless of the Logos being unaware of MY Fiery Presence for that precise moment, both YHWH and the Logos ("the Father" and "the Son") remained connected by the Holy Spirit. Because the Son was doing the Will of the Father in paying the penalty for all transgressions against ME, MY Spirit still rested upon him even though the Fiery Part of MY Being had to be hidden from him. Although this was somewhat similar to the way in which I covered Moses to protect him, the Fiery Part of MY Being[21] was totally eclipsed from MY Son as he bore your sins upon the cross, which is why he felt utterly and completely forsaken.

Since it was not the role of the Spirit to bear the iniquity and sin of mankind but was the role of the Son to do so, and since the Holy Spirit still rested upon the Son because he was doing the Father's Will, the Father remained connected — as the Father forever remains connected — to the Son by way of the Spirit. And the Son remained connected — as the Son forever remains connected — to the Father by way of the Spirit.

Earlier, I stated that I would solve the following riddle for you:

---

20 Matthew 27:46, King James Version (see also Psalm 22:1)
21 Exodus 33:21-23

"Which father is his own son, and which son is his own father?" and that I would explain MY answer. Here is the answer and explanation: I AM MY OWN SON AND I AM MY OWN FATHER! I AM WHO I AM! I AM WHO I WILL BE! I WILL BE WHO I WAS! I WAS WHO I WILL BE! I AM THE SELF-EXISTENT ONE! I AM! (It should stand to reason that understanding my true nature is difficult because I AM UNFATHOMABLE.)

The penalty for all human transgressions against ME had to take place in the flesh because the transgressions of Adam and Eve took place in their created flesh (which had a very different appearance in its original state than it does now). This explains the need for MY Logos not only to appear in flesh as a theophany, but, more importantly, for MY Logos to be born into flesh as a human being in order to carry the full weight of the penalty for the transgressions of immortal beings who had become mortal beings as a result of their transgressions. Transgressions against ME must always be paid for in the modality, or condition, in which they are committed.

Because Lucifer and the angels who rebelled against ME did so in a spiritual state of being, and they remained in a spiritual state of being, their penalty must be exacted in that modality. Because souls who rebelled against ME resulted in their current physical state of being, their penalty necessitates payment in that modality (which is to say, in physicality or corporeality). See? At this point, it is important to state again that your original flesh and your original state of being were vastly different from what you know and experience today.

If you blaspheme against MY Holy Spirit, the sin is unforgivable[22] because it is committed in your spirit (just like the transgressions of Lucifer and his angels are unforgivable because they were committed in their spirit). For the sake of clarification,

---

22 Matthew 12:31-32

"blasphemy against MY Holy Spirit" includes: (1) ridiculing MY Holy Spirit by calling MY Holy Spirit a liar and saying that MY Holy Spirit is reprehensible and evil, when the reality is that MY Holy Spirit is the only teacher of all truth[23] and provides the only way that human beings can know ME and MY Will as well as comprehend MY Compassion and MY Goodness while they are on Earth; (2) consciously choosing to return to the active life of sin that you had before you were saved; and (3) deliberately rejecting MY Plan of Salvation by renouncing MY Son all the way to your deathbed.

For the sake of clarification, (1) ignorance or lack of awareness of MY Plan of Salvation because you had never heard it explained to you or (2) taking your own life out of the darkness of emotional despair and mental depression does NOT constitute "blasphemy against MY Holy Spirit."

Although the blood of MY Son, the Lord Jesus Christ, covers all of the sins of the world (that is, sinning in the body), it does not cover spiritual sin (that is, sinning in the spirit). That is why "blasphemy against MY Holy Spirit" is unforgiveable.

The Fight

After I created specific spiritual strata (realms) and an order and hierarchy for spiritual beings in those strata, there was rebellion by some of the angelic beings under the leadership of Lucifer, MY one-time "Light-bearer." As MY "Light-bearer," Lucifer had a special place of honor within MY Spiritual Universe. However, chaos and confusion were introduced into these spiritual realms as Lucifer fell from his high position. Lucifer, a cherubic being created with the gift of free will (just like yours), became enamored of himself because of the sheer magnificence of his appearance, which magnificence was second only to MINE. And

---

23 John 16:13; 1 John 2:27

the more enamored he became, the more arrogant he became.

Make no mistake, arrogance is always born of self-pride and self-will, both of which are foreign to MY Nature, contrary to MY Character, and contradictory to MY Creation. I did not create any of you with arrogance. Arrogance is always a choice for all created beings with a free will. However, arrogance is never a choice with a good end.

Because "God is Love"[24] (which statement is true), some human beings like to think of ME only as "lovey-dovey," or saccharinely sweet. These fail to understand that I hate all things evil, and that because arrogance is always evil, I justifiably hate arrogance. These also fail to take into consideration MY need for divine justice and the intrinsic legitimacy of MY Wrath (that is, MY Justified Anger).

Although Lucifer "fell" to a spiritual level that he himself "created" through the introduction of arrogance into the spiritual realms over which he was given jurisdiction (more about that later), his appearance is still spectacular and his power to tempt mankind to go against MY Will still remains extremely strong. Nevertheless, Satan's power is not as strong as the power exercised through MY Logos. MY Logos overcame all evil for all time as the crucified and resurrected Christ. Nor is Satan's power as strong as MY Holy Spirit. MY Holy Spirit actually resides within those who believe on MY Son and in his mission.

Lucifer is now called Satan — which is to say, MY "Adversary" and MY "Enemy." It is Satan who created the conflict that I AM calling "the Fight." Lucifer was not content with his own magnificence and the delegated authority he had over his angelic followers. Satan heaped his grief (that is, he widened his separation from ME) by declaring an all-out war against ME in order to overthrow ME as Supreme Being. How? By trying to rob

---

24 1 John 4:8, King James Version

ME of MY Creation. Although you might see the impossibility of that happening, Satan's thinking became so clouded by his arrogance that he could not see the possibility (and certainly not the inevitability) of his defeat.

Although Satan has tried to rob ME of MY Creation, through MY Plan of Salvation I have guaranteed that all human beings who desire to return to ME are able to do so by calling upon the Name of Jesus the Christ, Y'shua H'Moshiach, as the only-begotten Son of God and their only Savior. ("Only-begotten" is used throughout this work to denote Jesus Christ as the only person on Earth ever conceived by MY Holy Spirit in consort with a human being.)

This so-called fight *is not* about you, yet it *is* about you. Fundamentally, the fight is really about ME, MY Power, MY Position of Exaltation as the Self-Existent One, and MY Creative Abilities, including MY entire Creation (which is where you come in). Satan wants to exalt himself by overthrowing ME. Despite Satan's calculating abilities and cunning nature, stupidity always accompanies arrogance. When Satan began his campaign against ME, he did not realize that overthrowing ME is an impossibility. Why is it an impossibility? Because I AM WHO I SAID I AM. AND I ALWAYS WILL BE.

During and immediately after his fall, Satan believed that he could shift power in the spiritual realms by having those with free will follow after him, obey him, and worship him. In his arrogance, Satan stupidly thought that he could cause ME to cease from being Creator by robbing ME of MY Creation. His premise was, and still is, fundamentally flawed, but arrogance *always* clouds one's interpretation concerning who is in charge.

Even now, despite Satan's realization that his end could be near, he continues to try to rob ME of MY Creation by setting up a counter-creation to MINE, complete with: (1) a final prophet, (2) a false Messiah (the final end-time Antichrist), and (3) religious worship. Because Satan likes to ape ME and MY Creation, he even has a moral code and houses of worship built into his end-time religion. Unfortunately, his moral code is a facade and the worship is directed only towards the primogenitor of all evil, Satan himself. Satan even has a so-called holy book through which he convinces his followers: (1) that "God" (not ME) cannot have an only-begotten Son, (2) that an only-begotten Son is not crucial to receiving eternal salvation, and (3) that so-called nonbelievers ("kafirs") need to be converted to Satan's way of thinking through the strategic use of fear — including economic, geopolitical, and physical threats of terrorism.

The truth be told, Satan cares not one iota, jot, or yod about his followers. To Satan, the ultimate fate of all human beings is inconsequential. That is why I stated earlier that the Fight is really not about you but about ME. Satan's stupid supposition is: "If HIS Creation is removed from HIM, then, by definition, HIS role as 'the Creator' is removed from HIM as well." Satan thinks (erroneously, of course) that the Creator will cease to exist, or not *BE,* without the Creation that defines HIM as "the Creator." In his own peculiar brand of nihilism, Satan thinks that I will become an imploded black hole in MY Spiritual Universe if MY Creation is stolen from ME.

I have permitted the Fight to continue until the pre-ordained time when MY Final Judgment will take place. Deliberation about the eternal salvation of souls who have accepted MY Only Plan of Salvation while they were on Earth is not part of MY Final Judgment. At that time, these "saved" souls will be judged according to their works on Earth,[25] which works will be judged righteously and fairly to determine the heavenly rewards they will each receive. In order to receive rewards for their works, their works need to have been motivated by genuine love for ME and for all of MY Creation.

---

25 Revelation 20:12-13, King James Version

At the time of MY Final Judgment, souls who have never heard of MY Plan of Salvation will be judged strictly on the presence or absence of earthly works[26] that were inspired by genuine love even though they did not know ME by MY Name. These souls will receive either eternal salvation or eternal damnation based on their works, the motivations behind their works, and the intended outcomes of their works. (For people who have never heard the gospel message, sacrificial selfless love always fulfills the Law because such Love is a Law unto itself.[27])

Finally, those who carefully (that is, deliberately) and consciously reject MY Plan of Salvation continuously until their earthly deathbeds can only receive eternal damnation.[28] Naturally, Satan and all his angelic followers belong to the last camp since they were beyond reclamation the first instant they departed from ME (for the reasons stated previously).

The Fall and the Curse

Although Lucifer and his angelic followers "fell" outside of MY Presence at the precise moment of their insurrection, and although Satan and his angelic followers "fell" by losing their dominion over the world at the precise moment that Jesus Christ bore your transgressions upon the cross, neither of these constitute the Fall of which I now write. The Fall of this titled section is the fall of mankind through its iniquity and sin by the actions of Adam and Eve. Adam and Eve not only represent all of humanity, they also represent all immortal beings with souls that I created. (For the sake of clarity, I AM not discussing a timeframe for the creation of souls in this section.)

---

26 Revelation 20:12-13, King James Version

27 Romans 13:8,10

28 Revelation 20:15

Adam and Eve fell the moment that they turned from obeying MY Will by acting on the temptations of Satan. Satan had tempted them: (1) to do what they had been commanded by ME not to do;[29] and (2) to try to become like ME by living forever with knowledge of both good and evil,[30] something of which created beings are not capable without losing their immortality. Although I can know both good and evil without becoming evil, created beings can only know both good and evil by experiencing evil through deliberate action in disobedience to ME.

Adam and Eve chose to dishonor MY Will with full knowledge of the consequence that they would die (that is, become separated from an intimacy with ME that I had originally intended to last throughout all eternity). When they transgressed MY Will, they found themselves in a state of being quite different from the one to which they had become accustomed. When they transgressed MY Will, MY Reflected Glory departed immediately from their flesh, causing their flesh to lose the luminescence that MY Reflected Glory imparted to them, and causing the living substance of that original flesh to crystallize and compartmentalize into what exists as protoplasm today. For the sake of analogy only, it was as if original DNA was three-stranded in the cells of the pre-Fall Adam and Eve but, as soon as they disobeyed ME, one of the three strands disintegrated instantly and completely. That disintegrated third strand figuratively represents MY Life Force. Additionally, such a loss caused them not only to lose their intimacy with ME but also to become mortal beings because of their newly-acquired, corruptible flesh. The corruption of their flesh was then transmitted to all of their progeny through the figurative "sin gene," which had become spliced into their genetic makeup through their act of disobedience. From that time onward, all souls in this newly-acquired, altered flesh were predisposed to

---

29 Genesis 3:3-4
30 Genesis 3:5

sin (that is, to miss the mark) as well as to suffer the debilitation, deterioration, death, and ultimate decay of their bodies.

The Adamic Fall not only included a type of self-imposed exile for Adam and Eve because of their disobedience, it also included MY Cursing the world I originally made. As Adam and Eve changed spiritually and substantively the moment that iniquity and sin entered their lives, so did the world change to their view. Not only had Adam and Eve changed to their view of themselves, the Universe changed to their view as well. Although your world and universe resemble the world and Universe that were originally created, what you now see does not compare to the beauty, splendor, and magnificence of MY Original World and Unaltered Universe. Indeed, your flesh, your world, and your view of the Spiritual Universe is altered from what I originally created. Paradoxically, MY Original Creation (symbolized in Genesis as "Eden") has remained intact, but you were expelled from it and cannot now see it.

Please remember that, like some hidden time bomb, a curse is embedded into every action that takes place outside of MY Will. But be of good cheer because, conversely, a blessing is in store for you every time you do MY Will. (Yes, every time!)

When Adam and Eve dishonored MY Will, I withdrew MY Spirit from them and they no longer had direct and immediate access to ME. Although I would communicate from time to time with humankind through MY Holy Spirit in the ensuing millennia, the relationship that I once had with MY Created was altered until the sacrifice of MY only-begotten Son reopened the free access of souls in dust to ME. This access is granted through MY Holy Spirit's residence within souls at the precise moment that they believe on MY Son and in his mission.

How do you obtain your free pass to Heaven? (Actually, it isn't free because MY Son had to pay for it with his life.) You acknowledge that you have sinned, or gone against MY Will, you repent of your sins, and you accept MY Plan of Salvation by believing on MY Son and in his mission as it relates to you specifically and all of mankind generally. Although it is rather simple, many do not accept MY Plan because acceptance requires humility on their part. Humility requires its practitioner to give up something that most people believe they cannot afford to give up: *control.*

Is it possible for you to lose your eternal salvation once you have received it? Although no external agency can rob you of your salvation, you can throw it away by returning to, or continuing in, a way of living that is foreign to MY Nature, contrary to MY Will, and contradictory to MY Creation. However, if you have returned to a disobedient way of living and genuinely feel remorse about such a return while you are still in the flesh, then you are not beyond reclamation. (Regrets and remorse after you die reverse nothing. You must repent while you are still in human flesh for any change to take place. This is MY Rule and MY Requirement.)

The Death Blanket

Spiritual death is best defined as "separation of the created from their Creator." When Adam and Eve sinned, a death blanket enshrouded MY Creation. This fog of death enveloped MY Creation at the precise moment that Adam and Eve "fell" to their newly-acquired, but previously nonexistent, corruptible state of physical being, which is hallmarked by debilitation, deterioration, death, and ultimate decay. In this way did MY True Creation become hidden from them and their progeny. Physical death not only accompanied spiritual death, physical death was the effect of spiritual death.

Although I had given Adam and Eve dominion over their world, they handed that dominion over to Satan by succumbing to his temptation for them to become like ME[31] (which is absurd because it is an absolute impossibility). Satan robbed them of the authority I had given to them by getting them to believe his lies (for the future, please remember that all temptation consists of lies and lies only). Adam and Eve ended up trading MY Truth for a lie. By going against ME, they chose to separate themselves from ME.

It was not until Jesus Christ won victory over Satan by resisting temptation all of the way to the cross that direct access to ME was restored. Through Christ's victory, all power, authority, and control in spiritual realms were removed from Satan by MY Logos (also known as MY "Word" and the Creative Part of ME). That was when Satan fell from Heaven. Yes, Satan's dominion has been removed forevermore by Christ's victory! The lost dominion of souls in dust over their world, which world is now under Christ's authority because of his victory, is imparted back to human beings when they believe on Jesus Christ (that is, believe in who he says he is, entrust their lives to him, and surrender their human wills to the Will of the Self-Existent Almighty One, ME).

Although the state of the world today might cause you to think that Satan still has dominion over it, any power he and his minions have is illusory and, at best, short-lived. I have permitted Satan to have access to earthly realms to test the sincerity of those who are returning to ME. Human beings can only pass this test by clinging to the cross of Christ, wherein they find MY Strength to overcome the world, their fleshly desires, and Satan's temptations. Indeed, if they cling to their own strength, they will fail.

Although the last enemy that is yet to be completely overcome is physical death,[32] restoration of MY Glory to the Earth will

---

31 Genesis 3:5

32 1 Corinthians 15:26, King James Version

remove this remnant of MY Curse. When I again infuse MYSELF into the fallen part of MY Creation, the last vestige of MY Curse will vanish. At that time, death shall be no more.[33]

Holy Scripture

Why do you think that the Holy Bible has continuity and complementarity throughout its entirety despite its multiple writers? Because I authored and inspired it through MY Holy Spirit! Although there is a missing yod or two within the current Tanakh (the Jewish Scripture or Christian "Old Testament"), the manuscripts of that complete work have survived relatively intact throughout the millennia mainly through the painstaking efforts of MY Jewish scribes and copyists, who reproduced each stroke of the Hebrew alphabet[34] in the Tanakh meticulously and faithfully. Likewise, the individual works of the established New Testament Canon have survived relatively intact from the time that the New Testament inclusions were originally written.

Although the genealogies listed in the Tanakh and in the Christian Gospels might be tedious reading, they are not frivolous because they help to trace (1) the human ancestry of Jesus Christ — who is "fully human and fully divine" and not "half human and half divine" — as well as (2) the origin of ancient peoples and their various migration patterns.

Much of MY Holy Scripture is written in narrative form (that is, "chronicled history") to help tell a true story in the most-engaging way possible. Just because certain events are reported within narrative form in MY Holy Bible does not mean that I endorsed their happening. *For example,* that it is reported that Lot offered his two daughters to the marauding residents of

---

33 Revelation 21:4

34 The word *alphabet* is derived from joining "aleph" and "beyt," the first two letters in the common sequence of Hebrew written characters.

Sodom does not mean that I endorsed the potential sacrifice of his daughters. MY Holy Bible simply records what happened. Similarly, many of the epistles (letters) of the New Testament contain incidental or anecdotal remarks to help them be more engaging to you as "living history."

Christian leadership has not often done a very good job teaching what the Tanakh (Old Testament) has for Christians. Here are eight reasons why Christians should read, study, and comprehend the Tanakh followed by one reason *not* to study it:

1. To understand the origin of the universe.

2. To understand the origin of mankind.

3. To learn the history of mankind since Adam and Eve as well as to learn the origin of iniquity and sin.

4. To understand the promises of God to mankind concerning the Jewish Messiah (MY Logos), who is the only Savior of the world.

5. To understand the prophecies of God that have already been fulfilled, that are currently being fulfilled, and that will be fulfilled at a later time.

6. To learn from the journey of the Children of Israel and how it mirrors the personal journey of individual Christians.

7. To learn basic spiritual principles and apply them to living today.

8. To better understand Old Testament quotations, references, and imagery used in the New Testament.

It is important to add here that Christians should NOT read, comprehend, and study the Old Testament in order for them to follow Levitical Law! Levitical Law was written at a different time for a different people who lived in a specific geographic location (Israel).

Am I finished with MY Jews? Of course not! Once I choose people, MY Call is irrevocable[35] unless they individually reject ME through the gift of free will that I gave to all created beings. Have MY Christians replaced MY Jews as MY Chosen People? Of course not! Both groups have been chosen by ME. I not only "juggle" Jews and Christians at the same time, I cause their paths to intersect periodically. To be sure, Christianity has been grafted onto the root of Judaism in the Tree of Life. Although I have never deserted (and will never desert) MY Jews because they rejected the Messiah I promised to send to them, they have returned to wandering (similar to the forty-year period during the Exodus). However, I used their rejection of MY Son as an opportunity to graft Christians into the Tree of Life. But after the Church Age is finished, I will re-graft MY Jews into the same trunk. Later, after human beings have been tested one last time and there is a final battle,[36] "the Son" will deliver unto "the Father" all "re-created" beings that have been placed under the Son's feet. Then, because all those who have chosen ME will have been cleansed and purified, I can then infill them with the Fiery Part of MY Being without their annihilation. At that time, I will again be *All-in-all* [37] and no longer need to have a triadic plurality (see the Foreword to this book for the definition of *triadic plurality)*. After that, I will never again partition MYSELF.

Although I have just stated that I will infill all "re-created" human beings with the Fiery Part of MY Being (just as I previously filled them with MY Holy Spirit when they accepted Jesus Christ as their personal Savior), please don't get pantheistic on ME. MY Creation will not become the Creator (ME); we will just be enjoined to one another in a reformed and reconstituted

---

35 Romans 11:29

36 Revelation 20:7-8, King James Version

37 1 Corinthians 15:28, King James Version

dyadic association. Although it sounds like quite a soup, I simply mean to say that I will infuse MY Re-Creation with the Totality of MY Being. Human eye has not seen and human ear has not heard what I have prepared for those of you who choose ME![38] The result will be both breath*taking* and breath*giving* at the same time.

Look for truth within MY entire Holy Bible, which consists of both Old Testament (Tanakh) and New Testament. Don't forget to use these principles when studying MY written word: (1) mentally hold the whole Bible while simultaneously attending to its various parts; (2) investigate the meanings that the words had when they were originally written; (3) study historical and literary contexts for the written words; (4) look for and identify major principles that you can apply to your daily living; (5) ask for MY Help in identifying the ideals that I have articulated within MY Holy Scripture; and (6) gradually strive to completely live up to MY ideals by asking ME for MY Help.

Grace

The Fullness of MY Grace is always extended to human beings, who are, in effect, woeful "souls in dust." However, although MY Grace is always extended to you, you receive it only to the degree that you live in contrition through a deepening attitude of sincere inner humility (as opposed to feigned outer pretense). Experiencing higher states of MY Grace is dependent on the depth of your contrition through humility.

Yes, there is only one Grace, but there are many states within it. And such states are only entered into, and MY Grace is only received, in proportion to your contrition through humility. That is why contrition through humility must be an obsession for those who are seeking to ever more fully live and move and have

---

38 1 Corinthians 2:9, King James Version

their *being* in ME. Although such an obsession is contrary to the human condition, without it souls in dust fall prey to the influence of evil in their daily activities.

Living in a state of contrition through humility is synonymous with living in a state of grace. You cannot have one without the other. Contrition through humility is your contribution, and grace is MY contribution, to the dyadic union of "Creator" (ME) and "created" (you) — which is to say, "Lover" and "beloved."

Contrition through humility is the attitude of a soul who acknowledges that its human life is not only born of, but also shaped by, iniquity and that this very same iniquity has produced vulnerabilities that, when acted upon, result in sin (or "missing the mark"). A true desire to please ME (that is, honor MY Will) and to gain, or regain, an intimate relationship with ME results in contrition. Your contrition through humility delivers you directly to MY Throne of Mercy. (The last statement presumes that you already believe on MY Son and in his mission.)

Contrition through humility is the condition of remorse in a soul who is painfully aware of the depravity of its human spirit as well as the poverty of its human condition regardless of its individual abilities and personal material possessions or lack thereof.

Grace, MY Unmerited Favor, is MY Gift to you. MY Grace is your opportunity to be fully returned to ME as you gradually and progressively learn to experience MY Being through MY Holy Spirit. To live in contrition through humility and, thus, to live in MY Grace is the "secret" to how you can experience MY Joy, which on Earth provides a true foretaste of Heaven. (Again, in this work, "Heaven" is completely synonymous with "MY Heavenly Consciousness," "MY Spiritual Universe," "the Kingdom of Heaven," "the Kingdom of God," "Paradise," and "Eden.")

You enter MY Grace the precise moment that you believe on MY Son and in his mission. You ascend its ladder in stages directly proportionate to: (1) your deepening contrition through humility; (2) your meditating[39] on ME, MY Written Word, and who you are in ME; and (3) your praying to ME as well as praising ME.

---

39 Psalm 1:2; 63:6; 77:12; 119:15, 23, 48, 78 & 148; 143:5

Chapter Two

There is a Famine in Your Land

Today, there is a famine in your land that has nothing to do with the cultivation of plants and the domestication of animals. Rather than being indicated by empty stomachs and emaciated bodies, this famine is demonstrated by the lack of spiritual substance within the souls of those who move through the earth plane of consciousness as "souls in dust" — who do not even think to question what or where their true nature once was and now *is*. These have accepted as their only reality the consciousness of self-pride and self-will that presently prevails within your sphere of activities.

Sad, but true, because most people do not look for what eternal verities can be found during their earthly sojourns, they are limited (simply by the limitations they have imposed upon themselves) from seeing the wider view of a horizon of thought upon which dawns the nature of a universal reality. That nature is invisible to the physical senses but visible, indeed, to the spiritually-enlightened sense of insightfulness, which is an inward-looking provided only when MY Holy Spirit resides within you.

To be sure, most people feel the pangs of spiritual emptiness, but, in trying to ease the discomfort that results from it, the overwhelming majority have chosen to work toward ideals that falsely hold up something within your Earth and its plane of consciousness as a standard for good. Even among those who profess to follow lofty conceptual frameworks are found many who believe that something, somewhere in the physical universe, is Good — or, at least, can be made to be Good. However, the supposition that good-in-itself (which is to say, "God") can be found within the confines of finitude and that absolute good is observable through mere mortal sense (which includes faulty human analytics and emotions in addition to the physical senses) is erroneous. As long as lives are based on such a weak supposition, they will never be joined to the only consciousness that provides true fulfillment, which is not just in your awareness of MY Being but in your actually living, moving, and regaining your being *in* ME.

Whenever people who are still spiritually alive align themselves with the systematics of any earthly belief — no matter if the belief is associated with politics, philosophy, sociology, or religion — they still feel a hunger gnawing from within, begging for something else. And, though they may turn by the droves to other belief systems for that "something else," they continue to feel unsatisfied, unfulfilled, and even lost because such feelings cannot begin to abate until those-who-seek realize that their true needs are filled from within only by spiritual substance. What is spiritual substance? Spiritual substance is the Essence of MY Being, imparted to you only through MY Holy Spirit at the precise moment that you believe on MY Son and in his mission.

Many of you, including those who have received good Bible training to interpret and resolve earthborn problems, are still unable to make the necessary connection between your true spiritual nature in Christ and the tiny Earth globe on which you live. I hung your planet in a space that is neither the center of a solar system nor the center of a galaxy or universe to drive home the point to you that you are neither the center nor circumference of the Universe where I reside. Although the tenets of an ethereality may ring true within you, you still lack the understanding that links the physical body in which you currently find yourselves with what you inwardly know is your true spiritual identity in and through Christ Jesus. Many of you, because you are unwilling to do the necessary work, leave the questions and their loose ends in the hope that the questions will somehow find their own answers and the answers will eventually tie themselves together.

The answers to all questions are already within you, waiting to be unlocked to your spiritual sense through an earnest, diligent, and prayerful search for truth within MY Holy Bible. Eventually, you must face the seeming incongruities between corporeality (physical being) and spirituality by regularly separating yourself from your world to study the Scriptures and search for truth within the sanctity of an inner peace. I provide you with such peace when your mind is focused on ME in prayer during Bible study. I provide you with such peace when you meditate on MY Written Word, WHO it says I AM, and who it says you are and what you can become.

If you turn toward ME, I will turn toward you[40] and, thereby, permit you a glimpse of the truth in a startling view, which will reveal to you that I *did* create the world — but my original creation is not the same one in which you are presently found.

Your spiritual identity is best understood only when I live within you through MY Holy Spirit, given to you at the precise moment that you believe on MY Son and in his mission. (If you still do not know ME, I ask that you take the first step toward ME right now by accepting Jesus Christ as your personal Savior as well as Savior of the world.) Your current physical identity is best understood by coming to know what happened when Adam and Eve fell to Satan's temptation, the details of which are presented in this book.

Since dependency on anything other than ME is a shaky foundation on which to build your life, it is MY Message to those-who-will-hear that if your individual faith in ME is only buoyed up by hearing a songbird, encountering someone with acceptable mannerisms, or seeing a blue sky — or, in short, by anything that is physically sensed, then that faith is found wanting and forever will be found wanting. Such faith will be insufficient to sustain you through the inevitable trials and

---

40 James 4:8

tribulations that you will encounter as you travel through the earth plane of consciousness. Sooner or later, if you are to progress to any higher realm of being, those-who-seek must come to an understanding that all earthly songbirds are parasite-infested, that all con artists have acceptable mannerisms (otherwise they would not be "artists" who fool others), and that people still starve for food under breathtakingly-beautiful blue skies. In short, you must eventually realize that your world is corrupt as well as corruptible. In the final analysis, regardless of what is said or done, the whole world in which you live (that is, where you have your physical being) is still subject to debilitation, deterioration, death, and decay. It is not my original creation.

Although the previously-cited are but a few of the many examples that could be given as evidence of the inadequacy of material existence to house and support the pure and perfect Life that I radiate, they nevertheless point to a veracity that exposes the spiritual emptiness of physicality and clears the way back to the Garden of MY Heavenly Consciousness for those who desire with all their heart, soul, mind, and might to return to it. (However, you cannot *will* yourself back to that "Garden.")

Because it is nothing more than spiritual immaturity that requires the fulfillment of earthly criteria for the demonstration of proof that there is a God, then bound to be upset is the faith of those who assume that their corporeality (that is, their physical being) is a manifestation of the Fullness of MY Glory (the Fiery Part of MY Being). These unwittingly seek to confine ME to their own image of ME, which image is the one they currently have of themselves.

If you reread MY Scripture, you will see that the original Adam was made in MY Image and Likeness and that Adam's son, Seth, was made in Adam's image and likeness,[41] which image was a

---

41 Genesis 5:1-3, King James Version

fallen one and not the one I originally created for Adam.

Now more than ever, "the joys of this world are temporal" needs to be stated without qualification and understood as such by those who are seeking amidst your earthly sphere of activities to find the Kingdom of God. Yet, in one way or another, most people insist on turning to that which is "of" the material universe for solutions to problems that are spiritual in nature. People just won't disbelieve their physical senses. Even most people who call themselves Christian would insist that God made the cloudless day (although they might not be as adamant about the stormy night) and that this world — including its heaven (that is, its sky) and its earth — constitutes MY Original Creation. However, such as these fail to realize that the physical universe is a manifestation of iniquity. Paradoxically, it is their own mass iniquity that hides MY True Creation from those who depend solely on human sense to give them a picture of reality.

Please do not misinterpret here that there is a duality between spirit and corporeality (which is to say, that spiritual *being* conflicts with physical *being*). That the physical universe in raw material form is a manifestation of iniquity does not mean that the physical universe is iniquity-in-itself. There is really only one duality, or conflict, that exists. It is between Good and Evil, not between spirit and matter. Matter is not the culprit. Matter is the effect, not the cause, of iniquity.

Scripture tells you clearly that you "wrestle not against flesh and blood."[42] Of course, that does not mean that you do not wrestle with your own flesh and blood in terms of raging hormones, brain chemistries, and physical addictions. It means that, if you are waging war against the world based on its appearances and your own physicality, then you are fighting needlessly and aiming your spiritual weapons in the wrong direction. Your target should be Evil, not corporeality, not physical being, and

---

42 Ephesians 6:12, King James Version

certainly not the physical universe. You do not really need to overcome matter; you need to overcome Evil.

Haven't you noticed that, when you open the window a crack to indulge your own parasitic behaviors, negative attitudes, and addictive desires (which include much more than just sexual appetites), it is difficult to close that window again? Because you cannot tame sin, all you can do is to not act on the temptation to sin and, if you have sinned, to quickly repent and ask ME for forgiveness concerning your sinful acts. Sinful acts are actions based on your own iniquity, which is responsible for your predisposition to sin. In addition to asking ME for forgiveness, you also need to ask ME for MY Strength to overcome future temptations. However, MY Son's life should be a lesson to you all. He was tempted all of the way *to* the cross, and even *on* the cross.

The concept that there may be twin worlds parallel and coincident in space may not be new to you. And the idea that time, space, and motion are relative to one another as functional coordinates of energy may not be new to you. What may be new to you is the idea that MY Perfect World is masked by corporeality, the visible sign of iniquity. (Remember, corporeality is not iniquity-in-itself and not the cause of iniquity, only an effect.)

MY Old Testament Prophets and MY New Testament Apostles were aware (some more than others) that an iniquitous mass consciousness had superimposed shadows of darkness over MY Spiritual Universe and that the physical universe itself was brought about by the fall of once glorious beings "like unto light." The fall of Lucifer and the angels who followed his lead introduced chaos and confusion into an outpocketing of MY Spiritual Universe with one big bang, a shot that can still be heard around your world.

Because I knew Adam and Eve would fall from the glorious estate that I gave to them (where they actually *reflected* MY Glory), I decided to stage their return, and the return of their progeny, to ME in this three-step process: physical birth, spiritual rebirth (vis-à-vis the salvation of their souls), and re-glorification of their bodies (which happens *en masse* in a most spectacular way at a later time). I wanted them to do their inevitable falling on Earth (although the Earth was vastly different then) so that payment for their sins could be exacted in the modality which resulted from their sins, and so that they and their progeny would eventually be free forevermore to have their habitation within ME without the possibility for another fall.

As soon as unfallen created beings (immortal beings) entertained ungodly thoughts and acted on them, their souls, spirits, and bodies became impure. Then, the vibrational rate of their once pure spiritual substance slowed to a level so heavy that it concomitantly manifested in the animate matter with which you are familiar today. MY use of "as soon as" is from the perspective of MY Perfect World and not from the space-time perspective of your world of appearances. When viewed from the core of iniquity, "as soon as" actually translates to "eons after," such units of measurement constituting the physical time that it took for chemical reactions to produce the aggregates with which those in corporeality are most familiar. In other words, of those who were tempted to exalt themselves above ME, all who succumbed to that temptation were catapulted over the billions of years of physical time that have elapsed since such time began. They were catapulted from MY Absolute Reality to the relative and spiritually unreal at the precise moment that they permitted unwholesome thoughts of self-pride and self-will to enter their individual and collective consciousness.

If you are having trouble fitting this in with the Adam and Eve account of creation, perhaps I can help you here. The Yahwist and Elohist accounts of MY Creation in Genesis[43] are there to illustrate that some spiritual truths are simultaneous rather than just linear and sequential. When they are simultaneous, spiritual truths are difficult to conceptualize, experience, and "know" by the human spirit through simple cognition and emotion. That is why you can only fully understand these things through MY Holy Spirit. *For example,* you can't conceptually merge such truths by illustrating them with a Venn diagram or by sequencing them perfectly in linear thinking. I know that there will be those who believe that this explanation is a cop-out, but, trust ME, it is accurate. If someone gave you two different beautiful glass marbles, you would not try to appreciate them by fusing them, you would best appreciate them side-by-side. This is how I would like you to appreciate the Biblical narrative concerning Adam and Eve and the accounts given here of the fall of eternal souls from immortality to mortality (that is, from "life" to "death"). The Yahwist and Elohist creation accounts in Genesis are not provided to give you double-vision, but, rather, to give you stereoscopic spiritual vision. So, too, are the accounts of Adam and Eve and the fall of immortals to mortality designed to give you true sight when viewed in tandem. In other words, you must use both of your spiritual eyes in order to have spiritual stereoscopic vision.

The thesis of the current chapter is this: What you in the earth plane of consciousness see as a universe is really a perverted (that is, bent or refracted) version of MY Spiritual Universe, which contains the Fullness of MY Glory (which is to say, "the Fiery Part of MY Being"). Although MY Spiritual Universe is eternal and changeless in truth, it appears altered to those who have themselves been altered by their own iniquity and who manifest their impurity as "the shadow of death." "The shadow

---

43 For this book, "Elohist" refers to Biblical passages that use the name of *Elohim* for Deity; and "Yahwist" refers to Biblical passages that use the name of *Yahweh* (YHWH or Y'hweh) for Deity. Applying these definitions to the creation accounts, Genesis 1:1 – 2:4a is "Elohist" and Genesis 2:4b-25 is "Yahwist."

of death," "corporeality," "physical being," "the shadow of turning," "corruption," "the visible sign of iniquity," "earthly flesh," and "the sin body" may all be used interchangeably to signify the outward manifestation of spiritual error when Adam and Eve first turned from ME. (Their "iniquity" was brought about by their turning from ME as they yielded to Satan's temptation.) Your corporeality as a purely physical state of being (which state *does not* reflect MY Glory) is distinguished from the spiritual reality of the corpus of redeemed souls in the Body of Christ (which state *does* reflect MY Glory).

Various philosophers and religionists have caught glimpses of this truth, but they usually ended up pitting Spirit against matter and not Evil. Evil is the culprit, not matter. Your major challenge is to overcome Evil and not to overcome matter. You waste precious time when you think that you must learn to transcend your own physicality. Instead, although Evil is undetected by your physical senses, you should be transcending it by resisting the Devil through the precious blood of MY only-begotten Son, Jesus Christ. As the blood of the lamb protected the children of Israel from the Angel of Death when it was applied to their door jambs just prior to their exodus from Egypt,[44] so does MY Son's blood protect you from Evil when it is applied to the lintel of your mind and the doorposts of your soul. (It is when you venture beyond the protected space that I have created for you through Christ Jesus that you get yourselves into trouble.)

What I have in store for those who believe on MY Son and in his mission is invisible and inaudible to those who indulge their own self-pride and self-will. And it will continue to remain unperceived by them in direct proportion to the level of such indulgence until the time of the end, when all — regardless of belief, disbelief, or unbelief — will confront the Nature of MY Absolute Reality in a celestial order whose spiritual hierarchy is based on faith in, and loyalty to, ME alone. Such faith and loyalty

---

44 Exodus 12:7, 21-23

are functions of genuine contrition for wrongdoing through humility as well as gratitude for everything that you now have and now have access to.

For the sake of clarity, here are the events that I have been detailing:

1. In MY Spiritual Universe, which you cannot now see, hear, or touch physically, I created a hierarchy of spiritual beings, including Lucifer, who had the special role of carrying, or bearing, MY Light (Glory, Spiritual Light, or Light-Energy).

2. As Lucifer and the angels who followed him decided to rebel against ME, they immediately fell.

3. Their fall caused matter to explode into existence from the Light-Energy that they carried. (This relationship of energy to matter is obliquely represented by your scientists in Laws of Thermodynamics, theories of relativity, and energy-mass conversion formulas. Metaphysically speaking, this event is represented by the following formula: $\Sigma E=0$, where Σ represents *the sum of*, E represents *fallen spiritual energy [i.e., iniquity]*, and 0 represents *absolute nothingness*.)

4. Out of the chaos, disorder, confusion, and "nothingness" that exploded into existence as matter, I made the physical universe. (In other words, I made order from disorder, sense out of nonsense, and "something" out of "nothing." I alone create *ex nihilo* and *de novo*.)

5. In MY Original Creation, I made Original Man ("Man," "True Man," or *immortal man*) in MY Image and Likeness. I imparted MY Life to Original Man. And I created Original Man to reflect MY Glory. (As stated earlier, your original "flesh" and created state were

quite different from what your souls inhabit today.)

6. Original Man ("Man," "True Man," or *immortal man*) fell by yielding to Satan's temptations, in effect, to join him in his fight against ME. (Throughout this book, *iniquity* is defined as "turning from God" and *sin* is defined as "action based on that turning.")

7. Because the apple that Satan offered was really a spiritual grenade, it exploded when Original Man ("Man," "True Man," or *immortal man*) bit into it. Then, at that precise moment, what you knew as MY Creation forever became altered to your view. (Although you might think that I may be playing a word game here, "forever" does not mean "throughout all eternity." In this usage, "forever" is a function of the dimension known to you as physical time whereas "eternity" is spiritual timelessness.)

8. With the fall of Adam and Eve came the curse of debilitation, deterioration, death, and decay that has plagued your world and its inhabitants ever since. *Immortal man* had fallen to become *mortal man*.

To summarize, MY Spiritual Universe (the place where I reside) has been obfuscated by the imposition of iniquity upon your view, and your forms have been altered from what I originally created in that your bodies no longer reflect MY Glory. However, although your view of MY Creation has changed, I have not changed because I do not change. I *do not* change because I *cannot* change. I AM THE SELF-EXISTENT ONE. I CHANGE NOT.[45] That I have partitioned MYSELF into "the Father," "the Son," and "the Holy Spirit" did not require ME to change. MY Essence and MY Substance did not change with MY partitioning and I certainly have never abrogated MY Will. I will never abrogate MY Will because I *cannot*. I CANNOT BE

---

45 Malachi 3:6, King James Version

WHAT I AM NOT. I AM ALWAYS WHAT I AM. And the changes that have occurred have been permitted by **MY** Grace and Mercy for the time being in order for you to be given the opportunity to return to **ME**.

Are you beginning to understand the magnitude of what **I AM** telling you?

Chapter Three

Your One True Origin

and Only Real Being

So you might better recognize the role that I, your Creator, intended for you within MY Perfect World (not the one you currently see), and, thereby, be better prepared to meet ME face-to-face, you need to try to remember the Source from which you have your one true origin and only real being.

Until now, I have not discussed the moment that I created your souls (the eternal souls that currently live in human forms). I did not discuss this within MY Holy Bible because the discussion would have gotten you off track. So, some of you may think that I create one soul at a time each time a human being is conceived; some of you may think that I create a soul sometime during the development of each human embryo and fetus; some of you may think that I create a soul at the time of childbirth; and some of you may not have given it much thought at all.

Before the beginning of the history recorded in MY Holy Bible, in order to reflect MY Pure and Perfect Being, I created channels of purity, which altogether constituted Original Man (capitalized here to keep MY Original Creation distinct from humankind). Confusion to the contrary often lies in human beings who believe that they are minuscule versions of their Creator. Unfortunately, your current state of being and present state of mind cause you to anthropomorphize everything: from invisible forces of nature all the way to your household pets (which is to say, you ascribe to them human emotions and rationality). You even try to anthropomorphize ME. How? You conceptualize ME in *your own image* rather than vice versa. You even refer to ME as "the man upstairs." Just how insulting is that? Such an epithet diminishes WHO I AM in the minds of the hearers. I know that many of you are embarrassed to use the word *God* or *Jesus* in front of others except as swear words. (Actually, the word *God* is not MY Name but more about that later.)

Because of the physical reality experienced through your human senses, human intellect, and human emotions, many of you walk in the belief that I inhabit the physical universe. Although I turned chaos into order after the Big Bang (when I brought order to the physical universe), I do not inhabit the physical universe in the way that you might think I do. Some of you think that I AM embedded in inanimate matter as well as all living forms as some type of impersonal and nebulous force. You might even state that you see ME in the physical universe, when it would be more accurate to say that you see evidence of ME throughout the physical universe, *for example,* in MY having brought order out of chaos in an Intelligent Design.

And some of you think that, because I set all laws of physics into motion at the time that I created order out of chaos, I have stepped away from you or that those laws are unalterable by ME. In your unbelief, you even try to explain all miracles detailed in MY Holy Bible with explanations based on physical nature. Although I stepped the Fiery Part of MY Being away from the physical universe so that it would not be annihilated, I AM still very much a part of your daily experience. I AM a Personal God, not an impersonal force of physical nature. You just don't see MY Being.

To those who depend on physical sentience alone, the data presented by the physical universe contributes to the swelling mass consciousness from which you must turn if you are to realize a state more nearly, and more perfectly, reflecting ME and manifesting MY Life. Although daily, earthly living may bombard you with worldly solutions — some blatantly (but most subtly) contemptuous of ME in their so-called answers — you must turn from them if you are to catch glimpses of ME in your current state of being.

Of importance to your apprehending MY Spiritual Universe — where the Fiery Part of MY Being resides — is: (1) your willingness to admit that you have been off-centered by self-pride and self-will; and (2) your desire for spiritual instruction that might enable you to grow back to ME. "Grow back" here does not mean that your salvation is dependent on works. It means that, although your salvation *is* instantaneous and *is not* a process, your sanctification *is* a process and *is not* instantaneous.

That you have even been allotted time for return to a spiritual network, whose fabric far surpasses in brilliance any materially-illuminated vesture, speaks not of your righteousness but of MY Infinite Mercy. I have never once stopped loving MY Offspring, wayward though you have been. As soon as a soul accepts that a life lived in self-pride and self-will just cannot *be,* that soul may commence to work more fruitfully to understand its spiritual heritage because it then will be facing in a different direction.

Souls in dust need to turn from thoughts of a lower, debased self to thoughts of a higher self (that is, their "supraself") and aspects of a common selfhood found only in ME. If a soul cannot confess, "By myself I am nothing and of myself I am less than nothing," it can have no part in MY Absolute Reality, where all individual souls are interdependent channels of MY Expression. What frightens most of you is your thinking that you are going to be swallowed up by some impersonal and nebulous life force and lose your individuality. To be sure, I created you as individuals meant to be parts, or members, of One Body with ME as the Head, but it is in the resumption of your place within MY Creation through Jesus Christ that you truly regain your individuality and are completely freed to be who I originally created you to be.

***

Perhaps I should write some type of disclaimer here. (Of course I should!) Regardless of the level of your understanding concerning what is written in this book, it is only important for you to accept: (1) that Jesus Christ is the only-begotten Son of God[46] as well as God in the flesh (God Incarnate),[47] (2) that Jesus Christ shed his blood on Mount Calvary for the remission of the debt for your sins,[48] and (3) that Jesus Christ rose again from the dead on the third day after his murder on the cross.[49]

I intentionally wrote MY Holy Bible so that its principal message could be understood by a diverse group of people with different emotional capabilities and intellectual means. For those of you who *do* understand what is written in MY Holy Bible, you should not pat yourselves on the back because what is personal brilliance to you may not be brilliance to ME. In actuality, I value true emotional commitment to ME through your demonstrated love for ME more than I do your intellectual understanding of ME. *For example,* some of MY Offspring who think more slowly reflect ME more brilliantly than many of MY Offspring with intellectual prowess (there are many forms of genius and many forms of ability). How? People with intellectual prowess are often impaired emotionally because they are unable to love anyone other than themselves or express that love without shame. Indeed, intellectual prowess can be a much greater disability, liability, and limitation than intellectual impairment.

***

---

46 Matthew 3:17; 17:5, King James Version

47 John 1:1, 14, King James Version

48 Matthew 26:28 & 1 Corinthians 15:3: King James Version

49 1 Corinthians 15:4, King James Version

Responding to the challenge of Christ Jesus to "be perfect even as your Father in heaven is perfect,"[50] those-who-seek must confront their own imperfections rather than ignore them. However, because of spiritual weakness, ignorance, or presumption, many who feel that they have embraced Christianity as a way of life have concluded that simple verbal negations of their own vulnerabilities and infirmities, or affirmations of their own self-perfection, are sufficient to dismiss wickedness in themselves as well as in others. Certainly, imperfections cannot exist within MY Perfect World, but they can and do exist within your world of appearances. Do not forget where you are and where you wish to be, for, though it may be difficult for you to admit that you harbor a false sense of self, no soul will be able to pass through MY Portal to Heaven as long as it willfully clings to excess baggage in the form of a cherished earthly personality or identity. That does not mean that you should not cherish your memories. It means that you should not look back like Lot's wife to find yourself frozen by your past.

Though the physical earth appears to be a reality-in-itself to those who people its globe, souls connected to human existence are actually located somewhere between MY Perfect World (that is, MY Sphere of Activities) and the world of self-pride and self-will (a world set apart from ME), how close or how far they are from one or the other determined by the lives that they lead and the attitudes they maintain. Since the two worlds of which I write are opposite and opposing in nature, they cannot comingle in one space, but they can (and do) exist coincidentally in two places at once.

It is impossible for Satan, who rules the world of self-pride and self-will, to occupy the same space where I AM. Depending on the sense, either spiritual or mortal, with which souls in dust make observations, they are exposed either to images in the light of Good or in the darkness of Evil. Here, you should not

---

50 Matthew 5:48, King James Version

misinterpret "in the light of Good" to mean that such Light (that is, Spiritual Light) makes things become "of God" when they are not, but, instead, should interpret that phrase to mean such Light exposes things for no more and no less than what they are. Additionally, you should not misconstrue that all "images in the darkness of Evil" will appear unpleasant because it is part of the serpentine nature of Satan to make look good that which is not good.[51]

I AM hoping you will understand that your current physical reality is somewhere in between MY World and Satan's world without concluding that you should hate corporeality. Remember, corporeality, or physicality, is *not* the culprit. Corporeality, although somewhat limited and limiting, should neither be feared nor loved. It is neutral. To help you conceptualize, perhaps you might think of the planet Earth and its plane of consciousness as a "quarantine zone."

Thus placed in proper perspective, the earth plane of consciousness contains both elements of Good and Evil: the overall force of the one (Good) having created a home in which the people of God are to dwell, and the other (Evil) having constructed a prison for the products of self-pride and self-will to inhabit. The former is substantive beyond human comprehension; the latter is weakness incarnate. Although the former is found in MY One True and Only Real Creation (invisible to the naked eye), the other is found in its parody, "the false creation" (which is false because Satan cannot really create *ex nihilo* or *de novo* but can only caste shadows and confabulate illusions).

"The false creation" is really no *creation* at all but, rather, made of images from an erroneous mass consciousness that obscure MY One True and Only Reality from those who indulge their own self-pride and self-will. And, although iniquity masquerades

---

51 2 Corinthians 11:14, King James Version

itself to the physical senses as absolute reality, and though it is interpreted as such by human analytics and emotions, all impurity is excluded from MY Perfect World. It is excluded according to MY Spiritual Law, which forever keeps the sacred separate from the profane — as they should be kept separate.

When chords harmonious with understanding MY True Creation are struck from within, the thought products of a swollen mass consciousness (which many have come to accept as their own thoughts) groan and respond: "Physical events, circumstances, and experiences have shaped us. Because human beings are products of heredity, training, and physical environments, they are dependent on physicality for their own survival and well-being. Why, then, should we disbelieve our senses?"

Whenever you overlook your one true origin and only real being, you displace your faith. In other words, you transfer your faith from the Source of Infinite Supply, in Whom you live and move and have your real *being,* to the black star of self-will, which casts its shadow over the truth to those who "see through a glass darkly,"[52] such filter imposed by their own iniquity, which is responsible for their predisposition to sin.

To further confound spiritual sense and compound the difficulty of progressing from mere mortal thought to thoughts of ME and MY Absolute Reality is the trust that souls in dust place in material acquisition. The claim, "I am content with what I have," is looked on today as insanity by the majority of those who passively accept or actively pursue self-gratification as the only release from their weary lives. Unfortunately, believing that there is no debate involved, such as these have turned to materialism, technology, and false ideology to solve all their problems and answer all their questions.

---

52 1 Corinthians 13:12, King James Version

Currently, there is such a pervasive ignorant reverence for empty knowledge and arcane lore that, at best, you are asked to believe that you are no more than evolving psycho-socio-biophysical units. However, although that conclusion may be based on reams and reams of so-called evidence, analysis, and speculation (which further support themselves with more of the same), the foundation of such a belief is, in truth, the pit of self-will, its so-called evidence is the snare, and the credibility that you ascribe to it guarantees your continued fall (in a form of spiritual suicide) from MY Grace through a spiral of lowered consciousness toward the "second death."[53]

So that they not become eclipsed by the darkness of self-will, souls in the earth plane of consciousness need to cease from all mental movements and physical actions that have their basis in iniquity (which has its foundation in a reality set apart from MY Absolute Reality) as well as to work to replace selfishness with selflessness. Yet most so-called shepherds in your earthly world (or *worldly earth,* if you will) neither teach by word nor by example such values. In fact, they turn many further away from ME by their pedantic litanies and controlling behaviors, which are irrational to spiritual sense and offensive to ME.

Because religious leaders have chosen to feed themselves rather than their sheep, the flocks are now "required at their hand," fulfilling this prophecy given by MY Holy Spirit through MY Prophet Ezekiel:

> Woe to the shepherds who do feed themselves! MY flock was scattered upon all the face of the earth, and no one searched or sought after them. Therefore, you shepherds, hear MY Word: I AM AGAINST THE SHEPHERDS, AND I WILL REQUIRE MY FLOCK AT THEIR HAND, AND CAUSE THEM TO CEASE FROM FEEDING THE FLOCK:

---

53 Revelation 2:11; 20:6; 21:8, King James Version

BEHOLD, I, EVEN I, WILL BOTH SEARCH FOR MY SHEEP AND SEEK THEM OUT.[54]

Because of their own selfishness and willfulness, it is not given for most souls in dust to understand the timeliness of the previous citation. To them, MY Holy Bible has little, if any, practical application to contemporary daily living and their own pursuits of happiness. They are unaware that the matrix that holds MY Absolute Reality together is a spiritual network that transcends their own space, time, and motion. They are unaware that "True Man" (the incorporeal, corporate Man that I originally created) can only *really* exist (that is, live, move, and have consciousness) within a universe unaltered by iniquity and sin.

Seeing that the interpersonal reality of which I write is not corporeal but spiritual, the personal worlds of self-will through which most souls in dust move are very far from MY Kingdom (that is, "Heaven"). Yet you were told by Christ Jesus that MY Kingdom is "at hand"[55] (Hebrew "al yod"), or "right next to you." You need to understand that MY Kingdom is "side-by-side" with your world of appearances but beyond your dimensionality or full comprehension.

How can Heaven be both far and near?

Heaven is a state of consciousness which is far from those who act on their own iniquity as if it constituted MY Absolute Reality but near to those who daily look for the true meaning behind their earthly life. Thus, those who seek MY Absolute Reality ponder its Nature within their hearts in full accord with this clarification by Christ Jesus concerning Heaven's locality:

---

54 Paraphrased from the King James Version of Ezekiel 34:2, 6-7, and 10-11
55 Matthew 4:17, King James Version

The Kingdom of God does not come with observation. Neither shall you say: "Here it is!" nor "There it is!" For, let it be known, MY Kingdom is within you.[56]

Unfortunately, many end up believing that, because they have an aspect of ME within them, they have the totality of ME within them or that they themselves individually are ME or will become just like ME, none of which is true because not one of you alone can hold the Fullness of ME. One day I will fill and infuse MY Re-Creation with the Totality of MY Being (including the Fullness of MY Glory), but that is yet to come.[57]

Because the consciousness in Christ Jesus was (and forever will be) of MY Holy Spirit, MY Children who are still scattered throughout your world need no longer feel separate from one another nor separate from ME. MY Holy Spirit is ever-available to all who regularly submit their self-pride and self-will to MY Honor and MY Will by believing on MY Son and in his mission.

Rather than depending on religious leaders, it is MY Own Holy Spirit that now seeks MY Flock. And, because the "Fullness of that Spirit" (the meaning of which is slightly different from the "Totality of MY Being" and the "Fullness of MY Glory") has already been demonstrated on this Earth in and through Christ Jesus, then (in order for them to answer the call to return to a Heavenly Consciousness) earthborn souls must open their doors of thought to the Reality of the One True and Only Real God and commit themselves to the demonstration of the Nature of MY Absolute Reality within their own lives.

---

56 Paraphrased from the King James Version of Luke 17:20-21
57 1 Corinthians 15:22-28

For earthborn souls not to remain earthbound, they must lay down the sense that would assign the quality of infinitude to the material universe.[58] Contrary to what many of you believe, the material universe is not infinite: it is a closed system. Ask any physicist, and he or she will tell you that the physically-observable universe is finite. Also contrary to what many of you believe, the cause of chaos and matter is neither in nor of ME. The cause of matter is an effect of self-pride and self-will and, as such, cloaks the Fullness of MY Glory from your view. Right next to your world is the world of MY Light. One day, I hope you will remember what you *were,* and *are,* and will again *be* in that Light.

As soon as souls in dust begin to wrest themselves from the shadows that have been thrown over the original land I created, they will rediscover that faith, and not dirt, is the common ground and substance of MY Original and Yet-to-be-Revealed Perfect World. As you become increasingly aware of the difference between true life (immortality) and real death (mortality), you who search for MY Absolute Reality will find that, as you yield your own self-will to MY Will, all your earthly days will merge into a time of gradual awakening from spiritual stupor and slumber.

Restoration to an integrity that is found only within MY Original Creation (where the Fullness of MY Glory shines forth) requires souls in dust to reach the level of spiritual maturity where they are willing to accept responsibility for their own undoing and for their own actions based on their turning from ME. In other words, they must accept that they, of their own free will, rejected the immortality that was set before them in exchange for a sham and state of disgrace that they have since come to accept, and have been taught to look at, as their only real life.

---

58 In this work, "material universe" and "physical universe" are used synonymously.

Souls who are passing through the earth plane of consciousness (headed either in the direction of Heaven or in the direction of Hell) must look at themselves differently (which is to say, in a Spiritual Light) if they are to recognize the emptiness in mortal self-sufficiency and again find their true reality in MY Love as well as find their only real identity within MY Christ, — MY Messiah, — MY Y'shua H'Moshiach. I add "MY Messiah" and "MY Y'shua H'Moshiach" to help remind you that "MY Christ" is not just some impersonal and nebulous life force but God-in-the-flesh (that is, the substance of MY Supreme Being in earthly flesh), the fullness of the Godhead revealed bodily.[59]

Considering the spiritual fact that a soul is either a channel for Good, the expression of God, or a channel for Evil, the expression of self-pride and self-will, it becomes easier to see that a human being does not make or create thought but, instead, opens or closes the door of its consciousness to either the Source of Infinite Supply or the source of confusion and destruction. To which one each soul in dust becomes most receptive depends entirely on its angle of inclination, the direction in which it is traveling due to its intent. Consequently, if a soul's mind — that is, its attention — is stayed on ME, it will be opened to MY Spirit of Truth (which is to say, to MY Holy Spirit), whose very nature of progressive enfoldment expands the consciousness of each soul that yields to its good. Such yielding souls are then connected to countless others who are already so elevated in thought to MY Mind, "the Mind of Christ."[60] Again, you do not lose your identity and individuality but, rather, gain your one true identity and only real individuality by being in ME.

Because I do not hide from those who seek ME, if a fallen being in the earth plane of consciousness seeks ME with a determination equal in intensity to that of a creature who quests for water in the desert, then that soul shall be filled with MY

---

59 Colossians 2:9, King James Version
60 1 Corinthians 2:16, King James Version

Holy Spirit. However, if a soul in dust is solely interested in the mundane, not only will that soul not find ME during its earthly experience, the profane will have gained that much greater of a hold on its consciousness, and self-pride and self-will will be that much closer to claiming complete control over yet another victim of mortal sense.

The idea that human beings are neither authors nor originators of thought but vessels for it will be difficult for most to accept because its truth stabs at the very heart of self-pride and self-will. Hence, those who fancy themselves as creators will be the first to reject it. Such souls have forgotten that one cannot really be creative unless one serves as a channel for the Creator. In truth, thoughts or feelings written, painted, enacted, or scored in musical note can have no lasting quality about them unless they are first conceived by "the mind that is stayed on ME."[61] Creative works only live on if they bring praise to MY Holy Name. In contrast, all works engendered in self-pride, self-will, and self-ignorance remain temporal, finite, and limited since such works bring no praise to MY Holy Name and, therefore, no permanent accolades to their so-called authors. This is especially true for people in earthly societies that forever search for what is new under the Sun. In short, seeking celebrity on Earth (or anywhere else, for that matter) is a waste of your precious time, effort, and energy.

Although it is plain to enlightened spiritual sense that "there is no new thing under the Sun,"[62] mortal sense would have you believe that the human mind itself is "the be-all and the end-all" and, therefore, capable of doing and accomplishing what has never been done before. But it is exactly through such self-delusion that history repeats itself over and over and over again because earthbound souls continue to make the same mistakes as long as they are involved in vain pursuits. As a result, not

---

61 Paraphrased from the King James Version of Isaiah 26:3
62 Ecclesiastes 1:9, King James Version

having learned from their world of appearances and its pathos what they need to know (so they will never again look to self-pride and self-will and their seeming reality as a suitable habitation for the Fullness of MY Glory), such souls remain caught within the earth plane of consciousness. In other words, souls who make little or no spiritual progress during their earthly sojourns restrict themselves in their movements even after the expiration of their physical bodies.

Although mortal sense would interpret that human parturition brings forth newly-created souls, such a conclusion is based on appearances only. Hence, those-who-seek must be careful not to accept a physical heritage as their original reality (the one in which they have their true identity), for, if they do, they will limit themselves to that view. Because, in the final analysis, you are as you see yourselves, all souls in dust who wish to ascend to a Heavenly Consciousness must extricate themselves from a material history, even from that part of history which is yet to come to pass — *the history of the future!*

If the etymology of the word *immortal* is considered,[63] the truth of the statement, "Immortality cannot be found in mortality," proves itself. In other words, that which is "without death" cannot be found within that which *is* "death" (or subject to death). Yet, despite this self-evident truth, souls in dust insist on believing that their existence in earthly flesh is indicative of true life and that the cessation of such existence is indicative of real death. They have blinded themselves to the spiritual fact that mortality is death and immortality is life. They have blinded themselves to the truth that the nature of mortality is antithetical to the nature of immortality. Immortality is deathless life and, as such, it is not experienced through the physical senses. See?

---

63 The prefix *im-* means "without" and the base word *mortal*, from the Latin *mors*, means "death."

In effect, your hearts, darkened by your own iniquity, have brought MY Curse upon you to exist in the living death that you now call "life." Your iniquity has brought forward a sin nature, from which you must escape, if you are to return to your true spiritual origin and really live in ME.

For those of you who have incorporated reincarnation into your belief systems, I WILL neither refute nor support your views in this book. I AM simply going to remind you that the current moment is the most important moment in your life and that physical existence is not MY ideal state of being for you. Although you are not to fear or hate corporeality, you are not to aspire to it either, for such aspirations can go nowhere. And hoping to deal with your spiritual weaknesses, vulnerabilities, and infirmities in some distant, imagined, and romanticized future is possibly the worst kind of procrastination you can indulge. Such indulgence has dire consequences.

So, then, what is your hope?

Despite where you are, you may yet have hope in ME, for I can, and will, remove this curse of death from off your souls. In other words, it is within MY Purview to turn the curse of death (that is, mortality) into a blessing for you individually and collectively. To be sure, through MY Infinite Grace and Mercy and the forgiveness of your sins, you can be washed clean again, or "white as snow,"[64] by the shed blood of Jesus Christ.

Because only I can remove your iniquity, requisite for such cleansing is that you learn the follies of self-pride and self-will and, as a result, come to depend solely on ME as the only source of your *real* being (and your *being* real). You must die to your own self-pride and self-will in order that you might be born again to MY World.

---

64 Isaiah 1:18, King James Version

Today, souls in dust have simply allowed themselves to become captivated by the world of appearances and, therefore, to be held captive by the propagator of the various lusts associated with it. That is why so many are selfish and willful and are materially-focused rather than spiritually-centered. Strident in their claims to an individual's self-importance, such as these are unable to hear MY Still Small Voice[65] that cries out to them in the wilderness and desert wasteland you call "Earth."

This work is written for those who are unsure, yet want to know, just why it is they live in an upside down world, — why it is they feel as if they do not belong here, — and why it is that no matter how hard they have tried, they still cannot get themselves to fit comfortably into the societies of men and women who are "at home" on planet Earth. This work is written for those who are willing to give up much of what they have thought is true about themselves and others to help them know how it is they are really pilgrims, foreigners, and strangers on Earth, and to help them articulate that understanding for themselves that they might be strengthened as well as strengthen others.

This work is committed to the lost children of God, such souls scattered throughout corporeality, to serve as a reminder to them that, having the same origin, they are not really separate unless they wish to be. It is only as you individually and collectively break the common perception that holds you in awe of mortality that you are able to understand your divine purpose as the Created of God. Then, recognize your golden moments and seize the opportunity to repent of your own self-pride and self-will. There is still time to recapture your one true origin and only real being in and through Christ Jesus.

In Whom and through Whom do you have your one true origin and only real being?

---

65 1 Kings 19:12, King James Version

Your Sole Eternal Purpose for Being

Your sole eternal purpose for being is to bless MY Name at all times and in all ways and in everything you think, feel, desire, say, and do. Your love for ME and your gratitude to ME should motivate you to bless MY Name through all forms of communication. It is in blessing MY Name that you glorify, worship, praise, and exalt ME.

While you are on Earth, you can bless MY Name by premeditating every action you take to ensure that it will please ME — including every gesture and body movement you make, every word you think, and every request you pray. You can bless MY Name in every step of your foot, in every movement of your eye, and in every inclination of your ear.

The phrase "bless the Name of the Lord" does not mean just saying the word "God." It means saying the Name that is "above every name," which Name is Jesus, "none other name having been given under heaven whereby you must be saved."[66] And it does not matter if you spell or pronounce that Name Yeshua, Yahshua, Y'shua, Yehoshuah, Yoshua, Yesua, Joshua, Jeshua, Jesus, Yesus, Hesus, Isa, or Isi. While you are on Earth, I do not care what language you use to bless MY Name. Besides, when you get to Heaven, you will learn MY New Name[67] and how to properly pronounce it there.

While you are on Earth, you can also bless MY Name by specifically referencing ME to others as the sole source of your salvation, faith, hope, joy, spiritual gifts, provisions, rewards, and blessings.

---

66 Acts 4:12, King James Version
67 Revelation 3:12, King James Version

Paradoxically, as human beings you have come to expect blessings from ME, but you must learn that you were created to bless MY Name. And *desiring* to bless MY Name is also blessing MY Name. THIS IS YOUR SOLE ETERNAL PURPOSE FOR BEING! This is what you individually, collectively, and corporately will be doing throughout all eternity. Your eternal joy is forever derived from blessing MY Most Holy and Sovereign Name.

Blessing the Name of the Lord your God involves all movement and every gesture, all actions and every reaction, all words and every vocalization, all thinking and every thought, all feeling and every emotion, all desires and every hope, and all posturing and every attitude.

Blessing the Name of the Lord your God involves all elements of your consciousness and every fiber of your being.

Blessing the Name of the Lord your God involves all premeditation and every meditation.

Blessing the Name of the Lord your God is contemplative yet action-oriented.

YOUR SOLE ETERNAL PURPOSE IS NOT FULFILLED BY WHAT I DO FOR YOU BUT BY WHAT YOU DO FOR ME!

Your love for ME and gratitude to ME provide the impetus for what you do throughout all eternity. And what you will do throughout all eternity will continually glorify, praise, and exalt ME by blessing MY Name.

Blessing the Name of the Lord your God is your sole eternal purpose for being.

Eventually, blessing MY Name will become as natural to your spiritual being as breathing is to your physical being.

The statement, "I will bless the LORD at all times,"[68] does not mean that you will bless the word "LORD" but that you will bless the NAME of the LORD.

You can learn more about blessing MY Name by finding and studying the Bible passages that reference "blessing the LORD" and "blessing the name of the LORD." (Find out what a Bible concordance is and use it.)

While on Earth, strive to bless the Name of the Lord your God always, even during grief, *for example,* at the physical death of your loved ones, at the loss of your job, upon abandonment by your friends, at the loss of your reputation, at the loss of your possessions, and at the loss of your physical abilities and life.

Let your love for ME motivate you to bless the Name of the Lord your God at all times and in all ways and in everything you do. Ponder how this is possible for your own life and eternal state of being. You won't regret it!

Always remember, you can bless MY Name by seeking to please ME. And "seeking to please ME" means praying that MY Will is done in all ways and in all places throughout all eternity.

If you have not found out already, you will learn that it is a blessing to bless MY Name!

---

68 Psalm 34:1, King James Version

Chapter Four

Less than Stellar Views of Corporeality

Iniquity is "turning away from God," and *sin* is "action based on that turning." Iniquity brings with it the predisposition to sin, or inclination to "miss the mark." Although iniquity is a state of being that is invisible to the naked eye, and although I AM invisible to those who live in an iniquitous state of being, I know all that goes on in iniquity, the mortal state of being. However, although I know all that goes on in iniquity, please remember that I withdrew the Fiery Part of MY Being (the Fullness of MY Glory) from all who exist in corporeality lest their flesh perish in MY Presence (that is, become consumed by ME).

Although the corporeality with which you are familiar is a sign of an iniquitous state of being, it is only one sign. Nevertheless, it is a sign that is visible to your naked eye. Corporeality is actually only one stratum within *mortality,* which is defined here as "the state of separation from GOD" (that is, separation of the fallen created from their Creator). Although corporeality is a physical sign of one's iniquity, corporeality is not "iniquity-in-itself." Evil is "iniquity-in-itself." Mortality is real death, and not just the transition you call "death." As a state, mortality includes discarnates (souls who are not now in a human body) and incarnates (souls who are in a human body).

"Discarnates" include pre-incarnate souls who are yet to be born in human form as well as post-incarnate souls who have not gone on to MY Paradise either because they have made the conscious decision to refuse MY Offer for Salvation or because they have not yet made up their minds to accept or reject it. Post-incarnate souls who have made the conscious decision to refuse MY Offer for Salvation become "unclean spirits," "demons," "devils," or "evil spirits" (all four terms are synonymous not only in this work but also in MY Holy Bible). The existence of "unclean spirits," "demons," "devils," or "evil spirits" does not preclude the existence of devilish fallen angels, some of whom are already in chains awaiting MY Final Judgment[69] and some of whom are still roaming spiritual realms under the direction of MY Enemy and Adversary, Satan. Because Satan is MY Enemy and Adversary, he is also your Enemy and Adversary, unless you do his bidding — at which time he becomes your warden.

To those who wear a garment of flesh (that is, a physical body), the globe called "Earth" appears to be a part of MY Ultimate Reality when, in fact, it is apart from MY Ultimate Reality. The only exception is if you live in a state of Grace. The precise moment that you believe on MY Son and in his mission, MY Grace is actualized for you personally. Then, as long as you are walking in faith, you are living in MY Grace.

Your material orb is a "stepped down" version of MY World. It is a lower sphere superimposed on and over, but not above, the real world that I made, such world only visible and audible to spiritual sense and only experienced in your plane of consciousness by the peace, joy, and hope I impart to those who are saved. (The "saved" are those who have received and accepted salvation through MY only-begotten Son.)

King Solomon's views on corporeality, as stated in *Ecclesiastes,* are certainly less than stellar. Though he stated his position clearly, few have been able to understand just what it was he was saying concerning the world of appearances. A recurring theme in *Ecclesiastes* is "all is vanity" — not the "all" that is to be found in MY Absolute Reality but the "all" of physicality and the world-system that existed during King Solomon's time and continues to exist even today.

---

69 Jude, verse 6 (there are no chapters in Jude), King James Version

"All is vanity" could have been rendered "all is emptiness," "all is transitory," and "all is unsatisfactory." To be sure, King Solomon was not referring to MY Original Creation, which is complete and permanent and satisfying but to the emptiness of creature existence without ME. King Solomon's *Ecclesiastes* is bound to be misunderstood by students of MY Holy Bible who assume that the Earth and its fleshly inhabitants constitute MY Original Creation.

King Solomon saw the emptiness of earthly cycles and the vanity in human labor. He saw the foolishness of human knowledge and human cunning. He remained unsatisfied by the things of the world and its world-system, most of which he had at his disposal and command. Unfortunately, a life of unchosen poverty is responsible for a disadvantaged existence beyond malnutrition and a poor quality of living. Unchosen poverty prevents many from concluding that material abundance is unsatisfying. Concerning the human creature, whom many of you have mistakenly come to think of as MY Glory, King Solomon set the record straight. Solomon viewed the "sons of men" (the Biblical epithet for "human beings") as "beasts"[70] who are unable to "find out the world that God makes"[71] because it is concealed from them by their hardened hearts, blind eyes, and stoppered ears.

King Solomon saw (1) that, on your Earth, wickedness reigns instead of judgment, which is the ability to discern between good and evil, and (2) that iniquity stands in the place of righteousness. He saw the futility and frailty of human life, the so-called life that is really death incarnate (when MY Holy Spirit is not living within you). He distinguished between "the spirit of man that goes upward and the spirit of the beast that goes downward"[72] — which is to say, he knew the difference between

---

70 Ecclesiastes 3:18, King James Version

71 Paraphrased from the King James Version of Ecclesiastes 3:11 and 11:5

72 Paraphrased from the King James Version of Ecclesiastes 3:21

the Essence of the Invisible God and the spirit of this visible error, the adulterated state in which you currently exist. He understood that all days of the lives of souls in dust are spent "as a shadow."[73]

Yes, King Solomon felt that you should not refrain from enjoying the fruits of your honest labor. But Solomon was not the jaded epicure that many would have you believe. He knew that it was "better to go to the house of mourning than to go to the house of feasting."[74] He understood that true wisdom is found in penitence[75] and that only such wisdom enables one to behold, as well as be beheld in, MY Perfect World, the true sphere where you really live, and move, and have your being.[76]

King Solomon understood the sinful and fallen state of souls in dust.[77] Yet he saw that your "face" (that is, your *appearance*) could be changed back to one reflecting ME through an increased understanding of where you are, what you are, and who you are in MY Absolute Reality.[78]

King Solomon foresaw that death, or mortality (which includes, but is not limited to, corporeality), would have its Judgment Day — when souls who are committed to Evil will have no discharge from their transgressions.[79] He also saw that, until Judgment Day, evil souls in dust would have it on their hearts and in their minds to continue in iniquity, especially since their punishment was not executed speedily.[80]

---

73 Ecclesiastes 6:12, King James Version
74 Ecclesiastes 7:2, King James Version
75 Ecclesiastes 7:3, King James Version
76 Ecclesiastes 8:16-17, King James Version
77 Ecclesiastes 7:20-29, King James Version
78 Ecclesiastes 8:1, King James Version
79 Ecclesiastes 8:8, King James Version
80 Ecclesiastes 8:11, King James Version

However, despite the disparity and the "time and chance" (that is, mere circumstance) that happens to you,[81] King Solomon was confident that, in due time, righteous souls in dust would receive their reward — if they honor MY Will. He knew that you are appointed to corporeality so that you might exercise a newly-bestowed faith in ME and, thus, be revived to the immortal life that can be found only in ME.

Besides King Solomon, another king gave report of the emptiness of your Earth and the fullness of the world that is to be found in the *Here-Beyond*. That king is your Sovereign Lord, Jesus Christ — the One Sent[82] — the one who proved his words with works.[83] Yet, as with King Solomon's testimony, few have understood the witness of King Jesus concerning the contrast between the world in which you are currently located and the one originally created by ME.

MY Logos, Christ Jesus, said:

> You are from beneath; I AM from above: you are of this world; I am not of this world.[84]

> ... he that hates his life in this world shall keep his life unto life eternal.[85]

> If you were of the world, you would be loved; but because you are not of the world, I have chosen you out of the world; for this reason, the world hates you.[86]

> I came forth from the Father and am come into the

---

81 Ecclesiastes 9:11, King James Version

82 John 3:16-17 & 17:21: King James Version

83 Matthew 4:23-25; Mark 16:20: King James Version

84 Paraphrased from the King James Version of John 8:23

85 Paraphrased from the King James Version of John 12:25

86 Paraphrased from the King James Version of John 15:19

world; again, I leave this world and go to the Father.[87]

In the world, you shall have tribulation; but be of good cheer; I have overcome the world [including the unique challenges from its corrupt world-system].[88]

I do not pray for this world, but for them which the Father has given me; for they are His.[89]

And now I am no more in the world, but these [the ones I am leaving] are in the world, and I come to You. Holy Father, keep through Your Own Name those whom You have given me that they may be one, even as we are one.[90]

I have given them Your Word; and the world hates them, because they are not of the world, even as I am not of the world.[91]

I do not pray that You should take them out of the world, but that You should keep them from its Evil.[92]

O Righteous Father, the world has not known You, but I have known You.[93]

My Kingdom is not of this world [nor its corrupt world-system].[94]

---

87 Paraphrased from the King James Version of John 16:28
88 Paraphrased from the King James Version of John 16:33 [Brackets mine]
89 Paraphrased from the King James Version of John 17:9
90 Paraphrased from the King James Version of John 17:11 [Brackets mine]
91 Paraphrased from the King James Version of John 17:14
92 Paraphrased from the King James Version of John 17:15 [Brackets mine]
93 John 17:25, King James Version
94 Paraphrased from the King James Version of John 18:36 [Brackets mine]

If I, the one true and only real God, the *Summum Bonum,* had created the chaos and corruption of this world, Christ Jesus would not have found it necessary to testify that he was not of this world and that he had overcome it. He would not have referred to the Adversary (Satan, the father of all lies[95]) as "the prince of this world."[96] Nor, for that matter, would the Apostle Paul have referred to Satan as "the god of this world"[97] or "the prince of the power of [its] air."[98]

Ask yourselves these three questions: (1) Would it be necessary to overcome your world if "carnal mind,"[99] your world's directing force, were *of*— or *from* — your Creator? (2) If your world were God's unadulterated, original creation, would St. James have stated that "friendship with the world is enmity with God"?[100] Finally, (3) would this world be destined to be removed — or "pass away"[101] — if it were the grand edifice of God? Children of God, you deceive yourselves if you believe that your Creator resides within mortality or its substratum of corporeality. Is it not written that no human being has seen the face (or appearance) of God and lived?[102] Your Creator cannot be seen face-to-face in dust. Yes, "the Word *was* made flesh,"[103] but the Word was also crucified in the flesh that you might be freed from the chains of iniquity and its carnal mind. So, too, are you to crucify your own flesh.[104]

To be sure, your corrupt "world-system" plays itself out in a world that is unreal, illusory, and not part of the world that I

---

95   John 8:44, King James Version
96   John 12:31, King James Version
97   2 Corinthians 4:4, King James Version
98   Ephesians 2:2, King James Version
99   Romans 8:6-7, King James Version
100   James 4:4, King James Version
101   Revelation 21:1, King James Version
102   Exodus 33:20; Isaiah 6:5
103   John 1:14, King James Version
104   Galatians 2:20 & 5:24, King James Version

originally created:

> Love not the world, neither the things that are in the
> world. If any person loves this world, the love of the
> Father is not in that person. For all that is in this
> world, the lust of the flesh [carnal desire], and the
> lust of the eyes [greed], and the pride of life
> [willfulness], is not of the Father, but is of this
> world.[105]

> Marvel not, my brothers and sisters, if this world
> hates you.[106]

> Greater is He in you, than he [Satan] that is in the
> world.[107]

> And we know that we are of God, and the whole
> world lies in wickedness.[108]

Here, it is important to point out that the declaration, "the whole
world lies in wickedness," might also be rendered from the
Greek as "the whole world is under the control of the Evil One,"
the same wicked being whose works Christ Jesus came to
"destroy" or "undo."[109] Thus, you need to, first, undo the works
of this world from your hearts that you might be found ready to
be received into MY World: (1) the world where all are one and
(2) the only *absolutely* real world.

The human body that you have is not the complete image and
perfect likeness of God. That is why you must learn to tame,
discipline, and overcome the creature in whose sin body you

---

105 Paraphrased from the King James Version of 1 John 2:15-16 [Brackets
     mine]
106 1 John 3:13, King James Version
107 1 John 4:4, King James Version
108 Paraphrased from the King James Version of 1 John 5:19 [Brackets
     mine]
109 1 John 3:8, King James Version

have come to reside and with whom you have come to falsely identify as your absolute reality. Please do not misinterpret these statements to mean that I want you to hate the animal kingdom, corporeality, or the material universe. I just want you to understand that the human body is an appearance quite different from the reflection of God and that human analytics and emotions do not permit you to fully comprehend MY Absolute Reality.

The human body is animated matter. It is subject to debilitation, deterioration, death, and decay. It is perishable. It is corruptible. It comes from dust and goes to dust. Because it is a biophysical machine, it can never be in a state of perpetual harmony — such state would be against MY decrees as well as contrary to the laws of physical nature.

Although many have sought to sustain the existence of their physical bodies, there have been — and always will be — limits to longevity within the earth plane for as long as corporeality exists. There must be limits. Corporeal bodies cannot become heavenly bodies. Physical creatures cannot become the metaphysical stars of God. After his death and resurrection (but before his ascension into Heaven), Christ Jesus showed himself in corporeal form to his disciples to help ensure that they not mistake him for a shade, spirit, or ghost and to prove to them, through his resurrected physical body, that he had power over the grave. Although the time will come when I translate and glorify your bodies, physicality can never be spiritualized. Physicality cannot be made into something that it is not. Those who labor under the premise that physicality can be spiritualized have their hopes displaced; they are deluding themselves. Your purpose for being in this world is not to immortalize the human bodies that you carry about but to re-immortalize your souls.[110]

---

110 Although all souls are eternal, in keeping with the language of this book, they are either in an *immortal* state of being (saved and restored) or in a *mortal* state of being (fallen and unsaved).

This means that your purpose is to transubstantiate your souls by allowing your faith in Jesus Christ to be tried, purged, and refined within the bounds of your world, which — except for MY Grace, MY Mercy, and MY Holy Spirit — is completely set apart from ME.

Souls in dust who are without Jesus Christ in their hearts are subject to control by carnal mind, your world's directing force. Sad to say, such souls are no more and no less than how they see themselves. Since they individually believe that they have no more than a physical identity and earthly personality, they condemn themselves to their own conclusions. Viewed in this way, all they can hope to be are physical beings subject to the limitations and lack associated with corporeal existence. In other words, they are earthly creatures controlled by the events of time and chance. They are beasts. They are toilers. And they are spoilers.

For any who would advance spiritually, it is important to put the human body in proper perspective so they are not fooled into believing (1) that a comely physique or an earthly form free from structural anomaly is an infallible witness of MY Love and (2) that physical unattractiveness or deformity is evidence of a just recompense for intergenerational or personal sin. It should be understood, first and foremost, that in MY Absolute Reality a perfect body is one that is free from iniquity and sin and, conversely, an imperfect body is darkened by transgressions against MY Will. It is legitimate to debate whether freedom from iniquity and sin — or, on the other hand, enslavement to iniquity and sin — is always expressed by the condition of one's physical being. Suffice it to say at this point, the physical body has never been an infallible testator of the presence or absence of MY Holy Spirit within a soul — unless, of course, the life that it holds is given up unreservedly in service to others or, on the other hand, given up intentionally to rebel against ME and sow discord. In either case, the physical body is not the "activator" of such works.

Physically speaking, what you have to work with on Earth is not much. Though the physical body is more plastic than most of humankind might think, it is still subject to debilitation, deterioration, death, and decay. Even though Christ Jesus healed multitudes, those healed were still subjected to other ills of the flesh. Lazarus' physical body was only raised up from putrefaction[111] to prove that Jesus Christ has divine power over all things. The raising of Lazarus was not for all time. It was not permanent. Later, the soul of Lazarus was to again pass from his physical body (as, indeed, you all must pass from yours).

When you pass from your mortal coil, what it is you pass on to depends on what you have done while in your earthly flesh.

If you have not mastered the flesh (meaning, if carnal mind is still master over you by the time you leave corporeality), then you are confined to an incorporeal substratum of mortality. I could say more about what this specific substratum entails, but it would prevent many of you from accepting the gist of what I AM trying to teach you through this book. I AM not trying to withhold "secret" information from you, I AM just trying to maximize the potential of this book to influence.

If you have mastered the flesh (meaning, if carnal mind is no longer master over you by the time you leave corporeality), then you rise above mortality and are returned to the Place where I LIVE, AND MOVE, AND HAVE MY SUPREME BEING. You are not only free to pass on to other experiences but free to pass over to the "the other side" of life through the portal made for you by the Lamb of God's blood sacrifice. Unfortunately, however, for most souls in dust, corporeality is a brothel where they further prostitute themselves, their ideals, their spiritual goals, and their divine purpose. These sell their true selves for a few moments of earthly pleasure.

---

111   John 11:39-44

To be sure, you have been appointed to corporeality that you might receive life — which is to say, have an opportunity to be saved by accepting MY Plan of Salvation.

The True Man and Perfect World I originally created cannot be seen through a retina, heard via a tympanic membrane, or felt by a nerve ending. Why? They are incorporeal — which is to say, they are beyond the realm of your current reality. What you witness in dust is a perversion (that is, an alteration or refraction) of the Glory of God. That perversion includes your own physical forms. (That DNA diffracts, or bends, light provides you with an excellent metaphor. Its substance cannot perfectly reflect the pure Light of God.) It is no accident that MY Holy Bible records Adam and Eve's expulsion from the Garden of MY Heavenly Consciousness in these terms:

> So God drove out the man; and God placed Cherubs at the east of the garden of Eden, and a flaming sword which turned every way, to prevent their access to the Tree of Life.[112]

Even the most conservative of literalists would hesitate to define the "flaming sword" in the above passage as a physical object. It is clearly an incorporeal object, and its Biblical meaning is metaphysical (and not figurative).

Speaking of corporeal versus incorporeal, souls in dust need to be reminded that the most important healing is spiritual, not physical. It is only the healing of your souls that brings restoration to your original state, or the place you were meant by ME to *be*. It is only the healing of your souls that can rejoin you to the family borne of MY Love. To be sure, the healing of your physical bodies may be instrumental in your recognition of MY Sovereignty over all things, but it is only through a true ego inversion (a "soular" event), which entails involution from the

---

112   Paraphrased from the King James Version of Genesis 3:24

spiritual darkness of self-will to MY Spiritual Light, that you are really revived and revivified. Why do you need such a healing? Souls in the earth plane of consciousness are shards broken from the original vessel that I, your Potter, made. They are parts scattered from their Creator's True Man (again capitalized to keep distinct from human beings).

Then, it should stand to spiritual reason (a process of the heart and not the head) that healing of the physical body through spiritual means may be withheld by ME if the healing would be detrimental to the advancement of a soul — that is, if it would prolong, or keep, a soul from being returned to ME completely. *For example,* Job was permitted to suffer as long as he pictured a false image of himself; it was only when he repented (that is, changed his mind) and was willing to accept and acknowledge that I AM Supreme Being during bad times as well as during good times that things began to change for him. He passed his test. Are you passing yours?

It is important for you to recognize that there is a plan greater than what you see or think you see. Why is it important? If you admit to a power higher than yourselves — a power that knows more than you know — you open yourselves up to the things of God and allow yourselves to be included within them. Then, you yield yourselves up to ME in a way that sets you apart from corporeality as you ascend toward MY Absolute Reality to rejoin MY Original Creation.

Those who think of healing only in terms of healing the physical body greatly limit their own sense and scope of the relationship of the created to their Creator. They fail to see the magnitude of the breach by humankind, which is a fallen race lost in an image of spiritual darkness. King David wrote:

> O God, You have cast us off. You have scattered us. You have been displeased. O turn Yourself to us again. You have made the earth to tremble. You have

broken it. Heal the breaches thereof, for it shakes. You have shown Your people hard things. You have made us drink the wine of astonishment.[113]

The human creature is not the Creator's original created. The physical form that you now have is not the form I originally created for you. Though substantive, your original form had diaphanous and translucent qualities. Its qualitative nature reflected MY Glory. Your original form cannot adequately be described in human terms. However, when MY Son returns for his Redeemed, your mortal bodies will then be translated and re-glorified.[114] You will then see for yourselves that you will be like him.[115] (You can't be him, but you can be "like" him — which is to say, "similar in appearance" to him.)

The danger of thinking of healing only in terms of the physical body is that you gloss over your most spiritually-glaring mistake, which is your errancy from ME. And, though the majority in your world may deny original sin from here to kingdom come, they will never be able to disprove the fact that souls in dust have been — and most still are — scattered from ME. Surely, that you are so well acquainted with "hard things" (not only things difficult but things corporeal) is a result of your transgressing MY Will. Lost souls, as mortals, further demonstrate that they have transgressed MY Will by becoming drunk with the wine of their love for a false self, which is their mistaken identity.

In its highest and truest sense, healing *is* salvation. To be so healed is to be saved from the abyss of selfishness, a very real pit of darkness. To be so healed is to be recalled by ME and, thus, re-membered to the Body of MY Christ. To be so healed is to be washed clean and raised up white as snow, like some holy thing. To be so healed is to dwell completely and wholly within ME,

---

113 Paraphrased from the King James Version of Psalm 60:1-3
114 1 Thessalonians 4:16-17
115 1 John 3:2

safe evermore.

Whenever primary emphasis is placed on the healing of physical bodies instead of the healing of sin-sick souls, mortals look away from the main purpose for MY Son having been sent to them. That is not to say they cannot pray expectantly to ME for release from physical affliction. The truth of the statement, "The effectual fervent prayer of a righteous person avails much,"[116] still holds true today. And that is not to say they cannot stay the plague from their door by right thinking, affirming right, and pleading the shed blood of Jesus Christ. Rather, that is to say that souls in dust need to understand just who they were meant to be and just how it is they have now come to be found in corporeality. They need to understand that the most important healing is the healing of their souls — individually, collectively, and corporately.

There are two categories of healing referred to in Scripture that I will now label with the terms "collective" and "individual." "Collective" refers to the restoration of souls to MY World and "individual" refers to the attestation of MY Truth of Being by proofs practical to corporeal experience, including the healing of physical bodies. Collective healing is spoken of conceptually in MY Holy Bible by these terms: "renewal," "deliverance," "binding up," "being built up," "repairing the breach," "revival," "salvation," "the taking away of iniquity," "returning to God," "coming together as members of the Body of Christ," and "the healing of the nations" (*nations,* in the language of MY Holy Bible, refers to Gentiles, or non-Jews).

In other words, the Holy Bible makes it plain to spiritual sense that there are divisions among mankind, and divisions between mankind and God, all of which need to be healed. What kind of divisions? Real defects of the heart, the kind that prevents the giving of yourselves in service to God and to others. Seen in this

116   James 5:16, King James Version

way, the healing of physical bodies by spiritual means is placed in proper perspective: The healing must work toward God's ends and not your own.

Hence, for the healing of a physical body to take place by spiritual means, such healing must result from, or contribute to, the recognition by souls in dust that I AM All-Sovereign. With regard to healing of the physical body, then, believers in Christian healing should be sure to keep these two things in mind: The healing of the physical body is not the primary healing. And it is neither MY Purpose nor MY Will to amplify the importance of earthly flesh, a substance that can never manifest nor reflect MY Glorious Light without temporary transfiguration or permanent translation.

The plane of existence in which immortals live is high above your orb of materiality. Its heavens are the fiery waters of God. Its earth is the common ground of faith in God. There, I AM the center and circumference of its Universe. There, the entirety of Heaven is MY Throne.[117] There, channels of purity walk in the Garden of MY Heavenly Consciousness and are bathed in the silver and golden rays of MY Light. There, souls reflect ME in all that they do. There, redeemed souls altogether constitute True Man, who is the only one made in MY Image and Likeness and found in the Body of MY Christ.

Are there stars in MY Heavens? Yes, they are the ascendants of Jesus Christ, souls aflame with MY Glory. They are virginal spirits and pure channels of MY Love. What do they look like? Like etheric snowflakes, each is unique. Multifaceted, everyone reflects their Creator in various ways. Stellated, each is six-pointed and yet is a point within a galaxy of stars. Just how many stars are there? Myriads upon myriads of stars comprise MY infinite and eternal Spiritual Universe (in contrast, the physical universe is a closed system and, therefore, finite and temporal).

---

117   Isaiah 66:1; Matthew 5:34, 23:22; & Acts 7:49: King James Version

Are the stars in MY Heavens male and female? No, male and female are corporeal frames of reference. The stars in MY Heavens are not gendered beings. "They are like angels, who neither marry nor are given in marriage."[118]

The immortals in Heaven do great honor to their Creator, I WHO AM LIFE-IN-ITSELF. As notes within creation's lay and words of its song, they praise ME. They sing out in profound humility: "Glory be to God in the highest!"[119] and "Worthy is the Lamb of God!"[120] and "Blessing, and honor, and glory, and power be unto Him — Who Sets Within All of Heaven, His Throne!"[121] and "The LORD is our Faithful Sovereign King!"[122] They never tire in their praise of ME. They rejoice in their wholeness, their completeness, and their peace. No longer scattered, they have finally come to hold their God above themselves individually, collectively, and corporately. These are the heavenly bodies whose lives revolve around ME. These are MY celestial beings, the spheres of God, and MY lights. These are MY real stars.

Read now, with understanding, the following verses from the Apostle Paul [amplified in brackets]:[123]

35. But someone will say: "How are the dead raised up? And in what body will they be found?"

36. You fool, that which you sow is not quickened except it die:

---

118 Paraphrased from the King James Version of Matthew 22:30 and Mark 12:25
119 Luke 2:14, King James Version
120 Revelation 5:12, King James Version
121 Revelation 5:13, King James Version
122 Deuteronomy 7:9; Psalm 36:5, 89:5; Isaiah 25:1, 49:7; 1 Corinthians 1:9; 2 Thessalonians 3:3; & Revelation 1:5: King James Version
123 Paraphrased from the King James Version of 1 Corinthians 15:35-55 [Brackets mine]

37. And concerning that which you sow you are not planting the body that it will become, but you sow bare grain, as if it were wheat (or some other grain):

38. But God gives it a body as it pleases Him, and to every seed its own [new] body.

39. All flesh is not the same flesh since there is one kind of flesh of men, another flesh of beasts, another of fishes, and another of birds.

40. There are also celestial [heavenly] bodies, and terrestrial [corporeal] bodies: but the glory of the celestial is one, and the glory of the terrestrial is another.

41. There is one glory of the Sun, and another glory of the moon, and another glory of the stars: for one star differs from another star in glory.

42. So also is the resurrection of the dead. The seed is sown in corruption; but it is raised in incorruption:

43. It is sown in dishonor; it is raised in glory: it is sown in weakness; it is raised in power:

44. It is sown a natural body; it is raised a spiritual body. Thus, there is a natural body, and there is a spiritual body.

45. And so it is written: "The first man Adam was made a living soul; the last Adam [Jesus Christ] was made a quickening spirit."

46. However, the immortal body [that you will receive] was not first, but the natural body was first and afterward that which is spiritual is formed.

47. The first man [Adam] is of the earth — in other words, earthly [a physical being]: the second man [Jesus Christ] is the Lord from Heaven [a spiritual being].

48. As is the nature of the earthly, such are they also that are earthly: and as is the heavenly, such are they also that are heavenly.

49. And as we have borne the image of the earthly, we shall also bear the image of the heavenly.

50. Now this I say, brothers and sisters, that your flesh and blood [the physical body] cannot inherit the Kingdom of God; neither does corruption inherit incorruption.

51. Behold, I show you a mystery; we shall not all sleep, but we shall all be changed [translated],

52. In a moment, in the twinkling of an eye, at the last trump [when Jesus Christ returns for us]: for, indeed, the trumpet will sound, and the dead shall be raised incorruptible, and we shall be changed [corporeal or natural bodies shall be permanently translated into incorporeal or spiritual bodies].

53. For this corruptible must put on incorruption, and this mortal must put on immortality.

54. So, when this corruptible shall have put on incorruption, and this mortal shall have put on immortality, then shall be brought to pass the saying that is written: "Death is swallowed up in victory."

55. O death, where is your sting? O grave, where is your victory?

Pleroma is a wonderfully useful Greek word that helps describe the state of eternal redemption. It transcribes to the penitent heart an understanding of the oneness, and "allness," of the Creator. When *pleroma* is used as subject, it means "that-which-fills" and when it is used as object, it means "that-which-is-filled." So, *pleroma* may be used effectively to describe the unity that is to be found in ME, which unity caused Christ Jesus to say:

"I and MY Father are one"[124] and "Holy Father, keep through YOUR own Name those whom YOU have given me, that they may be one, even as we are one."[125]

This is the same unity that prompted the Apostle Paul to use *pleroma* to denote MY Infilling the Church of God in Christ (not a religious denomination but a spiritual corpus), "which is his Body, the fullness *[pleroma]* of Him that fills *[pleromizes]* All-in-all"[126] and to denote the advancement of faithful souls to immortality: "Until we come in the unity of the faith, and of the knowledge of the Son of God, to the Perfect Man, to the measure of the stature of the fullness *[pleroma]* of Christ."[127] (In a spiritual sense, *pleroma* as subject is God the Father and *pleroma* as object is the Body of His Christ.) *Pleroma* especially symbolizes the nature of the Church of God in Christ in MY Absolute Reality, which, though corporate, is incorporeal.

Where is the *pleroma* of which I now write? Where is MY Fullness? It is on MY Right Hand, which is to say, it is within ME. Thus unlocked to spiritual sense for those who will hear, is the meaning of the following passages:

> The LORD [the Father] said unto my Lord [the Son]: SIT AT MY RIGHT HAND, UNTIL I MAKE YOUR ENEMIES YOUR FOOTSTOOL.[128]

> Jesus said: "Hereafter you shall see the Son of Man sitting on the right hand of power and coming in the clouds of Heaven."[129]

---

124 John 10:30, King James Version
125 Paraphrased from the King James Version of John 17:11
126 Paraphrased from the King James Version of Ephesians 1:23 [Brackets mine]
127 Paraphrased from the King James Version of Ephesians 4:13
128 Paraphrased from the King James Version of Psalm 110:1 [Brackets mine]
129 Paraphrased from the King James Version of Matthew 26:64

So, then, after the Lord [Jesus] had spoken to them, he was received up into Heaven, and sat on the right hand of God [the Father].[130]

But he [Stephen], being full of the Holy Ghost, looked steadfastly into Heaven, and saw the glory of God, and Jesus standing on the right hand of God, and said: "Behold I see the heavens opened, and the Son of Man standing on the right hand of God [the Father].[131]

If you are really risen with Christ, then seek those things which are above, where Christ sits on the right hand of God [the Father].[132]

. . . let us run with patience the race that is set before us, looking unto Jesus, the author and finisher of our faith, who, for the joy that was set before him, endured the cross, despising its shame, and is now set down at the right hand of the throne of God [the Father].[133]

To be *at* (or *on*) "the right hand of God" should not be misinterpreted. Spiritual truths are most often presented to you in terms and images that you can understand. Souls who sit at MY Right Hand are actually in MY Heavens, set as stars within the Consciousness of Christ Jesus. They are located within ME, as opposed to those who are located outside of, or apart from, ME — who are, in keeping with the language of MY Holy Bible, on MY "left hand." To be sure, the Fullness of MY Glory is hidden from those on MY Left Hand while I AM always evident

---

130 Paraphrased from the King James Version of Mark 16:19 [Brackets mine]

131 Paraphrased from the King James Version of Acts 7:55-56 [Brackets mine]

132 Paraphrased from the King James Version of Colossians 3:1 [Brackets mine]

133 Paraphrased from the King James Version of Hebrews 12:1-2

to those on MY Right Hand (which is to say, those who are in MY Grace and Glory). And I stay veiled to those on MY Left Hand until their individual hearts break and they prove themselves ready to receive ME by believing on MY Son and in his mission. When all who will submit themselves to the authority of Jesus Christ are under his feet, they will then be infused with Christ as the "all" of MY *All-in-all*.[134]

Having received eternal redemption, souls who have been returned to immortality are all monarchs (or "kings" in the language of MY Holy Bible). In what way? They each have received the crown of Life from ME. In other words, they wear MY Glory, the Brightness of MY Being. In short, immortality is MY Kingdom. It is MY Heaven and MY Throne. It is the place where all of MY Created live, and move, and have their being. It is, indeed, on the other side of your corporeality yet right next to you and within you.

Souls who are not immortal are mortal. However, depending on their individual degrees of reflectance or nonreflectance of ME, and their individual degrees of willingness or unwillingness to learn and to help others to learn, mortals are found in different strata within the state of mortality. (1) There are those who are advancing toward the *Godhead;* [135] these are the ones who are being received into the Fullness of MY Glory. (2) There are those who are falling farther from ME due to the faith they place in a false self and untrue self-identity. And (3) there are those who are past redemption — which is to say, beyond reclamation for having forfeited their spiritual energies to the Evil One. These are the "wandering stars to whom is reserved the blackness of darkness forever."[136]

---

134 1 Corinthians 15:28, King James Version
135 Acts 17:29, Romans 1:20, & Colossians 2:9: King James Version
136 Paraphrased from the King James Version of Jude, verse 13 (there are no chapters in Jude)

The object lesson to be learned in corporeality by souls aspiring to Heaven is not how to re-immortalize the human body, or how to have a "cellular awakening" but how to re-immortalize the soul. Great gains may be made in repurification (that is, sanctification) when souls in dust cease to worry about the fate of their temporal personal identities (which is to say, the corporeal images they bear) and the supposed status or reputation of their earthly visages. It is possible for souls in dust to become perfect by loving like their Master, Jesus Christ. He taught you how to love perfectly in forgiving others and by finding and feeding scattered sheep. To do this, you need to learn how to become "other-worldly" without becoming useless on Earth. (Becoming spiritually-minded does not mean becoming vapid or vacuous.)

Except for those who suffer for the sake of suffering, suffering is the mark of perfection for souls in dust:

1. Forasmuch then as Christ has suffered for us in the flesh, arm yourselves likewise with the same mind: for they who have suffered in the flesh have ceased from sin:

2. That they no longer should live their remaining time in the flesh to the lusts common to mankind but to the Will of God.[137]

Perfect beings are those who have ceased from sin, are unafraid of evil, and are at peace with God, with themselves, and with others. Every perfect being loves the Creator and all of the Creator's Offspring without measure. Each perfect being reflects MY Infinite Mercy by forgiving the hateful, the spiteful, and the abusive. Souls who have this mark of perfection cannot be touched by evil (though they may be tempted by it or injured by channels who subconsciously, unconsciously, or consciously yield to evil). These souls are sealed by ME — which is to say, found acceptable by ME. They are fully prepared to be received

---

137   Paraphrased from the King James Version of 1 Peter 4:1-2

into MY Kingdom through the spirit of adoption (which spirit is MY Grace, or "unmerited favor").

The length of your corporeal sojourn and the difficulties of your past and future experiences should not concern you. What should concern you is whether or not you are living for ME and for your fellow pilgrims here and now.

As souls in dust reflect more and more of ME, they become re-spiritualized in MY Light and their form begins to take shape in MY World. Here, there is a seeming paradox: Then, having obtained a foothold in MY Kingdom, they are both here and there (though they are farther from ME than those who are altogether in ME) until they are sufficiently advanced in ME to be one with ME completely.

As they progress, souls advance from death (unconscious of Jesus Christ) to sleep (subconscious awareness of Jesus Christ) to increasing wakefulness (conscious awareness of the presence of Jesus Christ in their lives) to true life (complete communion, companionship, and intimacy with ME through Jesus Christ).

For those of you who like to look in a mirror, it is easier to change appearances when you are dealing with the reflection. What does that mean? Though images in corporeality may change, and such images and forms may be influenced positively or negatively by physical activity — as well as by thoughts, emotions, and attitudes — souls in dust do not really change in appearance (in substance or in form) until they exchange the false picture they have of themselves (in which there is no reflection but only shadow) for their true image in God.

So, then, why are there less than stellar views of corporeality?

Chapter Five

The Control Gene

Lucifer fell because of arrogance born of narcissism (self-pride) and willfulness (self-will).[138] This arrogance precipitated his fight with ME for control of MY Creation. In the language of MY Holy Bible, control is "authority," "power," and "dominion." Satan sought, and still seeks, to wrest authority from ME, to seize all power in MY Creation, and to have all dominion over MY Creation. Although doomed to failure at its inception, Satan has been methodical in his takeover of various spiritual realms and regions. Nevertheless, I AM still Sole Sovereign even though I have granted Satan access to specific areas for the purpose of allowing MY Plan of Salvation to play out to rescue those who will return to ME.

If I were writing this book one hundred years ago, I would have restricted MYSELF to metaphors understandable at that time. If I were to write this book one hundred years from now, I would use metaphors that make the most sense to people of that future day. For this reason, I have entitled this chapter "The Control Gene" since DNA, genes, and viruses are understandable to many in your day. This is the reason I use them as metaphors to help describe the pandemic alterations that have taken place in areas of MY Creation that have fallen from their original state.

When Satan fell, he infected a number of created beings with the virus of control (that is, the desire for authority, power, and dominion). Metaphorically speaking, the virus of control is a retrovirus that inserts itself into the spiritual DNA of created beings who, at the precise moment that they indulge self-pride and self-will, become susceptible to its continued attack.

---

138 All arrogance is born of self-pride and self-will.

Infection from the control gene changed the predisposition of created beings from their original ascendant nature in ME to a selfish and prideful fallen nature set apart from ME.

Created beings susceptible to the attack of the virus of control were those who, although originally created complete and perfect, chose to indulge self-pride and self-will. Because arrogant traits and characteristics are foreign to ME and MY Creation, those beings who indulged such objectionable characteristics were excluded, ejected, and separated from MY Creation instantaneously. The choice was theirs to fall from their original, created state of being. I freely gave all created beings the gift of personal free will to do with as they would. To be sure, in this way — but not the only way — humanity is still made in MY Image and Likeness: MY Created have free will just like I have Free Will.

There are three reasons why I gave created beings the gift of free will. First, it is part of MY Nature to be generous and giving. There is no greater gift that I could give to created beings than the gift of free will. Second, I deserve to be worshiped because I AM WHO I AM. Worship from people who are captives, prisoners, or robots is really not worship at all. Forced obedience to ME brings ME no true honor, glory, or praise. I seek people to worship ME in spirit and in truth[139] because it is their choice to do so. Third, if the truth be told (and it is being told here), I want a Companion, someone with whom I can share MY Life. The "someone" of whom I write is not one soul, but One Person, or "True Man," collectively represented in the beginning by "Adam," and corporately represented in the end by the Body of Christ.

For those of you who tend to think in human terms only, I add this disclaimer plus affirmation: I do not desire to have sexual intercourse with MY Companion. Remember, in Heaven you are

---

139   John 4:23, King James Version

gender neutral, just as I AM gender neutral. Instead, I want to interface with MY Companion in mutual respect, mutual adoration, and free-will communion (that is, heavenly fellowship). In this way would you, collectively and corporately speaking, be a Companion to ME, and in this way would I be a Companion to you.

Yes, Adam was an individual human being, but "Adam" also represents the One Person, or "True Man," that I originally created to be MY Companion. MY Christ alone could not be that "someone" because "MY Christ" (MY Spoken Word or Logos) *is* ME. MY Spirit could not be that "someone" because "MY Spirit" *is* ME, too. However, redeemed souls as members of the Body of MY Christ, with Jesus Christ as the Body's Head, thus infused with MY Life through Christ, make not only a suitable Habitation for ME but also a suitable Companion for ME as well. When all things are subdued by Christ, I will then infuse all with MY ALL. (I AM the "All" and the Christ-filled Universe is the "all" in the phrase "All-in-all"[140]). After MY Infusion, Creator and Created will be inseparable as Lover and Beloved. This is why I told you that "human eye has not seen, and human ear has not heard, what I have prepared for those who love ME and wait upon ME."[141]

To those who would debate whether the Church of Christ or the Nation of Israel is MY Bride, let ME say this: Collectively and corporately, all the re-created beings within MY Creation constitute MY Eternal Companion. The Gentile-based Church of God in Christ (not a religious denomination) was grafted onto the Root[142] and the Trunk (that is, the Main Branch[143]) of MY Tree of Life after MY Jews (who are *still* MINE) rejected MY only-begotten Son, Y'shua H'Moshiach, as their promised

---

140   1 Corinthians 15:28, King James Version
141   Paraphrased from the King James Version of 1 Corinthians 2:9 and Isaiah 64:4
142   Romans 11:16-24, King James Version
143   Isaiah 11:1 & Romans 15:12: King James Version

Messiah. When the Church Age draws to a close, the Nation of Israel will then be re-grafted onto the very same Trunk from which it was cut (that is, from which it severed itself). Because the grafts of which I write are seamless, ultimately there will be no distinction in MY Creation as to who was first and who was second or even third — which is to say: first, MY Jews were grafted onto MY Root and Trunk; second, MY Christian Gentiles were grafted; and, third, MY Jews will be re-grafted again.[144]

It is written:

> The first man Adam was made a living soul; the last Adam [Jesus Christ] was made a quickening spirit.[145]

As a "quickening spirit," Jesus Christ reinvigorates, revitalizes, and re-creates those who fell from MY Original Creation. MY Logos has always been the Creative Part of ME. It should make spiritual sense to you, then, that MY Logos "re-creates" as well:

> {1} In the beginning was MY Logos (MY Spoken Word) and MY Logos was with God, and MY Logos was God. {2} The same was in the beginning with God. {3} All things were made by MY Logos; and without MY Logos was not anything made that was made. {4} In MY Logos was Life; and the Life was the Light of all created beings. {5} And the Light did shine in darkness, but the darkness could not comprehend the Light coming from MY Logos.[146]

> {11} MY Logos came unto his own [as the Messiah of the Jews], and his own [the Jews] received him not [that is, they did not accept him as their

---

144   Romans, Chapter 11, King James Version
145   Paraphrased from the King James Version of 1 Corinthians 15:45 [Brackets mine]
146   Paraphrased from the King James Version of John 1:1-5 [Brackets mine]

promised Messiah]. {12} But as many [Gentiles] as received him, to them gave MY Logos power to become the re-born of God, even to them that believe on his name [the Name of MY Logos, or Spoken Word, is "Jesus Christ"]: {13} who were born not of blood, nor of the will of the flesh, nor of the will of man, but of God. {14} And MY Logos was made flesh [as Jesus Christ] and dwelt among *you* — and *you* beheld his glory (the glory as of the only-begotten of the Father, full of grace and truth).[147]

The desire for control is seen not only in warring spiritual principalities but also in social distinctions made on Earth — from the extremes of totalitarian dictators seeking to exterminate MY Jews and MY Christian Gentiles all the way to supposedly innocent or seemingly benevolent extremes in which people try to manipulate and exploit each other with their: (1) age (youth or seniority), (2) physical ability (prowess or infirmity), (3) physical appearance (attractiveness or deformity), (4) intellectual capacity (abled or disabled), and (5) ranked positions in employment (including chief executive officers of international corporations as well as local attendants cleaning toilets).

For example, in the previously indicated categories, people at one end of the spectrum might try to control others through domination based on their rank, assigned authority, and supposed value to society. People at the other end of the spectrum might try to control others by seeking to engender sympathy for their seemingly-lower rank in the hopes of generating good-will toward them. To be sure, Satan's control virus has infected your entire global population.

In the final analysis, you are willing to control people by getting them to fear you or pity you. Whatever it takes to control, that is

---

147 Paraphrased from the King James Version of John 1:11-14 [Brackets and italics mine]

what you are willing to do.

There is no question that everyone tries to manipulate and exploit others; however, there is a question as to what degree and how often they do. Such is the nature of iniquity, the predisposition and inclination to sin. To be sure, the sin nature is a controlling nature.

In the case of unredeemed, or unsaved, souls in dust, they can do nothing but indulge their sin nature, sometimes even while employing exemplary standards of human protocol (as well as just the opposite).

With redeemed, or saved, souls in dust, it is quite different: It is as if each redeemed human being is conjoined with its old sin nature (that is, attached to its "old man" or "old woman"[148]). Unfortunately, redeemed souls in dust carry with them their old fallen selves, which are easily influenced by evil desires and fleshly interests. That is why redeemed souls in dust still have ungodly urges and desires — even though they (1) have committed themselves to ME by believing on MY Son and in his mission, (2) are "saved" from "eternal damnation"[149] and "the Lake of Fire,"[150] and (3) are "redeemed" to ME.

Sometimes, Christians view the rebirth process too figuratively. When they do, they fail to realize that they have been re-created through spiritual rebirth and not just cleaned up and polished. And, although the redeemed are reborn sinless, pure, and perfect, the "old man" or "old woman" is still right there with them, like a parasitic, conjoined twin. That old self serves as a vector for the control gene until your mortal coil is shed in your transition from corporeality to MY Paradise.[151]

---

148   Romans 6:6; Ephesians 4:22; & Colossians 3:9: King James Version
149   Mark 3:29, King James Version
150   Revelation 19:20; 20:10, 14-15; & 21:8: King James Version
151   Luke 23:43, King James Version

When "saved," you are not just restored but re-created. Your sin nature, its body of sin (corporeal form), and its carnal mind cannot be saved or salvaged. The Apostle Paul wrote:[152]

1. There is therefore now no condemnation to them which are in Christ Jesus, who walk not after the flesh but after the Spirit.

2. For the law of the Spirit of life in Christ Jesus has made you free from the law of sin and death.

3. For what the Law [of Moses] could not do, in that it was weak through the flesh, God [the Father] sending His own Son in the likeness of sinful flesh, and for sin, condemned sin in the flesh:

4. That the righteousness of the Law might be fulfilled in you, who walk not after the flesh but after the Spirit.

5. For they that are after the flesh do mind the things of the flesh; but they that are after the Spirit the things of the Spirit.

6. For to be carnally minded is death; but to be spiritually minded is life and peace.

7. Because *the carnal mind* is enmity against God: for it *is not subject to the law of God, neither indeed can it be.*

8. So then they that are in the flesh [bound to corporeality in fleshly desire] cannot please God.

How many people on Earth desire to control other people, situations, and ME? Everyone. Everyone? Yes, everyone. That "the whole world lies in wickedness"[153] is not hyperbole, or over-exaggeration. You might not want to control the whole world, but you might want to control the people whose lives

---

152 Paraphrased from the King James Version of Romans 8:1-8 [Italics, brackets, and underlining mine]

153 1 John 5:19, King James Version

immediately impact you. You might not want to control all the various social environments on the planet, but you might want to control your immediate situation and conditions. You might not want to control ME to make sure that all others are blessed, but you might want to control ME concerning what you desire to receive from ME (pleasant experiences) and what you desire to not receive from ME (unpleasant experiences).

How do you try to control ME? You threaten ME, and you make false promises to ME. You threaten ME with removing your faith in ME if you do not get what you want when you want it. You threaten ME with withholding your praise and gratitude from ME. You threaten ME with ignoring ME and the needs of MY people. You make false promises to ME by not following through with what you have said you would do. When you make false promises to ME, you blaspheme (that is, you ridicule and demean) MY Holy Name. You say that you love ME, but you treat ME as if I were dung. You find it convenient to lie to yourself, to others, and to ME in order to get your own way. You insult yourself, all others, and ME when you do this.

Some of you fancy that you are leaders. But all that you want to do is control other people and situations. You either think that leadership should be a benevolent dictatorship, or you think that leadership should be megalomaniacal (although you would purposely refrain from using that descriptor).

Spiritually speaking, church leaders can be worse than totalitarian dictators, especially when they try to justify their desire to control MY sheep by saying that MY ideal type of government is theocratic and, then, lying to themselves and others that they have been convicted by ME concerning what I really want for MY people under their autocratic rule. At least totalitarian dictators do not use MY Holy Name in vain. At least totalitarian dictators portray themselves as the wolves they are.

It should be of little wonder to you why MY Son said that "it is easier for a camel to go through the eye of a needle than for a rich person to enter Heaven."[154] He understood that rich people often trust in their riches[155] and that rich people often fool themselves into thinking that they are in complete control. When people believe that they are in complete control, it is more difficult for them to receive Jesus Christ as Personal Savior, Lord, and Sovereign King. Because many poor people already recognize that they are not in complete control, it is often easier for them to humble themselves and ask for forgiveness as well as to yield their individual wills more fully to MY Will.

Everyone under the Sun is vain, arrogant, and controlling. How much and to what degree is the question.

How, then, would you describe your own desire to control?

---

154   Paraphrased from the King James Version of Matthew 19:24; Mark 10:25; & Luke 18:25
155   Psalm 52:7; Proverbs 11:28; Mark 10:24; & 1 Timothy 6:17: King James Version

Chapter Six

Mythology about ME

Because so much mythology about ME has been devised and embraced, your understanding of ME is often very disappointing. Without asking ME, people have decided what I like and what I don't like. They have decided that symbols I have used to speak to MY People in MY Holy Bible should be ritualized, iconized, and worshiped. They have even fooled themselves into thinking that they do not "worship" these symbols but, rather, "revere" or "venerate" them. They play word games with themselves to convince themselves of what is not true.

Miriam (some of you call her "Mary" or "Maria"), the mother of Jesus, was a wonderful girl, tremendous woman, and authentic believer. She was the mother of Jesus but not the mother of God — even though Jesus *is* God ("God the Son"). Some of MY People take deductive reasoning, Aristotelian logic, and syllogisms to an extreme, vis-à-vis thinking represented by the following:

> "*If* Mary is the mother of Jesus, and Jesus is God,
> *then* Mary is the mother of God."

People who believe this do not realize that not all truth is linear in sequence (that is, reasoned in steps). Logic is a good device and helpful in critical analysis, but it cannot be used to understand everything or to know everything that is to be known. Some truths cannot be adequately represented in your space-time because either they are coexistent on different planes but not in the same space-time or they intersect in a circuitous way through dimensional portals that periodically align, merge, re-align, and then re-emerge with different absolute values and relational coordinates. With these two last statements, I have purposely tried to help you to conclude that things are not always as simple as you might like them to be and that not everything can be explained through human reasoning, logic, and critical analysis, respectable though they may be.

Miriam ("Mary") is your sister and not the mother of God. She should be respected, and I hope that you honor her, but I do not want you to worship her or devise any more fables about her being Coredemptrix, Mediatrix, or Theotokos.[156] There can only be One Redeemer, One Mediator, and One Eternal God. Remember, I AM Self-Existent and, therefore, have no parents. Like you, Miriam, mother of Jesus Christ, is a created being. Like you, she was created by ME. To be sure, you could not be more blessed than to have an earthly mother like MY Miriam. I AM so proud of her and was touched always by her humble, generous, and steadfast spirit during her earthly sojourn. But it is a blasphemy to MY Holy Name for you to worship any other created being, including MY beloved Miriam, who, as Christotokos,[157] is the most highly favored and blessed daughter of the Most High God.[158]

MY Son, Y'shua H'Moshiach, instituted the Christian communion meal as a bridge between the Old Testament Passover meal and his New Testament sacrifice upon the cross for the forgiveness of your iniquity and sin. The Christian communion meal is supposed to be a memorial to the fellowship that you have with ME through MY Son.

Transubstantiation?[159] Consubstantiation?[160] Memorialization?[161]

---

156 Greek *Theotokos* means "God-bearer" or "the one who gave birth to God."

157 Greek *Christotokos,* or "the one who gave birth to Jesus Christ," carries the correct nuance.

158 Luke 1:28, King James Version

159 *Transubstantiation* is the dogma that the bread and wine of the communion meal actually become the body and blood of Jesus Christ although they retain the appearance of bread and wine.

Memorialization! MY Christian Gentiles are just as bad as MY Jews who ended up worshiping the bronze snake upon the cross that I had MY beloved Moshe ("Moses") lift up to stop the serpentine plague.[162] Many of you refuse to think outside of the box because you can't even see the box! You do not realize that you imprison yourselves in your own thoughts and feelings.

Fables have emerged even about what I require for salvation. As you read or reread about the thief crucified next to MY Son,[163] I hope that you can see that I do not require water baptism for salvation. The thief upon the cross was saved without water baptism by: (1) his acknowledging that he was a sinner who deserved punishment; (2) his acknowledging that, though crucified like him, Jesus was innocent ("without sin"); (3) his acknowledging Jesus Christ as "Lord" by addressing him as such; and (4) his asking to be saved by requesting Jesus to remember him when he arrived in his Kingdom. MY Son assured the penitent thief of his salvation when he responded: "Today you will be with me in Paradise."[164] He did not make the thief get off the cross to get water baptized.

The meaning of the word *baptism*[165] includes "immersion." Whole body immersion into water represents four things: (1) a symbolic cleansing from iniquity and sin; (2) a dramatic re-enactment of the death, burial, and resurrection of Jesus Christ; (3) a public witness to others of one's identification with Jesus Christ as his disciple (that is, someone who is fulfilling Christ's personal request for his followers to be water baptized); and (4) a

---

160 *Consubstantiation* is the dogma that the actual body and blood of Jesus Christ are present at the same time with the bread and wine of the communion meal, but that the bread and wine have not themselves been changed supernaturally.

161 Luke 22:19; 1 Corinthians 11:24-25

162 Numbers 21:5-9; 2 Kings 18:4; John 3:14

163 Luke 23:39-43

164 Paraphrased from the King James Version of Luke 23:43

165 From the Greek *baptizo,* which means "to immerse or pour"

symbolic immersion into MY Holy Spirit (water often represents MY Holy Spirit) and concomitant access by the believer to all of MY Promises.

Rather than viewing the following two verses as complementary and equivalent to one another, many religionists and legalists of your day have created opposing formulas and divisive factions from these two verses in MY Holy Bible:

> [Christ Jesus said] "Therefore, go and teach [the gospel message] to all nations, baptizing them in the name of the Father, and of the Son, and of the Holy Ghost."[166]

> Then [the Apostle] Peter said unto them, "Repent, and be baptized every one of you in the name of Jesus Christ for the remission of sins, and you shall receive the gift of the Holy Ghost."[167]

The word *name* in both of the above verses is singular. Why? I have one Name! However, although one word may be the *center* of MY Name, one word is not the *circumference* of MY Name.

From the time of Adam's son, Seth, people first began to use the Name of "Yahweh."[168] From the time of MY Son's sojourn on Earth, people began to use the Name of "Y'shua" (Y'shua means "Yahweh *is* salvation"). And, in Paradise ("Heaven" or "the Kingdom of God"), MY Redeemed Children will use a Name for ME that is unknowable to you in your current condition of being:

> Each person who overcomes [Satan's temptations and his world-system] will I make a pillar in the temple of my God ["the Father"], and that person shall go no more out: and I will write upon each

---

166 Paraphrased from the King James Version of Matthew 28:19 [Brackets mine]

167 Paraphrased from the King James Version of Acts 2:38 [Brackets mine]

168 Genesis 4:26

person the Name of my God, and the Name of the City of my God, which is "New Jerusalem," which comes down out of Heaven from my God: and I will write upon each person my New Name.[169]

Please know that MY Name is not just one word. MY Name is comprised of all descriptors and declarations that acknowledge MY Nature and MY Character. MY True Name is conjugated in a dimensionless eternity that you cannot now fully comprehend. To be sure, MY Full Name is unknowable to you and unpronounceable by you on Earth. I tried to teach MY Old Testament Children that MY Name "Yahweh" is holy and should never be taken in vain, just as I have tried to teach MY New Testament Children that the Name "Y'shua" is holy and should never be taken in vain. "Taken in vain" here means "used in unholy contexts" as well as "taken for granted."

When authentic believers invoke ME by using the Name of "Yahweh" or "Y'shua," MY Presence is actualized in your state through MY Holy Spirit. Unless you believe in ME, invoking ME by using MY Name will be ineffectual. You must at least *begin* to believe, trust, and obey ME if your prayers are to be answered even though you might be using MY Name. Why would I respond to you if you are only going through motions, practicing rituals, and offering lip service to ME? I will not permit MYSELF to be played like a deck of cards.

In either of the "formulas" for water baptism noted previously, the key ingredients are the words "Son" and "Jesus," which are equivalent in sense and meaning when used by authentic Christian believers (who already know that "Jesus" *is* "the Son of God").

There are many people who know of ME as the "unnamed God"

---

169 Paraphrased from the King James Version of Revelation 3:12 [Brackets mine]

or the "unknown God,"[170] but they do not have an intimate relationship with ME because they do not know WHO I AM through hearing or reading MY Holy Bible. Theirs is not a faith relationship with ME. It can't be a faith relationship because they don't know that I have an only-begotten Son, let alone that he is MY Logos and that WE ARE ONE. And, unless these cry out to ME as "the unknown God" (not with those exact words) and ask ME to help them to get to know ME, I cannot respond to their requests. I "cannot" respond to certain prayer requests because I do not go against MYSELF and the divine protocols I have established for approaching ME in an acceptable manner. (That "I do not go against MYSELF" does not mean that I never change MY Mind in response to the prayer requests of authentic believers.)

I also do not permit MYSELF to respond to those who subscribe only to philosophies of religion — that is, those who study the belief systems of mankind but they themselves do not believe in Jesus Christ as the only-begotten Son of God (some of your theologians are earnest in their scholarship but not earnest in believing on MY Son and in his mission). These might get excited about the discovery of an ancient manuscript, but they are not really interested in discovering or experiencing ME. These have not "tasted"[171] ME to see that I AM good (which is to say, they have not consciously experienced MY Goodness directly through MY Grace and Mercy).

To be sure, I also cannot respond to those who believe that I do not, should not, and cannot have an only-begotten Son. I do not respond to those who are anti-Christ. That would be unseemly.

I only respond to those who believe on MY Son and in his mission as well as those who are genuinely uncertain what to believe about ME but want to find out what to believe. I *reveal*

---

170   Acts 17:23, King James Version
171   Hebrews 6:4-5 & 1 Peter 2:3: King James Version

MYSELF to all who want to believe, I *reveal* MYSELF to some nonbelievers who are being prayed for by authentic Christian believers, and I *manifest* MYSELF to — as well as answer the prayers of — all who believe on MY Son and in his mission. (To be sure, I do not always answer their prayers in the ways they might like or as soon as they might think I should.)

For those who might find fault with water baptism "in the Name of Jesus," I would reply to them with this Scripture: "The person who acknowledges the Son has the Father also"[172] (that is, "the Father" is implicit in the acknowledgement of Jesus Christ as MY only-begotten Son). I would also reply with the statement that people cannot acknowledge Jesus as Lord unless MY Holy Spirit is working in them and speaking through them (thus, "the Holy Spirit" is also implicit in the acknowledgement of Jesus Christ as MY only-begotten Son).

People who understand and readily accept that Jesus is the only-begotten Son of God but do not understand that Jesus is God have something yet to learn. People who understand and readily accept that Jesus is God but do not understand that Jesus is the Son of God also have something yet to learn. For those people who may be embarrassed to use the terms "Father" or "Son," I AM embarrassed by them.

For those who might find fault with water baptism "in the Name of the Father, Son, and Holy Ghost," I would reply to them that such a baptism honors ME in that it accurately proclaims WHO I AM. I would also add that people who believe in "God the Father," "God the Son," and "God the Holy Spirit" do not believe in three Gods: They believe in One God. I HAVE ALWAYS BEEN WHO I WILL ALWAYS BE. AND I WILL ALWAYS BE WHO I HAVE ALWAYS BEEN. MY BEING DOES NOT CHANGE.[173]

---

172   Paraphrased from the King James Version of 1 John 2:23
173   Malachi 3:6, King James Version

It does not matter if you are baptized by immersing or pouring (or even sprinkling). It does not matter if you are baptized "in" or "into" the "Name of Jesus" or the "Name of the Father, Son, and the Holy Ghost." I tried to teach you during Old Testament times that I do not look at outward appearances but, instead, at motives and intents.[174] However, your bent nature (as opposed to your divine nature[175]) causes you to try to regularly overturn this truth of MINE.

There are those legalists among you who quote the following verse to prove that I require water baptism for salvation:

> Jesus responded: "Except a person is born of water and of the Spirit, that person cannot enter into the Kingdom of God."[176]

Jesus was speaking to the Pharisee Nicodemus, who was already fully acquainted with water baptism as practiced by John the Baptist in the River Jordan but who did not know about spiritual rebirth through receiving Christ. When parsed correctly, the statement carries this meaning:

> Unless a person is [not only] born of water [but also] of the Spirit, that person cannot enter the Kingdom of God.

Water baptism legalists fail to counterbalance their understanding of the previous verse with the following verse that records what Jesus also said:

> The person who believes and is baptized shall be saved; but the person who does not believe shall be damned.[177]

MY Son did not say that the person who is not water baptized

---

174   1 Samuel 16:7
175   2 Peter 1:4, King James Version
176   Paraphrased from the King James Version of John 3:5
177   Paraphrased from the King James Version of Mark 16:16

shall be damned, but, rather, that the person who does not believe shall be damned. See the difference?

Many students of MY Holy Bible also fail to see the *double entendre* of "born of water," referring not only to the water of baptism but also to the bursting of the "bag of waters" when amniotic fluid precedes passage of the soon-to-be neonate (newborn) through the birth canal.

Finally, to end this chapter, there are those of you who think that I want every Christian believer to be wealthy, and there are those of you who think that I want every Christian believer to live in poverty. Both views are incorrect. I want what is best for you individually, collectively, and corporately to help you to become fully returned to ME and fully intimate with ME. Although simple to ME, your lives are more complex and multivariate than can be imagined in your corporeal condition of being.

Although it does not puzzle ME, it should puzzle you why people look for acts of nature to explain the supernatural events and miracles detailed in MY Holy Bible (thus viewing MY Holy Bible as inherently mythological) only to construct their own mythologies about ME by elaborating doctrines, rituals, liturgies, and requirements that do not have MY Sanction or Approval.

What myths do *you* still believe about ME? If you are unsure, then begin regular study of MY Holy Bible, and ask ME to grant you understanding, discernment, and wisdom through MY Holy Spirit.

Chapter Seven

Conflicting Natures

As you read the declaration of the Apostle John that "God is light in Whom there is no darkness at all,"[178] and couple it with the statement by Christ Jesus that "God is a Spirit,"[179] you can conclude correctly that MY Fundamental Nature includes Spiritual Light, or Glory.

Because the illumination of the beings I originally created was neither by way of streaming photons nor material glow, it is important to make the distinction here between Spiritual Light and physical light. Though souls in dust may view the light with which they are familiar as a nonmaterial substance, they err in such an observation. Although subatomic, the light-energy with which you are familiar is physical and not spiritual in nature. Indeed, the levels of organization to which the physical scientist includes elementary, or fundamental, particles and their component parts speak of the finite nature of those bits. And the characteristic of finitude is an obvious contradiction to MY Elementary, or Fundamental, Nature, which is Eternal.

The smallest building blocks of matter may be conceptualized as dense packets of light-energy, but they are exposed for what they are by the quality of being *dense*. Of course, when picking apart matter at the level of quarks and gluons, some of your modern theoreticians have already concluded that matter does not really exist. However, unless those who understand that conclusion are firmly grounded by placing their faith in ME, not even the greatest physical scientists will come to know how to interpret that information in a spiritual sense.

---

178 Paraphrased from the King James Version of 1 John 1:5
179 Paraphrased from the King James Version of John 4:24

Spiritually speaking, all physicality — including physical light-energy itself — is darkness. Physicality, as you know it, is not part of the Nature of MY Absolute Reality. Why? Without MY Life Force, all physicality is "the shadow of death" and spiritually inert. (Remember, your conflict is with Evil and not with matter.)

In view of the contrasting natures of Spiritual Light and physical light-energy, what should become clear to spiritual sense is the meaning of passages from MY Holy Bible that describe the source of illumination found in the Kingdom of God, the space where I live, and move, and have MY Being, and to which all MY redeemed will be returned one day:

> The Sun shall be no more your light by day ... but the LORD shall be unto you an everlasting Light.[180]

> There shall be no night there [in the heavenly city of New Jerusalem]; and they [its inhabitants] need no candle, neither light of the Sun, because the LORD God gives them Light [in other words, I AM the source of their Light].[181]

Viewed this way, it is easier to see that at the time of the end, when your "world languishes and fades away,"[182] I will reveal the Fullness of MY Spiritual Light, which is the Fiery Part of MY Being (or the Fullness of MY Glory). Although this revelation of MY Nature will be to the faithful and to the faithless alike, by accepting Jesus Christ as their Lord and Savior only the faithful will have made themselves acceptable for MY Radiant Presence to dwell within and among them — as well as be reflected by them. At that time, not everyone will be joyful that I have made

---

180 Paraphrased from the King James Version of Isaiah 60:20
181 Paraphrased from the King James Version of Revelation 22:5 [Brackets mine]
182 Paraphrased from the King James Version of Isaiah 24:4 (See also Revelation 21:1)

MY Face — that is, MY Appearance — to shine upon them.[183]

That MY Appearance is Spiritual Light should signify to those-who-seek that MY Spirit is intangible and, as such, cannot be held in their hands, heard with their ears, or seen with their eyes. In fact, physical sense organs are instruments that sense corruption (that is, corporeal conditions) and are themselves corruptible. Thus, not only can they not sense MY Presence, they would melt and disappear in the Absolute Holiness of MY Presence. The Purity of MY Spiritual Light is so powerful that it would dissolve all things impure with which it came into contact. That is one reason why I use angels to communicate MY Messages to you.

No wonder the Prophet Isaiah cried out in terror: "Woe is me! I am *undone* ... for I have seen the King, the LORD of Hosts."[184] Isaiah knew that — because "God is a consuming fire"[185] — no iniquity or sin, and certainly no earthly flesh, could stand in the Fullness of MY Presence. He understood the separate natures of mortality and God-indwelt immortality. Although Isaiah saw ME, he was not cut off from his people nor was his life expunged. Why? Isaiah was in a spiritual state when he saw ME. In concert with the Apostle Paul's description of his own experience, Isaiah was "out of the body."[186]

Although MY Spiritual Light is hell-fiery to corporeality and painful to those who love to live in spiritual darkness, the same Light is warm, gentle, and loving to those who have chosen to place their faith in ME. Indeed, MY Spiritual Light rekindles the still burning embers of souls who have not turned themselves completely over to self-pride and self-will.

---

183 Numbers 6:25; Psalm 31:16, 67:1, 80:3, 80:7, 80:19, 119:135; Daniel 9:17; Matthew 17:2; & 2 Corinthians 4:6: King James Version
184 Paraphrased from the King James Version of Isaiah 6:5
185 Deuteronomy 4:24 & Hebrews 12:29: King James Version
186 2 Corinthians 12:2-3, King James Version

In one of the Dead Sea Scrolls,[187] a scribe symbolized the inverted nature of mortal consciousness and the possible levels of enlightenment that can be achieved by souls in dust. Using a numerical light-to-darkness ratio based on the common denominator of nine, he described three individuals: (1) one "very wicked" with a light-to-darkness ratio of 1:8; (2) one "largely good" with a light to darkness ratio of 6:3; and (3) one "very good" with a light-to-darkness ratio of 8:1.

While I do not mean to suggest that there is a volumetric relationship between Spiritual Light and spiritual darkness in your souls, or that there is a bodily containment of an admixture of such Light and darkness, some profoundly simple truths may be apprehended in this ancient scribe's symbology, namely that: (1) souls in dust are exposed to conflicting natures; (2) there are different degrees of wickedness and goodness in the people around you; and (3) not one of you can be whole until he or she is fully reunited with ME in MY Spiritual Light and thus fully immersed in MY Love. If a soul is completely enblackened by spiritual darkness, the spiritual selfhood it once had in ME is totally eclipsed and that soul is removed from all possibilities for redemption. At the end of time as you know it, the soul who has completely separated itself from ME by rejecting MY Son and his mission is eternally damned and cast into the "Lake of Fire."[188]

It has always been glimmers, gleanings, and glimpses of MY Spiritual Light that have made clear the pathway of spiritual development for those who wish to be re-enlightened and, thus, restored to the Garden of MY Heavenly Consciousness. *For example:* It was in a flame of spiritual fire that an angel of the LORD appeared to Moses out of the midst of the burning bush that I might direct Moses to free the people Israel from their

---

187 Qumran Document 4Q186 from *The Dead Sea Scrolls: Qumran in Perspective* by Geza Vermes. William Collins and World Publishing Co, Inc., 1978, pages 84-85.
188 Revelation 19:20; 20:10, 20:14-15; 21:8: King James Version

oppressors.[189] It was in the "pillar of fire" that an angel of the LORD appeared nightly to the people Israel that they might be protected from Pharaoh's armies and be led far from their Egyptian captivity.[190] And it is in the Spiritual Light of Christ Jesus that many have been inwardly directed toward Heaven and, thereby, led far from the captivity imposed on them by iniquity and sin.

In MY Spiritual Universe, godly conditions reign. Godly conditions exist where you are, but they do not reign there. If MY Life is the Light of MY Creation, and "the true Light which lights every person that enters into the world,"[191] souls in dust who desire to be returned to MY World (the Sphere in which I live, move, and have MY Supreme Being) must examine their origin from the perspective of immortal sense rather than mere mortal sense. They must consider that if "True Man" was made in the exact image and likeness of God, then a certain incorporeality must apply to the created as incorporeality applies to their Creator. Those who are unable to see the light of that truth have simply confused "God's created" with "the creature" (the human being) in which they now find themselves.

Indeed, your multifaceted Creator was, and still is, reflected in HIS Creation, "True Man." In MY Holy Bible, you are reminded of the plurality of "True Man" in such concepts as "children of Israel," "sons of God," "children of light," "members of the Body of Christ," and "stars of heaven," but the Essence of the interpersonal reality in which I AM to be found is not within the multitudinous personalities and personas of human creaturehood. The Nature of MY Absolute Reality is spiritual, not material.

---

189   Exodus 3:4 to 4:17
190   Exodus 13:21-22 & 14:24; Numbers 14:14; Nehemiah 9:12 & 19
191   Paraphrased from the King James Version of John 1:9

When I spoke out of the whirlwind to Job, I referred to MY Original, and unfallen, Creation existing at a time "when the morning stars sang together and all the created beings of God shouted for joy."[192] Seen thusly, MY One True and Only Real Creation consists of created beings who, for their brilliance, are the stars of MY Spiritual Universe, where all such souls echo together praise for their Creator — from Whom they came to know life, movement, and being.

Please do not mistake that I AM claiming that you have no reality in your current state. I AM just making a distinction between the reality in which you find yourselves and MY Absolute Reality, wherein dwells the Totality of MY Being. If you are having a difficult time sequencing all the events about which I AM writing, it is because you are relying on linear thinking and not really appreciating that in MY Absolute Reality some of these events are superimposed upon one another (that is, they happened simultaneously) and, as such, cannot be apprehended or apperceived with your current sense of calendar chronology. *For example,* although you may sequence certain faith events chronologically, faith itself is independent of deductive and inductive reasoning or sequential linear thinking. If you recognize that some of your fellow created beings in your plane of consciousness process experiences more from an emotional or intuitive standpoint than from "if-then" frames of thinking, you can better appreciate the implication about which I AM writing. To be sure, some people know things without thinking about them. (This is somewhat foreign to those of you who come to know things mainly through deductive and inductive reasoning.)

That their Creator could push HIS Creation into being is understood by those who rely completely on ME as the Source of Infinite Supply, for they know ME to possess all-power and all-creativity. Such enlightened souls also apprehend MY Spiritual Universe as the all-conscious Mind of God and each other as MY

---

192   Paraphrased from the King James Version of Job 38:7

thoughts, verities, and realizations — the very "proofs" that not only AM I Supreme Being but also Creator. Knowing that from the Imagination of God exists the only Absolute Reality, there can be no doubt for those who live fully in ME (and I fully in them) that the Creator thought and it was, and is, so. Are you aware that I still create opportunities and conditions for you by just thinking and it becomes so?

Although you have fallen far from MY Glory, MY Supreme Being forever remains unchanged and always totally expressed. To be sure, MY Creative Expression is without end and changeless because there is no place within MY Spiritual Universe where I AM not or where I AM limited or less than MYSELF. I fill all space within the Totality of MY Being with the eternal movement of MY Life. As Creator, I always and completely express MYSELF through MY Creation. (What is true today is true tomorrow and what is true tomorrow is true today. Truth is eternal.)

In sharp contrast to the physical universe, time, space, and motion in MY Spiritual Universe are eternal. They are not finite and ending as they are in your plane of consciousness. Even though time, space, and motion are contingencies in the physical universe, even though they are cross-linked to form its apparent dimensions, and even though they thus overlap, your time and space and motion can never merge to form the unity of the absolute and inseparable all-time, all-space, and all-motion that is to be found within MY Spiritual Universe, a place in which where *is* when. Hence, time shortens and lengthens in your closed system of physicality, space bends, and motion decreases and increases according to temperature, concentration, and pressure. These physical changes are to no spiritual avail for souls caught within a corporeal web. You cannot depend on physical changes or the transformation of matter from one state to another to get you closer to your Creator. For you to draw nearer to ME, your changes must take place from within.

As long as souls in dust choose to make only physical observations, they will not be able to go further than relative frames of reference in understanding why they are on Earth. Admittedly, it is difficult for you to envision the upright, straight, and unbent nature of Spiritual Light when you yourselves are bent — that is, turned away from ME — and when any Spiritual Light within you is outwardly clothed with the garment of corporeality.

Unfortunately, because in your corporeal state you daily see shadows of darkness, you find it easy to conclude that the images with which you are presented happen to belong to a universal and absolute reality when nothing could be farther from the truth. Unaware that your Creator is "the Father of all lights, with Whom is no variableness, neither shadow of turning,"[193] unaware that corporeality and physical changes have no part within MY True Creation, and unaware that souls in MY World are actually dressed in ME, you *en masse* have set up an ill-defined pantheistic life force as your imagined creator and have assumed its transient emanations for your identities. Can't you see that you are the stars fallen from God's Heavens, continually held to Earth by your acceptance of the illusions of self-pride and self-will as your *chosen* reality?

Today, you are being called upon by ME to remember that every created being was intended to be an equally important part of the whole and that the integrity and harmony of MY Original Creation were established by ME in the spiritual pronouncement that all offspring altogether constituted the "True Man" I created through MY Logos and am re-creating through Christ Jesus (MY Logos and Christ Jesus are one and the same). However, to answer that call is an especially difficult challenge for those who live in this present earthly sphere of activities because you are

---

193   Paraphrased from the King James Version of James 1:17. "Turning" is iniquity and "shadow of turning" is the visible sign of iniquity (which is to say, corporeality).

mostly surrounded by others who are doubly mixed up and triply confused as to who they really are. So, most people do not really help to point you in the right direction.

In proportion to their willingness to learn, those-who-seek will find a number of spiritual keys in MY Holy Bible that will help them better understand (1) the Nature of the True Creation in MY Absolute Reality and (2) the nature of impurity in a universe that has been altered by iniquity and sin.

Because I AM "of purer eyes than to behold evil, and cannot look on iniquity,"[194] you may reasonably deduce that I AM incapable of containing iniquity, experiencing iniquity, or encountering iniquity without its annihilation. Hypothetically speaking, if I could know impurity, then I would be capable of not being MYSELF, and that is impossible. However, that I cannot know impurity is not to say that I do not know of it, because, knowing all things, I AM aware of the darkness that has been formed by the cumulative self-pride and self-will of souls who have fallen far from MY Glory.

As a spiritual diamond, purity is precious in all its ways. Purity alone allows MY Life and MY Love to pass through it with the force of a billion locomotives without explosion or implosion. Because I do not give rise to, nor dwell within, that which is impure and imperfect, it follows that transparent flawlessness, or purity, must be the Nature of the Creation that I originally designed to reflect ME. As you ponder that your souls were moved into being by MY Creative Impulse, it should become clear to you that both your spiritual heritage and your spiritual legacy are in a state of purity as members of God's "True Man," now being recast in the Body of Christ.

Though iniquity may be defined as "impurity," the word actually carries with it a weightier sense if you examine the Hebrew

---

194   Paraphrased from the King James Version of Habakkuk 1:13

word[195] from which "iniquity" is most often translated in the King James Version of the Old Testament. Besides "iniquity," the Hebrew word may also be translated into English as "punishment." Thus broadened to spiritual understanding, and in accord with spiritual law, iniquity *is* punishment — which is to say, iniquity is its own punishment. In other words, iniquity condemns itself. To be sure, that you have banished yourselves from MY Perfect World because of your iniquity is a just punishment.

To expand further upon the spiritual signification of *iniquity:* If you examine the other seven Hebrew words from which *iniquity* has been translated in the King James Version of the Old Testament, and if you combine their meanings, you will come to an understanding of *iniquity* as "an element of self-will, unrighteousness, or vanity that has afflicted the vessels who bear it, making them 'bowed down,' 'crooked,' or 'bent out of shape' from their originally-pure state."

Though most poetic devices in MY Holy Bible are only interpreted as figures of speech, many of them actually intimate to spiritual sense that corporeality is a function of iniquity. *For example,* phrases which describe that souls in dust have been "brought low," "cast down," and "clothed with shame," or that souls have "turned" and "fallen," imply the stepping down in consciousness of those who have directed their attention away from ME, such decelerating transformation resulting in their wearing the garment of corporeality that you call "flesh."

If you look for it, there is much evidence in MY Holy Bible that many of the righteous souls who contributed to the overall spiritual advancement of humanity were aware that the condensation of impure thought — the "concretioning" of

---

195   Hebrew *aw-vone´* [H5771] from the *Dictionary of the Hebrew Bible* in *Strong's Exhaustive Concordance of the Bible* by James Strong (Copyright 1890), Crusade Bible Publishers, Inc., Nashville.

iniquity, as it were — resulted in the physical forms in which you now find yourselves. However, although this evidence exists, it eludes those who have come to believe that they must not question what they see, hear, and feel with their physical senses. Most human beings take pride in a physical self, which, in the light of spiritual understanding, simply is the only picture they wish to have of themselves. Hence, undetected by those who are thus spiritually limited (by the limitations they have imposed on themselves) is the deeper meaning of these descriptive statements from MY Holy Bible:

> ... our days on the earth are as a shadow ...[196]

> ... our soul is bowed down to the dust ...[197]

> ... I walk through the valley of the shadow of death ...[198]

> Behold, I was shaped in iniquity ...[199]

> Such as [those who] sit in darkness and in the shadow of death ... because they rebelled against the words of God ...[200]

> All flesh is grass ... the grass withers ... surely the people is grass.[201]

> This is a people ... hid in prison houses ...[202]

> Are you not children of transgression, a seed of falsehood?[203]

---

196 1 Chronicles 29:15, King James Version
197 Psalm 44:25, King James Version
198 Psalm 23:4, King James Version
199 Paraphrased from the King James Version of Psalm 51:5
200 Psalm 107:10-11, King James Version [Brackets mine]
201 Paraphrased from the King James Version of Isaiah 40:6-7
202 Isaiah 42:22, King James Version
203 Paraphrased from the King James Version of Isaiah 57:4

... flesh and blood cannot inherit the Kingdom of God; neither does corruption inherit incorruption.[204]

For all that is in the world ... is not of the Father but is of the world.[205]

When created beings embraced elements of self-will and self-pride, and accepted them into their consciousness as their own, they became "polluted" by those elements and thereby "confused" (which is to say, no longer aware of who they were, and really are, in MY Absolute Reality). It is understandable to spiritual sense, though not excusable by it, that most souls in corporeality find it difficult to see beyond the mist, whose veil disguises and disfigures their one true and only real identity. The mist hides that identity not only from themselves but also from others so similarly-shaped in iniquity by a mind separated from ME.

Though the condition of iniquity should call forth great remorse within the souls of those who have become thus darkened by self-pride and self-will, there are few in your world of appearances who will even consider that flesh and blood are not the substances with which they were originally created. Such consideration would make many feel uncomfortable, especially in a state where people prefer to look for, and find, worldly pleasure. And, to further compound matters, because of the growing credibility that is now being given to the illusions of self-pride and self-will, directions for you to reach the creative, spiritual seed within you have become increasingly unclear. Indeed, most to whom you think you might turn for support would chide you into believing your physical senses when just the opposite is necessary for your spiritual growth and restoration to the Garden of Eden, MY Heavenly Consciousness.

---

204 Paraphrased from the King James Version of 1 Corinthians 15:50
205 1 John 2:16, King James Version

Those who seek to understand that the images and illusions of your world are delusions of self-will must combat the heaviness of the mortal thought with which they are surrounded and from which they themselves have drawn to construct their own belief systems. One obvious impediment to spiritual growth lies in religionists who misinterpret the statement, "the Word was made flesh,"[206] to explain that their own corporeality is indicative of MY Original, and unfallen, Creation. They have confused their own miserable existence with a very special event: the fulfillment of the promised Messiah through the birth of Jesus Christ, Y'shua H'Moshiach, to save souls lost in the throes of self-pride and self-will. Christ Jesus came to free all bound by iniquity from their only real grave, the grave of mortality.

And, on the opposite side of the spectrum, another impediment to spiritual growth lies in irreligionists who would crudely — or eloquently — mock ME for MY seeming ineffectiveness as Supreme Being in permitting a fallen state, or parody yet, of MY True Creation to exist. They simply do not understand the Nature of MY Infinite Grace and Mercy while I wait — even up to the appointed "time of the end"[207] — for tares to be separated from grains of wheat.[208] "Wheat" here represents the prodigal sons and daughters who will yet return to their heavenly home through the Christ-escape I have provided. (Though I have written "Christ-escape" here, do not mistake that I AM referring to anything other than MY only-begotten Son, Jesus Christ himself.)

The condition of iniquity is sad. But sadder still are the souls in dust who tenaciously cling to self-pride and self-will, on which basis they then conclude that what they are observing constitutes the one true and only reality. Such as these are not able to even imagine the crystal clarity of MY True Creation (original and

---

206 John 1:14, King James Version
207 Daniel 11:35, King James Version
208 Matthew 13:24-30

unfallen), let alone permit themselves to be restored to it.

Unfortunately, in your disgrace, many of you have come to view the hundred-plus elements of the physical universe and the unclear images that you have of yourselves as basic to MY Expression. This helps to prove that, as it is true "unto the pure all things are pure,"[209] so is it true that "to the impure all things are impure." Thus, unaware of the reality of MY True Creation because of their own spiritual darkness, many souls in dust remain content to wander through a thick "shadow of death" (that is, corporeality), willing to accept the misnomer "life" as descriptive of all aspects of their animate existence.

So that you do not misinterpret that corporeality is iniquity-in-itself, and erroneously conclude that it is *the* enemy, I must emphasize again that corporeality is only an image of self-pride and self-will — an image superimposed on souls who are themselves iniquitous — which is to say, "turned from God." To be sure, bearing the visible sign of their iniquity as a physical manifestation, souls in dust wear the shame of their self-imposed exile into mortality. However, it should also be noted that the birth of souls into corporeality is part of the Plan of Salvation that I worked out for those who, through their iniquity, turned from immortality to mortality. By accepting Jesus Christ as their personal Savior while they are in corporeality, souls end their bondage to "dust" and are freed from the grasp of mortality and, thus, become pure and perfect immortals again.[210] Such acceptance only "works" while souls are in corporeality. Accepting Jesus Christ as Lord and Savior after death does nothing to change things. Even the unclean spirits recognize Jesus Christ as the Son of God.[211] Their recognition does nothing to change their ungodly and unholy condition. A requirement of

---

209 Titus 1:15, King James Version
210 Although all souls are eternal, souls either *exist* in mortality or *live* in immortality.
211 Matthew 8:28-29

MY Plan of Salvation is that you accept Jesus Christ as your Lord and Savior while you are in corporeality in order for your acceptance to do you any good. You must demonstrate faith in ME while you are on Earth. Why? "Faith is evidence of things not seen."[212] You actually begin to take shape within MY Absolute Reality at the inception of your faith walk with ME and you continue to take shape as you progress in your faith.

In corporeality, all views of MY Spiritual Universe are obscured and distorted. But, because physicality is only a shadow — an "effect" of self-pride and self-will, as it were — all who hope to progress to any higher levels of being, and eventually be fully restored to MY Life, must commit themselves to learn that their own self-pride and self-will, not corporeality, was (and still is) the primordial wrong, their original sin, their first crime against God, the cause of their downfall, and the reason for their self-imposed exile into mortality.

In the single Biblical reference to Satan when he was "Lucifer" (Lucifer is the primogenitor of all fallen created beings), MY Holy Spirit spoke this invective against self-pride and self-will through MY Prophet Isaiah:

> How you are fallen from Heaven, O Lucifer [Light-bearer], Son of the Morning! How you are cut down to the ground, you who would weaken the nations! For you have said in your own heart: "I will ascend into Heaven, I will exalt my throne above the stars of God; I will sit also upon the mount of the congregation, in the sides of the north; I will ascend above the heights of the clouds; I will be like the Most High."[213]

---

212   Paraphrased from the King James Version of Hebrews 11:1
213   Paraphrased from the King James Version of Isaiah 14:12-14 [Brackets mine]

Thus unmasked to spiritual sense is the motivation of anyone who tries to set his or her star above others. In truth, the previously-cited message to the Lord of Confusion [or King of Babylon][214] is not only a remanding of the Prince of Darkness, the very leader of the rebellion which "made the earth to tremble ... and the world as a wilderness,"[215] it is a far-reaching reminder to all who have departed from MY Way that their punishment is already built into their crime.

It is divinely just that MY Perfect World is out of focus to those who were, and still are, caught by an illusion of grandeur in self-pride and self-will. Their own false egos cloud and befuddle their apperception of MY Spiritual Universe. Although MY Spiritual Universe is altered to them, in MY Absolute Reality it really remains unchanged. It is fitting that your apparent world (that is, your world of appearances) is a desert devoid of the water of MY Presence. MY Holy Spirit cannot, and will not, dwell within that which is flimsy, chimerical, and without spiritual substance.

For souls in your earth plane of consciousness to work more fruitfully toward understanding the Nature of MY Original Creation, they must question why it is that they are in corruptible bodies. Equally as important, they must be willing to hear the unpleasant answer to that question from within. Unless they willingly learn that the corporeal state is inherently iniquitous and, as such, is not the divinely-intended, eternal tapestry for the created of God, those who people your planet will continue to be fooled by appearances.

If you are not able to identify the real adversary of MY Will, you will have an increasingly difficult time working to be freed from the bonds imposed upon you by self-pride and self-will. And, unable to see through the darkness imposed upon them by a false sense of self (because they refuse to see), such souls prevent

---

214   Isaiah 14:4, King James Version
215   Isaiah 14:16-17, King James Version [Brackets mine]

themselves from catching glimpses of MY Perfect World. Further, unable to recognize ungodly elements in themselves and in others, these spiritually impaired are not only in danger of falling into the hands of those who would do them harm, they are in danger of actually losing the one true and only real identity that they can have in ME. Your belief in a false identity as your real identity has been perpetrated and perpetuated by none other than your own self-pride and self-will. You must take responsibility for your error.

Since men and women cannot cast out that which they are unwilling and, thus, unable to see, the inability to understand their true origin (and be returned, at least, in awareness to it) lies in those who have fallen so low that they no longer see that there is a foe to fight and a battle to be won. To be sure, your greatest foe is "the dragon, that old serpent, which is the Devil, and Satan."[216] But your next greatest foe is your own self-pride and self-will combined. That is why humility and gratitude should be obsessions to you. Without humility and gratitude, self-pride and self-will will overtake you and actually permit your greatest foe access to your individual spirit — your mind and heart, or cognition and emotion. Don't forget, that once slithering serpent is a swollen dragon, now gravid with evil.[217]

Somewhere between so-called Christian fundamentalism and so-called Christian metaphysics[218] is the delicate balance of understanding that permits identification of the source of all evil as a negative spiritual principle that operates through channels who have accepted for their reality the ultimate delusion of self-pride and self-will. The ultimate delusion is that true satisfaction can be found in sinful thoughts and actions. But in perilous deviation from that mark of understanding "the prince of the

---

216   Revelation 20:2, King James Version
217   Revelation 12:9, King James Version
218   *Christian metaphysics* refers to "a spiritual science and sense beyond comprehension by mere human science and sense."

power of the air, the spirit that now works in the children of disobedience,"[219] are those who would limit the cunning and cruelty of evil to one locality and one personality in the primogenitor of all evil, Satan. Likewise mistaken are those who think that evil can be disarmed and dismissed by ignoring rather than confronting the cause of it.

Many today minimize the influence that self-pride and self-will have within their own individual lives by attributing all evil to Satan. They assume no responsibility for the cause and effect of evil in their own lives. Others try to dismiss evil by speaking renunciations against evil and declaring affirmations of truth. These do not understand that, indeed, the source of evil is "nothing," but only when it is exposed to MY Light in your world. What is MY Light in your world? Christ Jesus himself![220] When confronting evil in the Name of Jesus Christ, souls in dust should take care that they themselves are walking in Spiritual Light and not darkness because, if they are not, they will be pulled farther from MY Source of Infinite Supply and closer to the bottomless pit, which is an abyss of spiritual darkness. You cannot cast out the effects of self-pride and self-will when you are harboring their cause within.

Because MY "works were finished from the foundation of the world,"[221] it is obvious to spiritually-enlightened sense that all who believe that they can change the order of things, or that they may add or subtract from MY Creation, cannot now really be a part of MY Creation because, if they were, they would not seek to change or alter it. Those living in the Spiritual Light of MY Son know that MY Creation cannot really be changed, although it may vary. Yes, MY Spiritual Universe has been altered by iniquity and sin, but MY True Creation remains forever unchanged and changeless. Your Creator is always completely

---

219   Paraphrased from the King James Version of Ephesians 2:2
220   John 8:12, King James Version
221   Paraphrased from the King James Version of Hebrews 4:3

expressed! Eden was not changed when Adam and Eve were expelled from it. Adam and Eve were changed.

As seen by those who never departed from MY World, as seen by those who have returned to it through MY Grace and Mercy (by believing on MY Son and in his mission), and as seen by those who have had a glimpse of its existence while on Earth, it is nothing more than the "nothingness" of self-pride and self-will that has been the downfall of souls in dust. Indeed, in this way souls have chosen to separate themselves from one another and from their Creator. And, for those who might question the use of "nothingness," that word is entirely appropriate to describe a false creation. Although the "false creation" may appear to be real, it is unreal and, hence, all for naught. To be sure, "false creation" is itself an oxymoron because there is only one Creator, ME, and, therefore, there can be nothing that can be "falsely" created. The so-called false creation is only an illusion. Certainly, that does not negate that I have made something out of nothing through MY Word, Christ Jesus.

To better understand where MY Spiritual Universe is in relation to the physical universe, it is important for students of truth to make an indelible note for themselves that their own self-pride and self-will are the only obstacles that bar them from seeing MY Spiritual Universe. In the light of this truth, the sole concern of those-who-seek should be that MY Spiritual Universe is hidden from their spiritual apperception and not that it is hidden from their corporeal sense. The view about which I AM writing is one of spiritual insight and not physical eyesight. Indeed, it is the view that you have when your eyes are closed to the confusive elements of your earthly sphere of activities. Although I must write about MY Spiritual Universe using frames of reference with which those in corporeality are familiar (for obvious reasons), it is MY Hope that the images that take shape in the reader's mind will be far beyond physicality and physical sense. It is MY Hope that these spiritual truths will impinge upon your consciousness the Essential Nature of MY True Creation.

I take issue with those who hold literalism responsible for perverting the inspired words of MY Holy Bible because true literalism moves into the realm of etymological word studies and parsing what has been written. In turn, etymology and parsing provide keys to deeper levels of understanding and richer meanings of individual words, phrases, and sentences. Instead of literalism, degree of adherence to physicalism in the interpreter should provide the index for measuring a perverted understanding of MY Written Word. As long as those who study the Scriptures are physicalists, matter-worshipers, and pantheists, they will be unable to see the real images within MY Inspired Word. Although the physically-minded might be able to concede the figurative meaning of Biblical statements like "... so pants my soul after You, O God,"[222] they will not be able to discern the deeper meaning of the Biblical keys that provide access to a fuller understanding of their own spiritual origin, fall, and present location nor see the way back to their true roots. Most people who believe in ME believe that I can be found in matter, thereby elevating matter in their minds to a place where it does not belong. For this reason, unfortunately, an understanding of MY Spiritual Universe is most often earth-bound by physicalism.

In working toward obtaining a glimpse of MY Spiritual Universe and grasping each glimmer of its truth, those-who-seek should come to understand that MY Written Word employs such literary devices as ellipsis, understatement, repetition, amplification, word-picture, word-portrait, deduction, induction, substitution, word exchange, hyperbole, paradox, simile, allegory, parable, symbolism, enigma, implication, *double-entendre,* irony, oxymoron, idiom, personification, and counter-questioning. The highest understanding of Scripture includes the spiritually-figurative and metaphysical sense of the divinely-inspired written Word. The earnest student, then, should examine her or his own interpretive stance and question whether he or she is mentally

---

222   Paraphrased from the King James Version of Psalm 42:1

reducing words, phrases, and verses to physical terms only when they would have greater significance translated as representative of spiritual truths and concepts.

Because MY Creative Nature is changeless, and because MY Offspring were made in MY Complete Image and Perfect Likeness, then the Original Nature of MY Created must also be changeless and incorruptible. MY Creation does not really have its true being in the physical universe, which is impure, imperfect, and full of change. The physical universe is actually the inverse of MY Spiritual Universe. The physical universe is an outpocketing of MY Spiritual Universe. The physical universe is MY Spiritual Universe turned inside out. The physical universe is an involution of MY Spiritual Universe. See?

My Complete Image and Perfect Likeness is not seen in that which is heir to the "cankerworm."[223] However, if I so choose, I certainly can express MYSELF *through*, as well as *to*, those caught in your corporeal web, despite its inherently corruptible nature. When I choose to do so, it always suits MY Purpose, generally and specifically.

Although the Kingdom of Heaven may be found within the God-given spark of life which those in the earth plane of consciousness still retain (except for those who have already given themselves completely over to self-pride and self-will), what those-who-seek are really seeking to be restored to is neither in material existence nor of matter. To be sure, MY Spiritual Universe is an elevated state set apart from material existence because it is, altogether and all-at-once, the abode and throne and mountain of God, where I Express MYSELF without measure. MY Spiritual Universe is the seat of MY Creative Consciousness, Christ Jesus. For those who might debate of its locality, please know that, though the Kingdom of Heaven may be the state without the place, it is never the place without the

---

223   Joel 1:4, 2:25; Nahum 3:15-16: King James Version

state.

MY Spiritual Universe is constructed on coordinates which are magnitudes of MY Creative Actualization, wherein I have pushed forth MY Thoughts upon those eternal axes in MY Statement of Being. The physical universe is constructed on coordinates which are magnitudes of iniquity, self-pride, and self-will that have cast their shadows of darkness over these finite axes in an illusion of falsehood. MY Spiritual Universe and the physical universe exist independently of one another. They are only linked when I choose for them to be linked. I choose for them to be linked through the blood of Jesus Christ and by MY Holy Spirit given to those who believe on MY Son and in his mission.

Because time is no more and no less than a sequence of related events, unrelated events cannot take place in the same time. (They can take place "at" the same time but not "in" the same time.) Therefore, because the events of MY Spiritual Universe are unrelated to, and not dependent on, the events of the physical universe, those two bodies of thought (the one pure, the other impure) exist in two different, albeit concurrent, times. The units of measurement that comprise time in MY Spiritual Universe are not interchangeable with, and they are forever separate from, those which comprise time in the physical universe. Although such times run alongside of one another, they are running forever parallel and, thus, can never be one. Similarly, because space is the area in which related events occur and motion is the rate at which they occur, events that occur in MY Spiritual Universe and events that occur in the physical universe can neither exist in the same space nor possess the same vibratory rate, momentum, or motion. In short, your outer space cannot be MY inner space.

Thus, seeing how MY Spiritual Universe is separate from the physical universe, I herewith make the distinction between the coordinates of the former as "spiritual time," "spiritual space," and "spiritual motion" and the coordinates of the latter as "physical time," "physical space," and "physical motion." It should be noted that "spiritual time," "spiritual space," and "spiritual motion" are wholly unified in MY Absolute Reality and are divided here only for the sake of discussion, comparison, and fine-focusing.

If you come to understand the separateness and division between the world in which you have come to exist and the world in which you have your real being, do not despair or be inconsolably grieved by it. Just remember that there is hope because a bridge exists between the two worlds through MY Infinite Grace and Mercy. For those who travail to be delivered from their iniquity and sin, I have provided an escape in and through Christ Jesus. He is the warp in space-time that connects MY Spiritual Universe to the physical universe. When you believe on Jesus Christ and in his mission, you undergo a spiritual involution by turning in humble submission from self-pride and self-will to MY Will. Through Christ, you are fully restored to MY Perfect World, where no less spiritual time exists for you than for any other whose re-entrance has either preceded or followed you.

Although eternity will always remain in MY Spiritual Universe, that is not to say that you have eternity to be accepted back into the bosom of MY Love. Unfortunately, most people in corporeality demonstrate through labored frivolity that they think they have all the time in the world to be reunited with ME. The portal of which I write, however, will only remain open until the time of the end, when the door to Heaven will be permanently closed, just as the door to Noah's ark was shut tight to prevent the godless and ungodlike from entering. From that point onward, it will no longer be possible for doleful creatures of the night to be released from the shadows of darkness that bind them. Even if they call out to MY Angelic Hosts, they will not be comforted since those called upon will be unable to do anything but reply: "... between us and you there is a great gulf fixed, so that they which would pass from here to you cannot; neither can they pass to us that would come from there."[224]

At what point did the physical universe come into existence? Studies of sidereal nature definitely indicate that the physical universe had a beginning, such genesis often referred to in your modern cosmology as the "Big Bang." However, the conceptual range of the Big Bang Theory is greatly limited. Although the theory takes into account that the origin of the physical universe is recorded in physical time, physical space, and physical motion by the eruption of an enormous, highly concentrated energy mass that produced matter, it fails to take into consideration that matter was sent hurtling out into the vacuity of a universe set apart from MY Spiritual Universe. But the limitation of that cosmogony is understandable since it is only through enlightened spiritual sense that one may gain a wider view of the origin of physicality. That view enables identification of the source that gave impulse to the physical universe and, revealing amidst the cumbersome skeins of physical time, when it all began.

Thus seen, the physical universe burst forth into existence with explosive force upon the introduction of self-pride and self-will into the consciousness of spiritual beings, beginning with Lucifer, who were then fallen from their state of being in ME. To avoid confusion, you should remember that the beginning of the physical universe is no more than a record of that event. It is an effect, and not the cause, of the Fall. In other words, earnest students should grasp tightly the knowledge that physicality is neither *self-pride-in-itself* nor *self-will-in-itself* but merely the evidence of self-pride and self-will.

Concerning these conflicting natures, a soul's standpoint and perspective are very important. Though the physical universe appears to those in corporeality to be substantive beyond belief, it is known as a shadow of the truth to those in MY Spiritual

---

224 Paraphrased from the King James Version of Luke 16:26

Universe. You should never confuse the startlement that gave rise to the physical universe with the ever-beginning in Spirit of MY True Creation, which, as one might think, is also ever-becoming.

Chapter Eight

The Guilt Complex

When created beings fell from MY Perfect World by turning from ME to act in self-pride and self-will, they condemned themselves to *death* (*death* is defined here as "separation from God") because of their guilt. They created a gulf between ME and them, which gulf I also think of as their grief. To be sure, if souls in dust "heap their grief" in the resolute decision to continue in *sin* (*sin* is defined here as "action based on iniquity"), they "widen the gulf" between MY Perfect World and their own personal world.

Because I AM Full of Grace and Mercy,[225] I sent MY Son into your world to bear your personal iniquity and sin so that those who would accept reproof for their sin might be restored and, thus, returned to ME. Ironically, MY reproof to sinners is subsumed in their free-will admission of self-guilt. In what way? It is painful for souls in dust to confess their sin by admitting that they are wrong. Embedded in their pain is MY reproof. It is painful to admit the profound harm that you have done to yourself, to others, and to your relationship with ME because of your self-pride and self-will. I AM not speaking about remorse only but, more importantly, repentance. Repentance includes actually changing your mind from wanting to indulge your sin nature to wanting to please ME. In the final analysis, your actions prove or disprove the sincerity of your repentance.

The only bridge over the gulf between your world and MINE is found in the cross of Jesus Christ. In John 3:16-21, MY Son said:[226]

---

225 Psalm 86:15, King James Version
226 Paraphrased from the King James Version of John 3:16-21

16. For God so loved the world, that He gave His only-begotten Son, that whoever believes in him should not perish, but have everlasting life.

17. For God sent not His Son into the world to condemn the world; but that the world through him might be saved.

18. The person who believes on him is not condemned: but the person who does not believe is condemned already, because that person has not believed in the Name of the only-begotten Son of God.

19. And this is the condemnation, that Light came into the world, but people loved darkness rather than Light because their deeds were evil.

20. For everyone who does evil hates the Light, neither is that person willing to come to the Light to be reproved [that is, rebuked] for sinful deeds.

21. But the person who is truthful is willing to come to the Light, that their deeds may be made manifest, that they are wrought in God.

Additionally, Christ Jesus said that "whoever believes my message, and believes on Him who sent me, has everlasting life, and shall not be condemned but be passed from death unto life."[227]

And the Apostle Paul wrote that "there is now no condemnation to those who are in Christ Jesus, who walk not after the flesh, but after the Spirit."[228]

Walking after the flesh and walking after the Spirit are clearly distinct from one another and carefully articulated as such in the

---

227   Paraphrased from the King James Version of John 5:24
228   Paraphrased from the King James Version of Romans 8:1

fifth chapter of Galatians. People who walk after the flesh are those who indulge their sin nature in:

> Sexual sin, uncleanness [impurity], lasciviousness [lustfulness], idolatry, witchcraft [including making false accusations against one another to manipulate situations and their outcomes], hatred, variance [quarrelling], emulations [jealousy], wrath [violence], strife [contentiousness], seditions [divisiveness], heresies [contrived disunity through denominationalism and sectism], envyings [spitefulness], drunkenness [active addictions], revellings [riotous behaviors], and similar things.[229]

In contrast, people who walk after the Spirit demonstrate their spiritual nature in Christ Jesus through:

> Love, joy, peace, longsuffering [forbearance with fortitude], kindness, goodness, faith, humility, and self-control.[230]

In all probability, you have indulged your sin nature [remember the "parasitic conjoined twin" that you still drag around[231]] by "walking after the flesh" in most if not all of the sinful ways indicated in the fifth chapter of Galatians. However, *if* you believe on MY Son and in his mission, and *if* you have confessed your sins to ME and asked for MY Forgiveness, *from that point onward* you can rest assured that I have forgiven you and that you remain forgiven. You can be certain not only that I have forgiven your sins but also that I have remitted (that is, cancelled) all your debts to ME because of those sins. Because of your reborn innocence, you no longer need to feel guilty. And you *should not* feel guilty. Why? MY Forgiveness is Absolute.

---

229 Paraphrased from the King James Version of Galatians 5:19b-21a [Brackets mine]

230 Galatians 5:22b-23a, King James Version [Brackets mine]

231 The conjoined allegory is first used at the end of Chapter Five in this book.

When your confessed sins have been forgiven, the only strategy Satan has left is to tell you that your sins are NOT really forgiven (remember, Satan is a liar[232]) and that you should still feel guilty because you *are* still guilty. If Satan is successful in getting you to feel guilty by reminding you of your past sins and your old sin nature, then he is also successful in getting you to doubt ME, to not trust in ME, and to not believe I AM WHO I SAY I AM. If you give in to Satan's attack, you will become incapacitated by false guilt. And, thus incapacitated, you will be an ineffective Christian (you are still a Christian, just ineffective). As an ineffective Christian, you cannot overcome Satan and his advancing forces. Satan will have you right where he wants you. As an ineffective Christian, you will not want to pray to ME and ask ME to correct situations and undo what Satan is doing to you, your life, and the lives of others around you. Satan wins battles (though not the war) by getting saved people to feel guilty. To be sure, because it is all based on a lie, Satan's attack is illegitimate.

Guilt is a powerful tool to Satan. The only legitimate inroad Satan has to authentic Christian believers is through unconfessed sin in their lives.[233] That is why it is important for you to be instantly honest with yourselves, with others, and with ME concerning the sins you commit. As quickly as you confess your sins to ME, I forgive them just as quickly. (This is not a license or an open invitation for you to sin.[234])

Part of the "Guilt Complex" addressed here also involves Christians accusing their Christian brothers and sisters of supposed crimes against them and ME. Christians regularly fall to this error when they have been wronged or perceive themselves to have been wronged. Then, they approach MY

---

232   John 8:44, King James Version
233   1 John 1:8, 10
234   Romans 6:1-2a, King James Version

Throne of Mercy[235] and conveniently forget that it is supposed to be a throne of mercy and not a throne of retribution and vengeance. They begin to castigate their Christian brothers and sisters by telling ME all of the other person's sins or trespasses against them and, supposedly, against ME. They ask ME to reprimand, punish, and/or pour down MY Wrath upon the perpetrators. They are also vehement in their self-justification as to why they are right and the other person is wrong and needs to be punished. They usually recount a detailed personal history with the accused to help justify their requests for punishment. They often ask ME to help get them out of the mess they think they are in. Also, in a bold move of mixed feigned benevolence, feigned martyrdom, and feigned sainthood, they often tell ME that, although they forgive the perpetrator, I should not. (However, they will deny that they have ever said this or that they feel this way.) They are almost gleeful in their anticipation of: (1) MY meting out punishment and (2) how sorry the accused will then be for the wrong committed against the accuser.

The operative word here is "wrong." The scenario just described is wrong, wrong, wrong! If you think that someone has trespassed against you, then you should first go to the person yourself to discuss the matter.[236] (Go alone to the person only if the trespass does not involve physical and/or sexual abuse.) As calmly and reasonably as possible, you should explain to the person why you think they have trespassed against you. Then, you should give them an opportunity to explain themselves, their actions, their motives, their intents, their attitudes, and their behaviors. Whether they can or cannot explain themselves to your satisfaction, you still have the following obligations (indeed, "debts") to them: First, you are required by ME to forgive them of all of their trespasses against you, just as I have forgiven you

---

235 Exodus 25:17-22, 26:34; Leviticus 16:14-15; & Hebrews 4:16, 9:5: King James Version. The "mercy seat" of the Bible represents God's heavenly throne of mercy.
236 Matthew 18:15-20

of all of your trespasses against ME.[237] Second, you are required to ask ME to forgive them (in other words, for ME not to hold their sin against them), just as MY Son asked ME to forgive his murderers as they were murdering him,[238] and just as the first recorded Christian martyr, Stephen, asked ME to not hold sin against those who were stoning him to death.[239]

You must remember always that "the Accuser" is Satan.[240] It is he who accuses the Christian brothers and sisters day and night before ME. When you accuse your Christian brothers and sisters, then you not only embolden Satan and his demonic forces but actually empower them by granting them dominion concerning specific interpersonal relationships. Why would you want to join forces with Satan? Why would you want to serve as Satan's tool?

Satan and his demonic forces hate forgiveness. The act of forgiveness actually takes power away from them because, like spiritual vampires, they feed on the by-products of self-pride and self-will, which include unforgiveness, discord, bitterness, and hatred. When surrounded by the spirit of forgiveness, Satan and his minions experience spiritual suffocation and panic attacks due to lack of inflow of negative energy from the evil motives behind unforgiveness, discord, bitterness, and hatred. Because forgiveness reflects MY Love perfectly, Satan and his demons shrink back to avoid contact with MY Light. Forgiving others is one way you are to resist Satanic attacks.[241]

Didn't you ever wonder why MY Son directed you to "be perfect even as your Father in heaven is perfect?"[242] Obviously, while in your corporeal condition, you can't be perfect by never sinning again. Indeed, unless you are suffering in the flesh, it is virtually

---

237   Matthew 5:23-24; 6:12, 14-15; 18:21-22, 35; Mark 11:25-26
238   Luke 23:34
239   Acts 7:59-60
240   Revelation 12:10, King James Version
241   James 4:7, King James Version
242   Paraphrased from the King James Version of Matthew 5:48

impossible for you to not sin in thought, in feeling, in desire, or in deed. (This last statement is not intended to grant you permission to sin.) However, you can be perfect by loving perfectly. Forgiveness is perfect love. So, in effect, MY Son was saying: "love perfectly by forgiving, even as your Father in Heaven loves perfectly by forgiving." How? By being kind to those who are unkind to you. And by biting your lip when others make hurtful, libelous, and slanderous comments against you.

In Matthew 5:44-47, Christ Jesus said:[243]

44. I say to you: Love your enemies, bless those who curse you, do good to those who hate you, and pray for those who despitefully use you and persecute you;

45. In order that you may be the children of your Father who is in Heaven: for He makes His Sun rise on the evil and on the good and sends rain on the just and on the unjust alike.

46. If you love those who love you, what reward do you have? Don't even tax collectors do the same?

47. And if you greet your brothers and sisters only, what are you doing differently than others? Don't even tax collectors do the same?

The spirit of unforgiveness is a controlling spirit. The spirit of unforgiveness causes you to rehearse hurts, remember wrongs, and recount trespasses against you. The spirit of unforgiveness is a damaging spirit. It damages you and others around you. You can break the cycle of damage by simply approaching ME and asking ME to heal the hurt you have sustained as well as help you to forgive. Some wrongs are so grievous that the hurt sustained from them takes a long time to heal, especially if the emotional wounds were deep, if they festered for a long time, and if thick emotional scar tissue has built up around the wound.

---

243   Paraphrased from the King James Version of Matthew 5:44-47

Thick emotional scar tissue must be excised by the scalpel of the Master Physician[244] before spiritual healing balm[245] can be applied directly to the wound.

Hurt is the primary emotion resulting from someone's trespass against you. Self-justification for your unforgiving spirit accompanied by anger are two major secondary emotions. Bitterness and hatred are the major tertiary emotions that develop as a result of your anger and unforgiveness. And revenge is in an uncharted territory that is treacherous to you as well as others around you.

If you are seeking revenge, or even if you have committed an act of revenge, there is still time to undo the harm that the spirit of unforgiveness has caused. You can slice through the spirit of unforgiveness with the sword of truth[246] by forgiving someone who has genuinely wronged you and by asking ME to forgive that person as well.

Forgiveness unbuckles the warp and heals the rift in spiritual space-time caused by unforgiveness. Forgiveness restores order and removes chaos. In MY Spiritual Universe, forgiveness not only reverses harm done but actually undoes it as if the cause for the harm had never existed.

You must have your causality in ME if you are to be fully restored to MY Spiritual Universe. Having your causality in ME necessitates your forgiving others. When you forgive others, you are reflecting ME without wrinkle and without spot,[247] demonstrating that you are, indeed, made in MY Complete Image and Perfect Likeness.[248]

---

244   Matthew 9:11-12 & Luke 4:23: King James Version
245   Genesis 37:25; Jeremiah 8:22, 46:11; Revelation 3:18
246   Ephesians 6:17; Hebrews 4:12; Revelation 1:16, 2:12, 2:16, & 19:15
247   Ephesians 5:27, King James Version
248   Genesis 1:26; Romans 8:29; 1 Corinthians 15:49; 2 Corinthians 3:18; Colossians 3:10

Please don't misconclude that I want you to pretend that a perpetrator has not wronged you. That would be dysfunctional and create its own difficulties. Again, I want you to use Y'shua and Stephen as examples. As MY Son was dying, he asked for forgiveness at the same time he acknowledged the crimes against him by saying: "Father, forgive them, for *they do not know what they are doing.*"[249] (Y'shua did not pretend that he was not being wronged.) And Stephen did the same when he said: "Lord, do not hold *this sin* against them."[250] (Stephen did not pretend that he was not being trespassed.) The trespasses against Y'shua and Stephen were not just simple murders (no murder is simple) but complex crimes that *cut to the quick* emotionally, mentally, physically, and spiritually for each victim.

For egregious wrongs, forgiveness can be a process and not one event recorded in a flash of time. Please know that as you forgive, your childlike innocence is restored, and you again become "MY darling boy" and "MY darling girl" (yes, you always remain MY sweethearts, MY babies, and MY dears). As MY Children, I dandle you upon MY knee,[251] press you close to MY spiritual bosom, and shelter you under MY protecting wing.[252] I enfold you with MY Love to comfort you. I quell your sobbing as you feel MY Love surround you. And I wipe away all your tears.[253]

To see others as I see them, you must look at them through the shed blood of MY only-begotten Son, Jesus Christ. When you look at others through that blood, you will not only be able to forgive the wrongs (which is to say, sins or trespasses) they have committed against you, you will also be able to forget those wrongs. Just as I do not see or remember your wrongs when I look at you through Christ's shed blood, in the same way will you not be able to see or remember the wrongs of others either.

---

249 Paraphrased from the King James Version of Luke 23:34
250 Paraphrased from the King James Version of Acts 7:60
251 Isaiah 66:12, King James Version
252 Matthew 23:37, King James Version
253 Isaiah 25:8; Revelation 7:17, 21:4

Looking at others through the shed blood of Jesus Christ is the only way that you can really forget as well as forgive.

You must also be willing to look at yourselves through the shed blood of Jesus Christ. This is the only way that you can move on with your lives and not be pulled down or held back by past mistakes. Looking at yourselves through that blood enables you to accept your own eternal salvation. Looking at yourselves through that blood, you are then not only fully persuaded of your own salvation but also no longer vulnerable to guilt, shame, and condemnation or to Satan's accusations of past or current wrongs as he rails against you. In the world of the invisible, demons see the wrongs you have committed because they do not look at you through the shed blood of Jesus Christ. I do not see or remember the wrongs that you have committed because I look at you through that blood. However, unless you are made holy by that blood, I do not look at you through that blood nor can you look at others through it. See?

Earlier, when I used Y'shua and Stephen as examples for forgiveness, please don't think that I AM equating the significance of their murders. Y'shua bore your iniquity and sin upon his cross of crucifixion. That cause brought to him untold added burden, which you now can scarcely comprehend. Stephen died because of the sins of others, but he did not die to bear anyone's sins. I AM not minimizing Stephen's death. I AM simply telling you that Y'shua's death was far more painful emotionally, mentally, physically, and spiritually than Stephen's death. It was the shedding of Y'shua's blood that operationalized MY Plan of Salvation to not only cover your sin-debt but cancel it completely.

Sometimes in feigned martyrdom, victims of abuse remain in abusive situations, and they erroneously quote MY Son's "turn the other cheek"[254] to help justify their unhealthy inaction.

---

254   Paraphrased from the King James Version of Matthew 5:39

Although Christ Jesus said to turn the other cheek, he did not say that you should run up to get your cheeks slapped over and over again. As soon as possible, remove yourself from the abuser's presence or have the abuser legally removed from your presence. And, in this and all other difficult circumstances, pray not that I grant you strength but cling to ME as your strength.

Although you might have a special love for someone (family member, friend, colleague, or spouse), you cannot carry someone else's burdens or pay their debt for sin. That does not mean that you cannot help them, support them, or try to influence them positively (the operative word here is "try"). It means that you cannot eternally rescue them from "paying the price" for their own errors in human judgment. (Human beings "pay the price" for their actions in both natural and supernatural consequences.) If you repeatedly rescue others to prevent them from paying the price for their actions, then you keep them from learning valuable lessons at the same time that you set yourself up as their "God."

Instead of encouraging others to seek and find ME during times of crisis, you often try to present yourself to them as "God." If you repeatedly rescue others, you set yourself up as their "Savior." And, if you find others "innocent" when they are really guilty, or when you want to see them punished for disappointing you (as they often will), you set yourself up as their "Judge." Ultimately, you do yourself, others, and ME a great disservice by not allowing everyone to develop — and then stand on — their own feet of faith. It is easy to prophesy what will happen if you continue to try to rescue others. First, you will become increasingly frustrated because they are not learning lessons and are not changing. Then, you will become increasingly weary, discouraged, and depressed as you realize that, no matter what you do, you cannot control them or their actions, behaviors, attitudes, or world views. Now ask yourself: "Who really needs to learn the lesson?"

You really need to learn the lesson! (1) You cannot change others or control what happens to them. (2) Only I can change people (who desire to be changed and who ask ME to change them). And (3) only I have the power, authority, and dominion to control events. Try as you might, you can never be God. Being God is not your responsibility. It's MINE!

In a near worst case scenario, as you learn that people are not responding to your efforts to control them, you may end up wishing they were dead, that you were dead, or both. ("Wishing" is the near worst case and acting on that desire is the worst case.) Regardless, in any situation, you can always have hope in ME. Even after decades of going in the wrong direction, you can always turn back by *re-turning* to ME. The solution is simple, but you make it complex. Don't be too hard on yourselves. Accept MY Grace and Mercy.

If you continually rescue others, — if you want to bear the burden of their sin-debt, — if you want to see others punished for their sin-debt, — if you are weary, discouraged, and depressed because of the harmful actions and negative attitudes of others, — if you wish others were dead, — or if you wish that you were dead, then please know that you suffer from the sinful desire to control. Please also know that you can never be in control because you can never be ME. I alone AM in control. I ALWAYS WILL BE IN CONTROL. BUT BE OF GOOD CHEER, I WILL ALWAYS BE YOUR HEAVENLY DAD! YOU ARE MY CREATION. HOW CAN I NOT HELP BUT LOVE YOU?

Sometimes I hear people tell each other that they must forgive themselves. However, if you trust ME as your God, then that action is moot. If you have asked ME to forgive you, and if you have accepted MY forgiveness, and if you believe that I AM God and have the power to forgive, then forgiving yourselves does not really enter into the equation (except, perhaps, as a "feel good" exercise of questionable value). Moreover, if you look at yourself through the shed blood of Jesus Christ (as I look at you), then you will see there is no need to forgive yourself.

In closing this chapter on the "Guilt Complex," it is important to add that, to ME, all unconfessed sin stinks like manure. Most of you think that your unconfessed sin does not stink or that it stinks less than someone else's. But it stinks all the same. Likewise, you should not look at yourselves as "less guilty" of unconfessed sin than someone else because your sin is not as bad as theirs. Why? If you have transgressed one of MY Commandments, then you have transgressed them all.[255] By the way, burning all the sweet incense[256] in the world cannot mask the stink from your unconfessed sin. And, although you might think that you can avoid personal repercussions from your unconfessed sin, please know that your unconfessed sin will always hit a moving fan blade and be thrown back at you.

To rid yourself of unnecessary guilt, please tell ME what unconfessed sin you have left in your life. Now is just as good a time as any to tell ME and to ask for MY Forgiveness. Do this daily. (You can always make a written list to help you focus, but you must always destroy that list immediately after you make it.)

255 James 2:10
256 Exodus 25:6, 30:1, 7-8; Psalm 141:2; Luke 1:9-10; Revelation 8:3-4

Chapter Nine

After MY Own Heart

Your *iniquity* (your "turning from ME") resulted in your *sin nature* (your "predisposition to sin"). Your iniquity also resulted in your individual and collective *corporeality* ("sin body," "body of sin," "shadow of turning," "mortal body," or "flesh"), which was, and still is, appointed by ME as the visible sign of your iniquity. *Sin* is "action based on iniquity," which occurs, first, by your entertaining ungodly desires and, only after that, by enacting those desires in your actions. Your actions do not precede your desires. Rather, your desires precede your actions. Scripture[257] records that:

14. Every man or woman is tempted when drawn away by his or her own lust ...

15. Then, when lust has conceived, it brings forth sin: and sin, when it is finished, brings forth death ["death" connoting both supernatural as well as natural consequences].

That Jesus the Christ, Y'shua H'Moshiach, was made "in the likeness of sinful flesh"[258] when "the Word was made flesh"[259] was for the purpose of condemning through his sacrificial and sinless offering that which condemned you to *mortality* (the supernatural consequence denoted by your "separation" from God and the natural consequence denoted by the "death" of your physical body). Indeed, through his sacrificial and sinless offering, Christ Jesus led captive your once-permanent captivity to sinful desires and actions.[260] He won the victory by

---

257 Paraphrased from the King James Version of James 1:14-15
258 Romans 8:3, King James Version
259 John 1:14, King James Version
260 Ephesians 4:8, King James Version

overcoming the world. His victory now permits you to win yours by placing your faith in him alone.[261]

Ideally speaking, you should be freely offering your eternal gratitude, humility, thanksgiving, and praise for the sacrificial sinless offering that Christ Jesus made for you. "Freely" here refers to your self-sacrifice of worshiping ME. I should be worshipfully approached through your gratitude, humility, thanksgiving, and praise because I AM WHO I AM. I do not force you to worship ME even though I deserve to be worshiped. Indeed, I deserve your very best consciously-chosen attitudes and efforts. ("Consciously-chosen" does not mean that you can feign them.)

As a Christian, when you entertain and indulge fleshly desires,[262] you are actually entertaining and indulging your old fallen sin nature.[263] At the same time, you are opening the floodgates of your consciousness to thoughts, feelings, ideas, and images from demonic realms. How far you open those floodgates — and, therefore, how powerful are the demonic thoughts, feelings, ideas, and images you receive — depend on how often you entertain and indulge sinful fantasies and how vulgar and heinous they are. Yes, except for the unforgiveable sin of blasphemy against MY Holy Spirit, all sin is sin to ME, but not all sin is qualitatively the same in the demonic realm. Distinctions exist there. Portals for demonic influence are greater the more vulgar and heinous the sins you entertain, envision, and enact.

In the world of the invisible, actions based on sinful thoughts, feelings, ideas, and images are open invitations for increased demonic involvement and activity in your lives, especially in the

---

261   John 16:33, King James Version
262   Romans 6:6; Colossians 2:11
263   Romans 7:5, 18, & 25; Romans 8:4-5, 8-9, & 12-14; 1 Corinthians 5:5; Galatians 5:13, 16-17, 19-21, & 24; Galatians 6:8; Colossians 2:11 & 13; 2 Peter 2:10 & 18

areas of the sins you emotionally entertain, mentally envision, and physically enact. The carnal mind that still tries to parasitize you is where all sin begins. The sin is committed by your old carnal mind first before you act it out in corporeality. The more vulgar the sinful fantasy and heinous the crime, the more vehement and violent will be demonic involvement in your earthly experience (during wakefulness as well as during sleep). The door to the demonic realm is unlocked by your entertaining ungodly desires, cracked open through your envisioning the enactment of those desires, and swung wide open by your acting them out in the physical.

What you attract and what you produce all begins and ends with the state of your heart. Both godly and ungodly desires originate in your heart, which is the core of your soul. Your King, Christ Jesus, said:

> {33} Either make the tree good, and its fruit good; or else make the tree corrupt, and its fruit corrupt: for the tree is known by its fruit. {34} O generation of snakes, how can you, being evil, speak good things? for out of the abundance of the heart the mouth speaks. {35} A good person out of the good treasure of the heart brings forth good things; and an evil person out of the evil treasure brings forth evil things.[264]

> {18} ... those things which proceed out of the mouth come forth from the heart; and they defile the person. {19} For out of the heart proceed evil thoughts, murders, adulteries, fornications, thefts, false witness, and blasphemies: {20} *These* are the things that defile a person ...[265]

---

264 Paraphrased from the King James Version of Matthew 12:33-35
265 Paraphrased from the King James Version of Matthew 15:18-20

At MY request, MY Prophet Samuel evaluated the sons of Jesse to identify who would be the next King of Israel after Saul. Samuel assumed that Eliab, the first of the sons presented to him, would be chosen by ME because Eliab was tall, dark, and handsome. As Samuel made this assumption, I quickly rebuked him:

> Do not look on his countenance or on the height of his stature because I have rejected him: for the LORD does not see as man sees; man looks on the outward appearance, but the LORD looks on the heart.[266]

I measure the stature of a person based not on your three dimensions of physical height, breadth, and depth but, instead, based on the three spiritual dimensions of sincerity, purity, and love.

1. Sincerity. Is the person sincere in seeking to please ME (that is, yield his or her own will to MY Will)? To be sure, sincerity alone does not enlarge a person's stature. Many misguided people have been sincere in their pursuit of vain philosophies and false religions. In the final analysis, sincere people seeking to please ME should be willing to lay down all of their theological misconceptions and religious malpractices. Please take note that laying down "all" theological misconceptions and religious malpractices usually takes place one at a time. (I encourage you to be patient with one another, just as I AM patient with you.) Sincerity adds height to your spiritual stature, depending, of course, on the degree of your sincerity.

2. Purity. Is the person seeking to live a holy life? If so, holiness should permeate the person's attitudes and activities. Purity has tremendous benefits. People who are pure in heart both see ME and understand MY

---

266   Paraphrased from the King James Version of 1 Samuel 16:7

truths.[267] Purity adds breadth to your spiritual stature, depending, of course, on the degree of your purity.

3. Love. Does the person love ME with all of his or her heart, soul, mind, and might?[268] Does the person love others as much as himself or herself?[269] Does the person love perfectly by forgiving others of their trespasses against him or her?[270] If the person is a mature Christian, does the person feed (that is, nurture) MY lambs and sheep?[271] Here, *love* is an action verb and not a noun. It is only through love for ME and MINE that souls in dust are returned to their original purpose and primary state of being. Love adds depth to your spiritual stature, depending, of course, on the degree of your love.

For those who might be swept away by an immature religious zeal, true Christian martyrdom includes daily sacrifice in the self-immolation of insincere motives and intents, impure thoughts and feelings, and selfish "love" (which really is not love at all).

Your spiritual stature in ME grows over time depending on your faithfulness to ME throughout your daily experiences and during your periodic testing. Your every success and failure are used by ME to grow you through the well-watering of MY Holy Spirit. However, you will only grow and produce fruit if you are attached to the Vine. Who is "the Vine?" Almost two thousand years ago, Christ Jesus answered that question:

> {1} I am the true vine, and My Father is the cultivator. {2} Every branch in me that does not bear fruit, He takes away: and every branch that bears fruit, He purges it, that it may bring forth more

---

267   Matthew 5:8 & Titus 1:15: King James Version
268   Deuteronomy 6:5 & Mark 12:30: King James Version
269   Leviticus 19:18 & Mark 12:31: King James Version
270   Matthew 5:44-48, 6:14-15, King James Version
271   John 21:15-17, King James Version

fruit.[272]

Ironic, isn't it, that I appointed you to till the ground[273] and here I AM the ultimate sodbuster?

It is recorded in MY Holy Bible that King David had a heart "after MY own:"

> {22} And when the LORD had removed Saul, He raised up David unto the children of Israel to be their king; to whom also He gave testimony and said: "I have found David the son of Jesse, a man after MY own heart, who shall fulfill all of MY Will."[274]

How do you receive and keep a heart that is "after MY own?" You begin and end in penitence.

Penitence is the one factor in spiritual development most often neglected by souls in dust. Yet, without penitence, you cannot even hope to apprehend spiritual matters. Unless hearts are penitent, you will be unwilling to give up human opinions and mortal beliefs that you hold to be true. In effect, with an impenitent heart, you demonstrate your unwillingness to be taught by MY Holy Spirit.

Without penitence, there is simply no room in your heart for spiritual truth. *For example,* all of the etymologists and exegetes in your world could be gathered together to interpret various meanings within MY Holy Bible; however, without penitent hearts, their individual and collective interpretations of Scripture would be void of depth, and their scholarly utterances would be little more than vain babblings. If Christ Jesus himself were standing in front of you, and your impenitent heart refused to

---

272 Paraphrased from the King James Version of John 15:1-2
273 Genesis 3:17-19, 23, King James Version
274 Paraphrased from the King James Version of Acts 13:22; see also 1 Samuel 13:14, King James Version

soften and melt in his presence, you would not be able even to comprehend what he was saying to you (until, perhaps, it was too late).

To be sure, Christian men and women should not confuse their ability to reason with their having "the mind of Christ."[275] Oftentimes the divine Logos defies human logic. Spiritual reasoning is dependent on penitence. (More about that later in this chapter.)

You alone may freely choose penitence for yourself when it is offered to you by ME, but you cannot achieve a state of penitence without ME. I alone grant repentance to you in response to your desire to please ME. I alone soften your heart.[276] I alone create within you a new heart.[277]

If you desire to have a penitent heart, all you need to do is ask ME for one. (You need not do anything alone anymore if you have a mind to ask ME.) All that asking ME requires is your humility. All that keeps you from asking ME is your arrogance. To be sure, arrogance is pushy, but there is no greater push against arrogance than penitence. Your penitence pushes your arrogance aside and lets you see ME. Your penitence opens the eyes of your heart.[278] And the more penitent you are, the more enlightened your heart becomes.

The crucifixion of a thousand Christs could not rend the veil that covers an impenitent heart because that curtain can only be parted by ME in response to your desire to please ME. Penitence cannot be forced on anyone through corporal punishment or by confinement because the reformation of a life must begin as the conscious, inner decision of that life to live differently.

---

275 1 Corinthians 2:16 & Philippians 2:5: King James Version
276 Job 23:16, King James Version
277 Psalm 51:10, King James Version
278 Ephesians 1:18, various translations

It is only in penitence that you open your heart to ME and permit ME to come and reside within you through MY Holy Spirit. It is only in penitence that you are released from the shackles of your world and its world-system. It is only through penitence that you can be reclaimed to the family born of God's love. And it is only through penitence that your soul can be healed:

> The Daystar yet shall gleam,
> Throw down its treasured beam!
> It yet shall touch upon your soul,
> And mend its troubled seam.[279]

True penitence is past compunction and beyond grief. It is the mark of a soul that has turned itself right about face toward ME. It is a gift to ME of the highest order. It is the continued state of submission to MY Will. It is a demonstration of your eternal gratitude for MY efforts on your behalf.

Everyone on Earth knows how difficult it is for them to say: "I am sorry." Perhaps you find it uncomfortable to place yourself in a bad light in front of others. Perhaps you are embarrassed for having done something wrong. Perhaps you do not want to diminish the image you are seeking to project to others. Perhaps admitting that you are wrong would then require you to make a change that you are unwilling to make. Regardless of the reason or reasons, so difficult is it for souls in dust to say "I am sorry" that those three words often go unsaid. How much more difficult, then, would it be for a soul, not only to say "I am sorry," but also to live the words "I am sorry" every day of its earthly existence? Yet, if you are to enter and remain in active spiritual recovery from self-pride and self-will, such a continuing *metanoia* (or "mind-state of repentance") is required of you.

It is nothing less than your own hardness of heart that prevents you from admitting that you have done anything wrong. And it is

---

279   Copyright 1975 by Joseph Adam Pearson.

nothing less than your own denial of wrongdoing that would prevent you from entering MY Holy of Holies,[280] the place within where you meet ME, your one true and only real Self. Unfortunately, however, because most souls in dust look to find the Divinity without, the last place they venture to look for ME is within.

I must say that I hesitated to tell you that I AM your Self because you might decide that you are destined to become ME. [Everyone in Heaven still laughs at that notion.] Although one day I will infuse you and all other members of the Body of Christ with the Totality of MY Being, you can never become ME. When I say that I AM your Self, I mean that only in ME do you have your one true identity and only real being. I state that I AM your Self in the same way that Iochanan the Baptizer ("John the Baptist") said of MY Son: "He must increase and I must decrease."[281] I state that I AM your Self in the same way that Christ Jesus said: "In order to gain your life, you must first lose it."[282] I AM the Creator. You are MY Created. I AM your Spouse. You are MY espoused. I AM your Lover. You are MY beloved.

I WILL eternally remain your Creator. You will eternally remain MY Created. Yes, I AM your Life, and I AM your Self. To be sure, if you have given yourself completely to ME, then it is no longer you who live but I Who live within you.[283]

Why should you be penitent?

Penitence is the only way for souls in dust to get to MY Glory-land. Where is MY Glory-land? It is *over there,* across the river, and to the east — in an overworld far above your current plane of consciousness. Without penitence, no one is allowed to cross the

---

280   Hebrews, Chapter Nine
281   Paraphrased from the King James Version of John 3:30
282   Paraphrased from the King James Version of Matthew 10:39
283   Galatians 2:20, King James Version

bridge between your world and the next. Penitence is the fare required for your passage over the bridge. Your penitence is the toll. For those who might interpret this to mean that salvation is based on works (that is, requiring the "payment" of penitence) instead of depending solely on the sacrificial sinless offering of Christ Jesus, please remember that it takes a willing heart to receive salvation. I certainly do not force salvation on anyone, and not everyone is going to be saved even though salvation is offered to everyone through the sacrificial and sinless offering of Christ Jesus. I do not compromise MY Integrity. In effect, penitence separates the sheep from the goats.[284]

Penitence is the only thing on Earth that can keep you in love with ME. (Arrogance certainly cannot do that!) Penitence prevents the "prince of the power of the air"[285] from holding his power over you. (Through penitence, you will always find the strength necessary to overcome Satan's temptations.) Penitence prevents you from becoming embittered by the unpleasant circumstances in which you may find yourselves. Penitence keeps you from judging others and from being judged.[286] Penitence prepares you for Heaven.

Instead of fear concerning the loss of the false image you have of yourselves, there should be great joy among you that I consider penitence sufficient as your contribution to the salvation process.

The more penitent you are, the brighter you become. To be sure, there is a direct relationship between your penitence and the degree of your reflectance of MY Glory. From MY spiritual vantage point, the more you submit yourselves to ME in contrition, the more you increase in brilliance until your brilliance eventually equals that found within MY Glory-land. In MY Glory-land, you are brilliant because you reflect MY Glory in

---

284 Matthew 25:32-33, King James Version
285 Ephesians 2:2, King James Version
286 Romans 2:5, King James Version

all of your facets (somewhat like a spiritual diamond).

Let ME explain.

When souls are fully returned to ME as MY complete image and perfect likeness, they no longer carry around the darkness of self-pride and self-will. Because their souls are thus freed from iniquity, they are then enabled, once again, to reflect ME without blemish. When a soul receives its "crown of glory"[287] in Heaven, the garment of self-pride and self-will that it has worn since it first turned from ME (which is to say, the soiled appearance that has been a sign of its iniquity) is forever removed and permanently replaced with a new mantle, such robe an investment of ME. The appearance of a soul who lives in ME is bright as I AM bright, giving Light not as the Source of Light but, rather, as a vessel bearing MY Light, magnifying the Source for all to see.

Glory is what the children of God wear in Heaven. It is what makes them white.[288] It is an aura of goodness. It is a circle of Light. It is a radiant beauty and splendor that is incorruptible and unchanging. A very apparent luminosity, the Glory of God is what sets MY Children apart from the children of darkness. Thus, "glorious" is not only descriptive of MY bright appearance but also of the appearance of those who live fully in ME. As you wait patiently for that change to take place, please be reminded that all Glory belongs to ME!

Earlier in this chapter, I stated that spiritual reasoning is dependent on penitence. Indeed, spiritual reasoning is a process of the heart and not the head. When the caul of darkness has been removed from off the heart, when the heart has been circumcised of its self-pride and self-will, when the

---

287   1 Peter 5:4, King James Version
288   Matthew 17:2, 28:3; Mark 9:3; Luke 9:29-31; John 20:12; Acts 1:10; 1 John 3:2; & Revelation 3:4-5, 4:4, 6:11, 7:9, 7:13-14, 19:8: King James Version

commandments of God have been inscribed upon the fleshly tablets of the heart, and when a soul seeks out ways for MY Love to be expressed through its heart, then, and only then, is a soul ready to apprehend divine ideas, spiritual facts, and truths of being. Until that time, a soul in dust is either dead (as one of the "walking dead") or asleep to the purpose and meaning of life.

How do you get spiritual reasoning?

It begins with the softening of your heart. Such softening occurs in mortals when they come to believe on MY Son and in his mission. Mortals must become open to the world of Spirit before that world's elements can be both seen and heard. It ends — no, continues — in your love for ME and genuine concern for the well-being of others.

If you are a person after MY own heart, then you demonstrate generosity by sharing your love, affection, encouragement, knowledge, experiences, and resources with others. You do not withhold these things from others. You freely share the things that are most dear to you with ME and with all others who belong to ME.

If you are a person after MY own heart, you are childlike without being childish. If you are a person after MY own heart, you are as harmless as a dove at the same time that you are as wise as a serpent.[289]

Are you a person after MY own heart? If not, you can be one. All you need to do is ask ME.

---

289   Matthew 10:16, King James Version

Chapter Ten

Knowing Who You Really Are

If *mortality* is "death," and *corporeality* is "the shadow of death," what can souls who pass through dust hope to accomplish during their earthly sojourns?

Although you are presently tied to corporeality, you may refrain from acting on this visible sign of iniquity as if it constituted your one true and only reality. In other words, you can cease from acting on corporeal appearances as if they provided you, or could provide you, with a true picture of what MY Absolute Reality is like. And you can free yourselves from the shackles of sin, the "sting of death,"[290] in accord with the admonition of Christ Jesus that you be not "of" the world (and its world-system) even though you are found "in" it.[291]

Although you banished yourselves from the Garden of MY Heavenly Consciousness, — although physical bodies are the "coats of skins"[292] that cloak the naked consciousness of your bent souls, — although corporeality now hides the Nature of MY Absolute Reality from you, — and although you have refracted the Spiritual Light with which you were originally endowed, you need not view corporeality (the "shame" that you now wear) as the only frame of reference available to you as you make your way through its darkness. Instead, by looking to the Light[293] that is in Christ Jesus, you may turn toward your Creator, and thus toward your true home in Heaven. In this way, you can come to know who you really are in ME.

---

290 1 Corinthians 15:56, King James Version
291 John 17:11-17, King James Version
292 Genesis 3:21, King James Version
293 John 1:9, 8:12, & 12:46; 1 John 1:5: King James Version

By ceasing to act on physically-related images of unwholesome wants and desires (such action constituting sin), souls in dust refute the power that self-pride and self-will have in their lives, reopen themselves to the Light of God's "perfect day,"[294] and, as a result, see through all physical things to all spiritual things (gradually, of course). Unfortunately, however, those who do not struggle to remove the evil that has visited their souls — because they will not believe that they themselves are sinners or that there is a power greater than that which causes them to sin — cannot see MY Light. Since not even the faintest glimmer of spiritual truth reaches those who cling to their iniquity by consciously and deliberately continuing to sin, all things to them must remain inverted and out of focus for as long as they indulge, and to the degree that they indulge, their own self-pride and self-will.

Unknown to many of you, it is only by *not* succumbing to the temptation to sin that you are let go from the hypnotic hold that "the god of this world"[295] has on you and are, thereby, able to triumphantly proclaim these words as you march toward MY Glory-land: "O death, where is your sting? O grave where is your victory?"[296] Yes, refraining from sin allows those still caught in the web of carnal mind and corporeality to keep from becoming further entangled in iniquity so that they might begin the inward journey to that bright land which seems so far away and yet is so near. It is only by shutting yourselves off from the cause of divisiveness (which is to say, action based on iniquity, or "sin") that you start to sense the unity of all real life, a unity that was not bred by a flash of lightening upon some volcanic ash but born of MY Love. It is upon seeing such a common ground that you advance more closely toward MY Glory-land, where you will meet the rest of your spiritual family in Christ and find that you are, in truth, the rest of them.

---

294   Proverbs 4:18, King James Version
295   2 Corinthians 4:4, King James Version
296   Paraphrased from the King James Version of 1 Corinthians 15:55

Mere imagination cannot provide the breathtaking — no, breath*giving* — view that is obtained when you subjugate your human creature in self-sacrifice to MY Love. Though at first "the creature" whines and shudders with self-pity that it is being denied (1) the celebrity of its imagined glamour and (2) the comfort from its self-proclaimed speciality — it is in such restraint that the animal slowly dies while MY Holy Spirit within your soul quickens[297] the real you. Then, when "the creature" is finally thrust through with the sword of truth, it gives up the ghost and the soul that it once held condemned is freed to soar upward on its now unfurled wings of faith to greater heights thereafter. Although seemingly contradictory, the statement of Christ Jesus, "whoever loses his or her life for my sake shall find it,"[298] expresses the necessity for souls in dust to move through corporeality in surrender, yielding themselves up to ME in all that they do. In this way are you fully released from the false image you have of yourselves.

From "only begotten Son of God"[299] to "first begotten of the dead,"[300] it is fitting that Christ Jesus is the only Head of the Church of God. As "high Priest,"[301] and sole "Mediator of the New Covenant"[302] between God and humankind, it is also fitting that he is first over those who were once dead (that is, "mortal") but are now made alive (that is, "immortal") in him.

Although Christ Jesus is "the *only* begotten Son of God," Christ Jesus is not the *only* "begotten of the dead." Thus, it is necessary

---

297 *Quicken* means "impart life to" or "revive." See Psalm 71:20, 80:18, 119:25, 37, 40, 50, 88, 93, 107, 149, 154, 156, 159, 143:11; John 5:21, 6:63; Romans 4:17, 8:11; Ephesians 2:1, 5; Colossians 2:13; 1 Timothy 6:13; & 1 Peter 3:18: King James Version

298 Paraphrased from the King James Version of Matthew 10:39

299 John 1:14, 18; John 3:16, 18; & 1 John 4:9: King James Version

300 Revelation 1:5, King James Version

301 Hebrews 3:1, King James Version

302 Hebrews 12:24, King James Version

for "those who hunger and thirst after righteousness"[303] to understand that, when they seek to do MY Will, they are, though not Jesus, also *of Christ.*

How so, "though not Jesus, also *of Christ"?*

It is the mystery of faith that joins those who seek to do MY Will to the consciousness of MY Christ and, hence, to the one and only originator of all truth. Such a spiritual consanguinity traverses all apparent boundaries to include (1) those who are struggling to be freed from the grip that self-pride and self-will currently exercise within their lives as well as (2) those saved who have gone on ("passed on") before them. Remember, I created one Body of whom all saved souls are members. In MY Absolute Reality, all saved people are interdependent channels of MY Supreme Being. They do not constitute or comprise MY Supreme Being. Rather, they are channels for it.

Sooner or later, it becomes obvious to each one travailing to be delivered from mortality that, because I AM Love,[304] you must already be loved to the uttermost. Yes, you are already loved to the last element of MY Supreme Being. Hence, you cannot ever be loved any more than you currently are, neither at present nor at some distant point in your cosmic future. Concerning such spiritual intimacy between Creator and created, it is important to emphasize to souls in dust that if you wait for ME without (outside of yourselves), I WILL BE a long time in coming, but if you wait for ME within (inside of yourselves), it will eventually dawn on you that I AM already there waiting for you. (Please note, waiting for ME "without" is not referring to the return of MY Son to Earth, which return, most assuredly, will occur.)

As I see it, one of the greatest obstacles to understanding the Nature of MY Absolute Reality — and, thereby, knowing who

303 Matthew 5:6, King James Version
304 1 John 4:8, King James Version

you really are — is overcome as you apprehend that I actually reside within you when you are fitting channels for MY Love. In MY Absolute Reality, I cannot be separate from those who are MY Created (who include MY "re-created" through Christ Jesus) nor can they be separated from each other or from ME. Of course, earthly appearances would lead you to believe otherwise, but you must keep in mind that such appearances are not part of MY Absolute Reality. Corporeal images prove nothing about MY Perfect World and who you really are. Although one day you will receive a glorified body, and although that body has some similarities to your current body, your glorified form is not corporeal. It is not physical. It is incorporeal and spiritual. And, albeit incorporeal and spiritual, it is substantive beyond mere mortal understanding.

That I live in you only to the degree that you prove MY qualities and attributes should be frightening to those in your earthly sphere of activities who profess to do MY work but do not demonstrate the single most important quality by which I laid down MY entire Spiritual Universe, which quality is love. Every soul who has tried to exist outside the framework of unselfish love has ended up negating itself — that is, phasing itself out of the one true and only reality it can have in ME. All such souls end up cutting themselves off from ME (the Source of all real *being*) and, hence, from communion with all saints (those who are eternally conscious of the spiritual truth that they live in ME only through the sacrificial and sinless love offering of Christ Jesus).

For those who might protest that MY Creation must contain impurity as well as purity, let it be known that MY all-time, all-space, and all-motion include by excluding. Boundaries do exist for MY Perfect World. Although MY Creation is infinite, those who live within it and contribute to MY Glory do not experience both good and evil, right and wrong, and purity and impurity; nevertheless, they most certainly can distinguish between the contradistinct characteristics in each pair.

For souls in the earth plane of consciousness to become spiritually renewed and restored in purity to what I originally intended for them, they must rekindle MY fire within through their efforts to remove the illicit power of self-pride and self-will that now sits enthroned within their souls. (Although salvation is not dependent on your efforts, the process of sanctification relies on them.)

If souls in dust are to re-enter MY Kingdom, they must be willing to wake from their sleep of death to sacrifice the illusive pleasures and pains that have kept them bound to self-pride and self-will. King David came to such an understanding, which inspired him to write:

> Sacrifice and offering You did not desire; my ears have You opened: burnt offering and sin offering have You not required.[305]

> For You do not desire animal sacrifice. Otherwise, I would give it. You do not delight in burnt offerings. The sacrifices of God are a broken spirit: a broken and contrite heart, O God, You will not reject.[306]

Like King David, you also must come to the spiritual recognition that I neither expect nor exact false sacrifices from you. Instead, I require the most difficult offering: sacrificing yourself daily in gratitude, humility, and penitence. If you "press toward the mark for the prize of the high calling of God,"[307] then you will daily place yourself on the altar as "a living sacrifice."[308]

To be sure, I AM worthy of the only offering that gives true evidence of contrition in those who have gone astray, which evidence includes the sacrifice of your self-pride for MY Pride and your self-will for MY Will. For those who would glean merely

---

305 Paraphrased from the King James Version of Psalm 40:6
306 Paraphrased from the King James Version of Psalm 51:16-17
307 Philippians 3:14, King James Version
308 Romans 12:1, King James Version

half a truth here and then try to press another soul physically, emotionally, or mentally into submitting to ME, please know that such action has no foundation in truth. Feelings of genuine thanksgiving, selflessness, and contrition cannot be forced from without when they do not exist within. Unless an offering is presented of one's "own voluntary will,"[309] it means nothing to anyone, least of all to ME.

In your world of appearances, many people have taken the defeatist attitude that an unblemished life (which is to say, a Biblically-perfect life) simply cannot be lived by those who dwell in fleshly vehicles. And some of these same people have additionally concluded (as demonstrated by the lives they lead) that all indulged weaknesses, vulnerabilities, and infirmities will be forgiven without any natural or supernatural consequences. Unfortunately, choosing those mindsets as backdrops for living on Earth is a mistake since they provide scenarios for one spiritual failure after another. In direct opposition to such negativism, not only is Biblical perfection attainable, it is your challenge from ME:

> I AM THE ALMIGHTY GOD. WALK BEFORE
> ME AND BE PERFECT.[310]

Unfortunately, some religious people have decided that what will do the trick is the emphatic mouthing of verbal affirmations, like "I am whole," "I am perfect," "I am made in the image of God," and "I am healed." Undoubtedly, however, these paroxysms are insufficient without genuine gratitude, humility, and penitence to back them up. Your fellow citizens may not recognize the difference between genuine and feigned, but I do. *(For example, a smile that is "sweet" to you could be sincere, saccharine, or sardonic to ME.)*

Although the word *perfect* may call to mind visions of physical

---

309 Leviticus 1:3, King James Version
310 Genesis 17:1, King James Version

beauty, youthful vigor, and intellectual excellence, those images are but poor shadows of the attractiveness, dynamism, and brilliance that are found in MY True Creation, where beauty in one another is perceived from within, action is the result of spiritual forethought, and luminosity depends completely on degree of reflectance of MY Glory. Spiritually elevated in thought and looking beyond mortality, it is easier to see that, as the work of God, MY Children are altogether lovely and, thus, the true luminaries, or stars, of Heaven. And, regardless of what those on Earth might think, believe, and/or say, a perfect body is, first and foremost, one that is free from sin.

By searching through the multiple meanings of the Hebrew and Greek words from which the word *perfect* has been translated in the King James Version of the Old and New Testaments, students of truth will gain a greater sense of what a state of Biblical perfection entails. In such an undertaking, one would not only find "unblemished" but also "without spot," "whole," "complete," "finished," "of full age," "replete," "fulfilled," "satisfied," "at peace," "peaceable," "established," "upright," "undefiled," "clean," "returned to one's former condition," and "showing one's true self." However, despite the wider view that might be obtained from such a search, and in spite of additional words that might be used to round out an even fuller sense of what it means to be Biblically perfect, unless souls in dust are willing to have the tarnish removed from off their souls, they will not be able to understand firsthand the significance of "Biblical perfection." (What you have just read is not intended to be in contest with the truth that the salvation of your souls is provided solely by the sinless blood offering of Jesus Christ "once for all."[311])

To be restored to the consciousness that is in Christ Jesus, which consciousness is described in MY Holy Bible as "the mind of

---

311   Hebrews 10:10, King James Version

Christ,"[312] souls in dust should have an unquenchable thirst for MY Holy Spirit. It is in the searching for — as well as in the finding and drinking of — such "living water"[313] that you early rise to an awareness that MY Created are sojourners of purpose in the "waste howling wilderness"[314] of Earth and that only the spiritually disinherited, walking in the ways of the world, travel its purposeless paths. Since "carnal mind"[315] continually tries to convince you that a state of existence in dust is natural for the created of God, it makes it difficult for you to want to accept that there can be no permanent dwelling, no real rest or pleasure, and no true glory in your current plane of consciousness. (You are buffeted daily to believe that you should make yourselves at home where you are and win the acceptance of at least some forms in humankind.)

How many on your globe could honestly say: "There is nothing here for me" or "There is nothing — neither love of sin nor pleasure in physical sentiency — that holds me to this world of appearances"? And, of those who could, how many have reached the point in their spiritual advancement where they have maximally objectified their current condition by putting off their lower, abased self, which operates on the animus of corporeality, so they might be, right now, "present with the Lord"?[316]

"Absent from the body"[317] and yet present with the Lord? In dust and yet "in the Spirit"?[318] How can that be? How is it possible to exist in corporeality and yet "live, move and having your being"

---

312   1 Corinthians 2:16 & Philippians 2:5: King James Version
313   John 4:10, King James Version
314   Deuteronomy 32:10, King James Version
315   Romans 8:6-7, King James Version
316   2 Corinthians 5:8, King James Version
317   2 Corinthians 5:8, King James Version
318   Romans 8:9; 1 Corinthians 5:3; 1 Corinthians 14:2; Galatians 3:3, 5:16 & 25; Ephesians 6:18; & Revelation 1:10, 4:2, 17:3, & 21:10: King James Version

in ME?[319] These questions are not silly to broach nor unanswerable. Although you are in corporeality, those of you who seek to know who you really are will not be denied. MY Truth does not hide from those who seek it. However, the answers to all your questions still must come from within you — which is to say, even if you are studying MY Holy Bible, unless you are willing to accept it as truth, you will not be able to learn from it. Thus, repetition and increased time on task are not successful teaching methodologies for the spiritually unteachable. For those who believe they already know everything there is to know, there is no room within them to "get understanding,"[320] especially not the kind whose torch lights the way from your world, finitely finite, to the one "without end."[321] Ironically, those who are caught in the looking glass of vanity are damned by their own convictions because they *do* know everything they can ever hope to know (as long as they cling to such a view). As a result, they remain spiritually incapacitated, unable to flee to ME because of their ignorance of who they really are. (Most often, spiritual ignorance is due to the lack of an inquiring mind.)

Concerning the uncertainty of "here and yet there," an exclamation used by Abraham, Jacob, Moses, Samuel, David, and Isaiah sheds additional light on the topic: Their exclamation to ME of "Here am I!"[322] intends much more than their verbalization of the self-evident or their announcement of an existential moment. "Here am I!" states their purpose of being. Through its exclamation, their souls gave open testimony that they no longer were willing to view their selfhood independent of MY Life, Love, and Light. It is the statement of souls yielding themselves back up to ME consciously and willingly, receptive to all instruction from ME that they might receive the "re-

---

319 Paraphrased from the King James Version of Acts 17:28
320 Psalm 119:104; Proverbs 3:13, 4:5-7, 15:32, 16:16
321 Ephesians 3:21, King James Version
322 Genesis 22:11, 31:11, 46:2; Exodus 3:4; 1 Samuel 3:4; 2 Samuel 15:26; & Isaiah 6:8: King James Version

reward"[323] of MY hereafter there-ever-after. In short, "Here am I!" is the response of souls surrendering to their Creator, WHO has been saying, and continues to say, "HERE I AM!"[324]

It is important for the spiritually-minded to grasp tightly that their true home is wherever I AM — which is to say, that their real being is in ME: not their imperfect, or human, being (which is their current appearance in mortality) but their perfect, or glorified, being (which is how they appear in immortality). Because you cannot "be" where I AM not, souls in dust need to apply unceasingly that understanding to the shadows, dreams, illusions, and nightmares they meet while homeward bound. Souls in dust who let down their spiritual defenses, though but for a moment, are often found spiritually weakened enough to be attacked and controlled by self-pride and self-will. Unfortunately, whenever souls in dust forget that they are only in transition within the earth plane of consciousness — that is, merely passing through its corporeality either *to be* or *to be no more* — they are unwilling to relinquish the false image they have of themselves. As a result, they are unable to find the strength that is necessary for them to step from death to life at the end of their earthly days.

Because the Kingdom of God is within you,[325] and because you can only have your one true identity and only real being in ME, souls who fail to supplant physically-based views of existence with spiritually-enlightened views of life greatly err. Since you are how you see yourselves, such souls condemn themselves to remain "bound in fetters and held in cords of affliction"[326] — which is to say, tied to mortality in one form or another. Indeed, many in corporeality take no responsibility for their individual actions, preferring instead the license of viewing themselves as autonomous from one another. This license permits them to do

323   Isaiah 58:8, King James Version
324   Isaiah 58:9, King James Version
325   Luke 17:21, King James Version
326   Paraphrased from the King James Version of Job 36:8

as they please without the burden of a guilty conscience. Since the apostate make Christ's mediation of null effect for their own lives, the platform of mortality on which they stand becomes their way station to Hell. Hell does nothing but open its gates and enlarge its borders to receive them into eternal damnation.

Without knowing who, what, where, and when they really *are,* it is easy for souls in dust to accept their low, fleshly estate as existing within the schema of MY eternal handiwork and, thus misguided, to continue to try and dig a home in dust farther away from ME. It should stand to spiritual reasoning (a process of the heart and not the head) that, if I AM incorruptible and immortal (and I AM), then MY Creation, which is made in the image and likeness of ME, also must be incorruptible and immortal. As recorded in the wheels of mortality and in the skeins of physical time, all who have clung to their encarnalized condition, as if it were a desirable state, were on the road to spiritual extinction (that is, eternal separation from ME).

From the first moment of the appearance of souls in dust, physicality has always been unfit to hold the Essence of MY Being. That is why I declared: "MY Spirit shall not always strive with humankind because [in addition to what else it is] humankind also is flesh."[327] In other words, there will be a point in physical time when MY Life, Love, and Light will be totally withdrawn from those in corporeality who remain intent on glorifying themselves. If only you would take the time to look within yourselves, you would find that I AM the ONLY Cause of all real being. It is only in ME that you know who you really are.

I continue to lament because:

> MY people have changed their Glory for that which does not profit. MY people have committed two evils: they have forsaken ME, the Fountain of Living

---

327   Paraphrased from the King James Version of Genesis 6:3

Water, and hewed them out cisterns, broken cisterns, that can hold no [living] water.[328]

"Knowing who you really are" does not mean that you need to get in touch with yourselves physically, psychologically, or philosophically. Rather, it means that you need to discover fundamental truths about your first estate.

Early Christians were challenged by this query from the Apostle Paul: "Do you not know your own selves that Jesus Christ is in you unless you are counterfeits?"[329] Likewise, contemporary Christians should be challenged by the inner call to investigate that which is spiritually substantive and, through such investigation, come to rediscover who they really are in their Creator's species of thought.

If corporeality were the eternal work of the Most High God, then there would be no need for ME to call you home because you would be there already.

It is not sufficient for ME to tell you in order for you to fully comprehend the insignificance of who you think you are and the significance of who you really are. Souls in dust must discover that for themselves. (Such self-discovery is the true sign of a quickening spirit.)

It is only when you each come to the point at which corporeality and its false images of "individuality" and "separateness" seem altogether unnatural for you that you are willing to extricate yourselves from the tight grip that self-pride and self-will have had on you. Then, fully awake from the dead, "you will know even as you also are known."[330]

Are you ready to learn who you are in ME?

---

328 Paraphrased from the King James Version of Jeremiah 2:11 & 13
329 Paraphrased from the King James Version of 2 Corinthians 13:5
330 Paraphrased from the King James Version of 1 Corinthians 13:12

Chapter Eleven

The Dissolution of Corporeality

Few people realize that corporeality is a curse. Fewer people realize that corporeality is a curse imposed upon them by their own iniquity. It is your iniquity that has brought you from immortality ("true life") to mortality ("real death"). And it is your continued falling, or action based on your iniquity, that keeps you tied to the substratum of mortality called "corporeality." Acting as if corporeality is all that there is, many souls in dust bind themselves to a flesh that is not the eternal substance of God and to a place that does not hold God's Glory. In so doing, they destine themselves to remain in mortality (although not necessarily in corporeality).

If you exist in corporeality without MY Holy Spirit residing within you,[331] then you are one of the "walking dead." You have an eternal soul, but you are not immortal in the sense that the word *immortal* is being used in this book. To be sure, all souls are eternal. Christ Jesus addressed the eternal nature of all souls when he spoke of "eternal life"[332] (or "life eternal"[333]) for some and "eternal damnation"[334] (or "everlasting punishment"[335]) for others. However, only some eternal souls are "immortal." The others are "mortal." In this book, "immortal souls" are saved souls who have either gone on to be with the Lord in Heaven or who are still in corporeality and have not made their transition to

---

331 God's Holy Spirit indwells a soul when that soul accepts God's only-begotten Son by believing on him and in his mission. ("Believing on" connotes *trusting*.)

332 Matthew 19:16; Mark 10:17-25, 10:30; John 3:15, 5:39, 6:54, 10:28, 17:2: King James Version

333 Matthew 25:46 & John 4:36, 12:25, 17:3: King James Version

334 Mark 3:29, King James Version

335 Matthew 25:46, King James Version

Heaven yet. And, in this book, "mortal souls" are unsaved souls either in corporeality (in a flesh body) or in incorporeality (not in a flesh body).

Despite what people think about the longevity of corporeality, it is not eternal. Most souls who are at home in corporeality find it difficult to imagine that one day all corporeality will be removed suddenly and unexpectedly:

> {10} But the day of the Lord will come as a thief in the night, at which time the heavens shall pass away with a great noise, and the elements shall melt with fervent heat, the earth also and the works that are therein shall be burned up. {11} Seeing, then, that all these things shall be dissolved, what manner of persons should you be in all holy conversation and godliness, {12} Looking for and advancing toward the coming of the day of God, wherein the heavens being on fire shall be dissolved, and the elements shall melt with fervent heat? {13} Regardless, according to His promise, we look for new heavens and a new earth, wherein dwells righteousness.[336]

For you to get more accurate bearings on your current location, you will need to become better acquainted with MY Holy Scripture, wherein lies the basis for understanding the view of the eventual dissolution of all corporeality. In addition to the explicit view just quoted, this dissolution is presaged, allegorized, analogized, alluded to, symbolized, and prophesied throughout MY Holy Bible.

When the cities of Sodom and Gomorrah reached the fullness of their iniquity, I consumed them by raining upon them "fire and brimstone from heaven."[337] Because the children of the Exodus complained, it is recorded that "the fire of the LORD burned

---

336 Paraphrased from the King James Version of 2 Peter 3:10-13
337 Luke 17:29, King James Version (See also Genesis 19:15 & 24)

among them, and consumed them...”[338] MY Holy Bible also records that when Korah lead the rebellion against MY servant Moshe (Moses), “there came out a fire from the LORD and consumed the two hundred and fifty men that offered incense.”[339] And, each time King Ahaziah sent “a captain of fifty with his fifty”[340] to take MY Prophet Elijah, “the fire of God came down from heaven and consumed the captain and his fifty.”[341]

A very important concept concerning MY Nature and its capabilities are contained in the previously-cited Bible passages. MY Wrath (that is, MY Justified Anger) can be so kindled by the sinful actions of those in humankind that it can consume, expunge, and remove them from physical existence. As I told Moshe: “You cannot see MY face [that is, MY Appearance] because no human being can see ME and live.”[342] Thus, although MY Spiritual Light is radiantly warm and awesomely beautiful to those pure and perfect heavenly beings who fully and completely “live and move and have their being”[343] in ME, that same Light, as a “consuming fire,”[344] would annihilate corporeal beings if they were exposed to it.

Why have I permitted corporeality to continue without interruption since its inception? Because I love MY Creation, I have withheld the Fiery Part of ME from breaking forth upon the fallen until the time of the end (that is, the end of relative time). When the last souls who belong to ME are finally sealed and eternally separated from those who do not belong to ME, MY Glory will then burst forth upon all physicality. At that time, all souls (saved and unsaved alike) will acknowledge that I AM

---

338 Paraphrased from the King James Version of Numbers 11:1
339 Numbers 16:35, King James Version
340 2 Kings 1:9, King James Version
341 2 Kings 1:12, King James Version
342 Paraphrased from the King James Version of Exodus 33:20
343 Acts 17:28, King James Version
344 Deuteronomy 4:24, 9:3 & Hebrews 12:29: King James Version

God.[345]

Many times I have been tempted by the sins of souls in dust to destroy your world. But "being full of compassion, I did not destroy you; indeed, many times I turned MY Anger away from you, and did not stir up all of MY Wrath."[346] Instead, I reserved infusing the physical universe with the Totality of MY Being and carrying out MY Final Judgment until the end of physical time. MY Final Judgment and MY Infusion[347] will not occur until after the one-thousand-year reign of Christ Jesus on Earth[348] (that is, at the end of *the Millennium*). Until that time, "it is of MY Mercy that you are not consumed because MY Compassion is consistently unfailing."[349] However, make no mistake, I WILL not wait beyond the time that I have set. This is consistent with what MY Prophet Daniel wrote concerning another end-time event: "for yet the end shall be at the time appointed."[350] MY Compassion is not without principle. I WILL not allow MY Spiritual Law to be disregarded throughout eternity. Yes, I AM compassionate, but I also require justice.

As already indicated, at various times in Bible history I have dissolved the corporeality of those who have displeased ME. It is also recorded that I have dissolved the corporeality of people who have greatly pleased ME. How? I stepped up their consciousness and "translated" (quickened) their physical bodies so they might ascend to Heaven without experiencing physical death.

---

345   Romans 14:10-12, Philippians 2:10
346   Paraphrased from the King James Version of Psalm 78:38
347   1 Corinthians 15:28, King James Version (See also Ephesians 1:22-23.)
348   Revelation 20:7-15, King James Version
349   Paraphrased from the King James Version of Lamentations 3:22
350   Daniel 11:27, King James Version

Concerning Enoch, MY Holy Bible records and explains his unusual earthly departure as follows:

> And Enoch lived sixty and five years and begat Methuselah: And Enoch walked with God after he begat Methuselah three hundred years and begat sons and daughters: And all the days of Enoch were three hundred sixty and five years: And Enoch walked with God: and he was *not* [found]; for God took him.[351]

> By faith Enoch was translated that he should not see death; and was not found because God had translated him because before his translation he had the testimony that he pleased God.[352]

It is also recorded that, as he talked with his fellow prophet Elisha, Elijah departed in a most unusual way:

> ...there appeared a chariot of fire, and horses of fire, and the two of them were separated; and Elijah went up by a whirlwind into Heaven.[353]

Both Enoch and Elijah were removed from physicality and glorified. (That they were glorified is implied in MY Holy Bible by the appearance of Elijah "in glory" at the time of the Transfiguration of Jesus Christ.[354]) Because MY Forgiveness of their iniquity was so complete and so instantaneous, they literally stepped from the earth plane of consciousness to MY Perfect World. It is not that their physical flesh became spiritual flesh. Instead, their filthy garments of corporeality were dissolved and their iniquity was removed, freeing them to directly enter MY Kingdom.

---

351 Genesis 5:22-24, King James Version
352 Hebrews 11:5, King James Version
353 Paraphrased from the King James Version of 2 Kings 2:11
354 Luke 9:29-31, King James Version (See also Matthew 17:1-3 & Mark 9:2-4.)

Both Enoch and Elijah were *translated:* (1) because of their extraordinary righteousness[355] as well as (2) to serve as prototypic examples of the resurrection of your bodies during "the Rapture." For the sake of clarification, "the Rapture" is the first *en masse* bodily resurrection of saved souls *(the first resurrection);* it occurs before the beginning of *the Millennium.* A second, and final, *en masse* bodily resurrection of saved souls *(the second resurrection)* takes place at the end of *the Millennium.*

The English word *rapture* is derived from: (1) the Latin noun *raptus/rapti,* whose meanings include "caught up" or "seized and taken away" and (2) the Latin verb *rapto/raptare,* whose meanings include "to catch up" or "to seize and take away."[356] The Biblical Rapture (Greek *harpazo* [357]) is the great "catching away" of Christians *before* Jesus Christ sets foot on Earth during his Second Coming (Greek *parousia* [358]). Regardless of when you think that the Rapture should occur or the specific time that it actually does occur, the operative word in the last sentence is "before." In other words, the Rapture will occur sometime *before* Christ Jesus sets foot on Earth. ("Sometime" here means, though undetermined by you, predetermined by ME. And "before" even includes immediately preceding Christ's Second Coming as the first step in a two-step process.) Unless Christians get rigid, controlling, and legalistic about their conclusions, the debate between and among them as to *when* (not *if,* but *when*) the Rapture will occur is healthy. Debating helps them to learn MY Scripture.

---

355   In the Holy Bible, "righteousness" refers to placing one's faith in God (Y'hweh in the Old Testament and Y'shua H'Moshiach in the New Testament) and walking in that faith daily.

356   The noun is used in St. Jerome's Latin Vulgate of the Holy Bible in 2 Corinthians 12:2, 4 and Revelation 12:5.

357   Greek ἁρπάζω

358   Greek παρουσία

The Rapture is described accurately by the Apostle Paul as follows:

{13} But I would not allow you to remain in ignorance, brothers and sisters, concerning those which are "asleep" [believers who have already physically died and whose souls have gone on to be with the Lord] that you not be sorrowful like others who have no hope, {14} For if we believe that Jesus died and rose again, even so [the souls of] those who "sleep in Jesus" will God bring with him. {15} For we say to you what we have received directly by the word of the Lord, that we who are alive [believers who have not yet physically died] and still remain [on Earth] until the coming [Greek *parousia*] of the Lord shall not take precedence over those who are "asleep" [in him]. {16} For the Lord Jesus himself shall descend from heaven with a shout, with the voice of the archangel, and with the trumpet of God: and the [bodies of those already] dead in Christ ["asleep in him"] shall rise first: {17} Then, we who are alive and still remain [on Earth] shall be "caught up" [Greek *harpazo*, Latin *rapiemur*] together with them in the clouds, to meet the Lord in the air: and so shall we ever be with the Lord. {18} Therefore, comfort one another with these words.[359]

{49} And as we have borne the image of the earthly, we shall also bear the image of the heavenly. {50} Now this I say, brothers and sisters, that flesh and blood cannot inherit the Kingdom of God; neither does corruption inherit incorruption. {51} Behold, I am showing you a mystery: We shall not all "sleep," but we shall all be changed, {52} In a moment, in the twinkling of an eye, at the last trumpet: for the

---

359 Paraphrased [and amplified] from the King James Version of 1 Thessalonians 4:13-18

trumpet shall sound, and the [bodies of the] dead shall be raised incorruptible, and we [who are still alive] shall be changed. {53} For this corruptible must put on incorruption, and this mortal must put on immortality. {54} So when this corruptible shall have put on incorruption, and this mortal shall have put on immortality, then shall be brought to pass the saying that is written: "Death is swallowed up in victory."[360]

The Rapture is a time when souls travailing on Earth will be delivered from their iniquity and the power of death at the Second Coming of Christ Jesus. The Rapture will be like the departures of Enoch and Elijah. At that time, souls in dust who have committed themselves to doing MY Will — by believing on MY Son and in his mission and striving to act accordingly — will be "stepped up" to MY Consciousness. All together, and at the same time, they will be carried away. From that point on, they will be enwrapped eternally in MY Glory, and each will receive a new somatic identity. In other words, it is during this event that all saved souls will receive their glorified bodies. Souls who are caught up "to meet the Lord Jesus in the air"[361] will not retain their physical identities. (Something so unlike ME cannot be made to have a part in MY Spiritual Universe.) This does not mean that you will not have form and substance or that you will not have bodies in Heaven. It just means that your heavenly bodies will be incorporeal and, therefore, quite different from the ones that you now have. Describing what your future bodies will look like, the Apostle John wrote:

> ... it does not yet appear what we shall look like: but we know that, when he [the Lord Jesus Christ] shall appear, we shall be like him; for we shall see him as

---

360 Paraphrased [and amplified] from the King James Version of 1 Corinthians 15:49-54, including quote from Isaiah 25:8.

361 1 Thessalonians 4:17, King James Version

he is.[362]

Although Jesus Christ has his own unique somatic identity, you will look like him to the extent that you will then be enwrapped completely by MY Glory. Your new bodies will have the same basic form, substance, and function as his.

When will the Rapture take place relative to the dissolution of all corporeality? The Rapture of MY Church shall precede the dissolution of all corporeality by one thousand years. (Chapters Twenty and Twenty-One of the Book of Revelation articulate what will occur in chronological order.)

Is it so far-fetched for you to believe that corporeality is not the "be-all and end-all" of existence and that corporeality has never been, is not now, and never will be found in MY Absolute Reality?

You cannot cling to particulate matter and its seeming reality throughout eternity. When will you be ready, willing, and able to give up the false image you have of yourself? Tomorrow? The day after tomorrow? The day before your earthly sojourn comes to an end?

Souls in dust have come to believe (more in demonstration through their actions rather than in their conscious thinking about it) that corporeality will be perpetuated throughout eternity. They fail to see that corporeality is a temporal and transitory state. They fail to see through the illusions of its appearances. And they fail to see the allusions in MY Holy Bible to the dissolution of corporeality.

Concerning Biblical references to the dissolution of all corporeality, concepts expressed by certain key words in Scripture are most helpful in providing insights to the end of all

---

362 Paraphrased from the King James Version of 1 John 3:2

physicality. In the King James Version of the Bible are found these key words (in their various grammatical forms): "dissolve," "consume," "fall," "burn," "move," "remove," "shake," "melt," "flee," "devour," "languish," "fade," "vanish," "depart," and "pass."

Although many Biblical passages relate to the dissolution of all corporeality, the following are some of the clearest on the subject:

> A fire goes before Him and burns up all of His enemies. His lightning enlightens the world: the earth saw and trembled. The hills melted like wax at the presence of the LORD of the whole earth. The heavens declare His righteousness, and all the people see His Glory.[363]

> Therefore, I Will shake the heavens, and the earth shall be removed out of her place in the wrath of the LORD of hosts, and in the day of His fierce anger.[364]

> The earth is utterly broken down, the earth is clean dissolved, the earth is removed. The earth shall reel to and fro like a drunkard and shall be removed like a temporary dwelling; and the transgressions thereof shall be heavy upon it, and it shall fall, and not rise again.[365]

> You will be visited by the LORD of hosts with thunder, and with earthquake, and great noise, with storm and tempest, and the flame of devouring fire.[366]

---

363 Paraphrased from the King James Version of Psalm 97:3-6
364 Paraphrased from the King James Version of Isaiah 13:13
365 Paraphrased from the King James Version of Isaiah 24:19-20
366 Paraphrased from the King James Version of Isaiah 29:6

Lift up your eyes to the heavens and look upon the earth beneath: for the heavens shall vanish away like smoke, and the earth shall wax old like a garment, and those who dwell therein shall die in like manner: but MY Salvation shall be forever, and MY Righteousness shall not be abolished.[367]

The mountains quake at Him, and the hills melt, and the earth is burned at His presence, yes, the world and all who dwell therein. Who can stand before His indignation? And who can abide in the fierceness of His anger? His fury is poured out like fire, and the rocks are thrown down by Him.[368]

Therefore, wait upon ME, says the LORD, until the day that I rise up to the prey: for MY determination is to gather the nations, that I may assemble the kingdoms, to pour upon them MY indignation, even all of MY fierce anger: for all of the earth shall be devoured with the fire of MY jealousy.[369]

And this shall be the plague wherewith the LORD will smite all the people who have fought against Jerusalem: Their flesh shall consume away while they stand upon their feet, and their eyes shall consume away in their sockets, and their tongues shall consume away in their mouths.[370]

And the earth departed as a scroll when it is rolled up; and every mountain and island were moved out of their places.[371]

---

367 Paraphrased from the King James Version of Isaiah 51:6
368 Paraphrased from the King James Version of Nahum 1:5-6
369 Paraphrased from the King James Version of Zephaniah 3:8
370 Paraphrased from the King James Version of Zechariah 14:12
371 Paraphrased from the King James Version of Revelation 6:14

> And I saw a great white throne, and Him who sat on it, from whose face the earth and the heaven fled away; and there was no place for them.[372]

> And Death and Hell were cast into the Lake of Fire.[373]

> And I saw a new heaven and a new earth: for the first heaven and the first earth were passed away …[374]

That the Earth melts like wax in MY Fiery Presence, — that the Earth is removed in the day of MY Anger, — that the heavens shall vanish like smoke, — that the Earth shall be devoured by the fire of MY Jealousy, — that I will pour out MY indignation upon the Earth, — that all flesh will be consumed by ME, and — that the Earth and her heavens shall flee and not be found: *altogether should paint a clear picture for the spiritually-minded.* All corporeality is going to dissolve. Only that which is eternal is indissoluble.

All physicality must pass away if you are to behold — and be beheld in — MY Glory. As the flood of waters came during Noah's time to cleanse the Earth of the apostate, so, too, must the infusion of MY Fiery Presence come to blot out all iniquity as well as its various manifestations. At that time, the Light of God will cause all shadows to flee — even "the shadow of death"[375] (corporeality). If only literalists had thought more literally, they might have seen this coming.

---

372 Paraphrased from the King James Version of Revelation 20:11

373 Paraphrased from the King James Version of Revelation 20:14

374 Paraphrased from the King James Version of Revelation 21:1

375 Psalm 23:4, Isaiah 9:2, Amos 5:8, Matthew 4:16, & Luke 1:79: King James Version

Afterword

Views expressed in this book are not based on consensus reality or the reality of any one individual. They are based on the present author's perceptions of God's absolute reality as he understands it and can best articulate it. When in doubt about any view, regardless of whether it is expressed by the present author or any other person, always consult God's only written Word, the Holy Bible, and ask for wisdom from God. If you ask aright, God will not withhold His Wisdom from you:

> [5} If anyone lacks wisdom, let that person ask of God, who gives to all people liberally, and does not reproach; and it shall be given. {6} But let each person ask in faith, not wavering. For the person who wavers is like a wave of the sea driven with the wind and tossed. {7} That person should not think that he or she will receive anything of the Lord.[376]

We cannot save ourselves. We are saved solely through the shed blood of God's only-begotten Son, our Lord Jesus Christ. That is why all creation bows at his feet. We can only blush in shame at the purity of his innocence. When we see each other in Heaven, it can only be through his shed blood. If you study God's Holy Bible, I know that you, too, will be able to catch a glimpse of God's absolute reality while you are still on Earth. To understand the Holy Bible, all you need to do is look through the holes in the precious hands and feet of Jesus Christ as you read.

Grace and peace to you in the Name of Jesus the Christ, Y'shua H'Moshiach!

---

376   Paraphrased from the King James Version of James 1:5-7

Appendix

Incarnates and Discarnates

Definitions

Incarnates (incarnate souls) are souls residing within human bodies that have been assigned to them individually (that is, one soul is appointed to each human body by the Creator). *Discarnates* (discarnate souls) are souls who are not inhabiting human bodies assigned by God. The operative word here is "assigned" because some discarnates — as unclean spirits, demons, evil spirits, or devils (all Biblically synonymous terms) — possess, inhabit, or control human bodies that are not assigned to them by God. For the sake of clarification, no unclean spirit is assigned by God to possess any human being. Also, for the sake of clarification, possession of one human being may be by one unclean spirit, a group of unclean spirits, or groups of unclean spirits. (More about demonic possession later in this Appendix.)

Discarnates are either *pre-incarnate* or *post-incarnate:*

Pre-incarnate souls are awaiting the time when they will enter the physical realm in tandem with the conception, development, and birth of a new human body that is assigned to them (i.e., appointed by God for them).

Post-incarnate souls are in one of three possible states of existence: (1) already in Paradise because of their open, committed, and confirmed acceptance of Jesus Christ as their Personal Savior while they were on Earth; (2) in between human incarnations because they have neither completely accepted nor completely rejected Jesus Christ as their Personal Savior while they were on Earth; or (3) as the unclean spirits, demons, evil spirits, or devils referred to previously, roaming the netherworld (underworld, hell, Hades,[377] or Sheol[378]) until the time of the Final Judgment by God.[379] (The words *netherworld, underworld, hell, Hades,* and *Sheol* are all interchangeable here.)

Unclean Spirits

Unclean spirits, demons, evil spirits, or devils (all Biblically synonymous terms) are souls beyond reclamation. They are discarnates who have consciously rejected the Will of God after they have come to know and understand what the Will of God is. *For example,* there are people who understand the gospel of Jesus Christ and the significance that it has for them personally but who have made a conscious decision to not only not forgive others but also to hate others who have trespassed against them. The previous statement might generate debate between those who believe that saved souls can lose their salvation and those who believe that saved souls cannot lose their salvation (or that anyone who "loses" salvation was not really saved to begin with). Resolution for that debate is intended by the following statement: Saved souls cannot be robbed of their salvation, but, because they are free will agents, they can throw their salvation away. Unforgiveness for perceived or real wrongs committed against you and hatred of other human beings are identification marks of the Devil. Unforgiveness for wrongs committed against you and hatred of others open human beings up to demonic attack and, therefore, are the most dangerous emotions any human being can indulge. To be sure, those who entertain these

---

377 Greek ᾅδης
378 Hebrew *sheh-ole'* [H7585] from the *Dictionary of the Hebrew Bible* in *Strong's Exhaustive Concordance of the Bible* by James Strong (Copyright 1890), Crusade Bible Publishers, Inc., Nashville.
379 Revelation 20:10-13, King James Version

dangerous emotions separate themselves from God's protection. However, incarnate souls who repent of their unforgiveness and hatred of others before their transition to a post-incarnate state are restored to God's protection.

Souls become unclean spirits, demons, evil spirits, or devils: (1) because of their open, committed, and confirmed rejection of Jesus Christ as their Personal Savior while they were incarnates; or (2) because of their refusal to re-enter corporeality when appointed to do so by God. In effect, refusing to re-enter corporeality is spiritual sin, or blasphemy against the Holy Spirit — and is, therefore, an unforgiveable sin (a damnable offense against God) — because it is the rejection of God's Will while one is fully conscious of God's Will.

The only option for unclean spirits to re-experience physical pleasure is for them to possess souls on Earth and inhabit their human bodies. Inhabitation enables unclean spirits to regain physical sentience (an opportunity that they would never have through legitimate means) and even permits them to feel rushes of pleasure from, *for example,* substance abuse, fulfillment of lustful earthly desires, and perpetrating criminal acts against human beings (especially creating trouble for human beings whose souls belong to God). Possession really refers to the control that unclean spirits exercise over the soul of a human being. But pleasure for unclean spirits extends far beyond just re-experiencing physical sentience and enacting crimes against God and humanity. Unclean spirits derive their greatest pleasure as they bring additional souls into their predatory ranks.

Unclean spirits grow in strength and power by growing in number. To ensure that souls are added to their ranks, unclean spirits direct much effort toward claiming souls in spiritual suicide ("self-murder"). Here, suicide does not include people who have killed themselves because of exogenous depression, endogenous depression, and/or brain disorders related to improper synaptic transmission, chemical imbalances, or lesions.

Here, spiritual suicide includes those who die in sin because they have consciously chosen to not forgive others and to hate others despite full knowledge of the forgiveness of sins by the Lord God Almighty (especially after having experienced the Lord's forgiveness first-hand). If unclean spirits are successful in getting possessed human victims to kill themselves before they can repent of their heinous sins of unforgiveness and hatred, then they are successful in entangling others in their horrible dark clouds of condemned souls. There are many such clouds free-floating in the netherworld as individual groups of enblackened souls "to whom the mist of darkness is reserved forever."[380]

A Case for Possibilities

Biblical Christians (it is most desirable to be a Biblical Christian) flatly reject reincarnation because the Holy Bible does not introduce it as a construct for a Biblical worldview. Possibly the most damning verse in the Holy Bible used against reincarnation is Hebrews 9:27:

> {27} And, as it is appointed unto men once to die, but after this the judgment: {28} So Christ was once offered to bear the sins of many; and unto them that look for him shall he appear the second time without sin unto salvation.

Biblical Christians fail to consider that Hebrews 9:27 is referring to all souls collectively suffering *spiritual death* at the time of their original "separation from God" because of iniquity and sin (which death is the "first death") and is not referring to individual human death. Seen in this way, the "first death" (spiritual mortality or separation from God) was appointed to all souls collectively because of their iniquity and sin (not to be

---

380   2 Peter 2:17, King James Version (See also Jude, verse 13.)

confused with the Biblical "second death").

The Biblical "second death" is not appointed to all souls but, rather, only to those souls (1) who completely reject Jesus Christ as the Son of God, as the promised Messiah of Israel, and as Personal Savior and (2) who have no Messianic expectancy. References to the "second death" are found in the Book of Revelation in the following verses:

> He that has an ear, let him hear what the Spirit says unto the churches; he that overcomes [through faith in Christ Jesus] shall not be hurt of the second death.

> Revelation 2:11 [brackets mine]

> Blessed and holy is the person that has part in the first resurrection: on such the second death has no power, but they shall be priests of God and of Christ and shall reign with him a thousand years.

> Revelation 20:6

> {14} And Death and Hell were cast into the Lake of Fire. This is the second death. {15} And whoever was not found written in the Book of Life was cast into the Lake of Fire.

> Revelation 20:14-15

> But the fearful, and unbelieving, and abominable, and murderers, and whoremongers, and sorcerers [including drug dealers], and idolaters, and all liars, shall have their part in the lake that burns with fire and brimstone, which is the second death.

> Revelation 21:8 [brackets mine]

> *For the sake of clarification, the "second death" (or "Lake of Fire") is not synonymous with "nether-world," "underworld," "hell," "Hades," or "Sheol."*

Reincarnation cultists, who do not respect the authority of the Holy Bible, often invent places in the Bible that supposedly refer to reincarnation. *For example,* they might incorrectly use specific Bible verses[381] to "prove" that John the Baptist (Iochanan the Baptizer) was a reincarnation of the Old Testament Prophet Elijah (Greek *Elias*). Reincarnation cultists also try to revise history to help support their position that certain leaders in the early Church conspired to suppress and remove access to all information concerning the validity of reincarnation.

The Holy Bible does not refer to reincarnation. However, just because the Holy Bible does not refer to reincarnation does not mean that reincarnation does not occur. (Similarly, just because the Holy Bible does not refer to electricity does not mean that electricity does not exist.) There are those who will say that statements supportive of reincarnation cannot be God-inspired because such statements would be contradictory to the Holy Bible and God does not contradict Himself. To be sure, God does not contradict Himself. However, reincarnation is not contradictory to any truth in the Holy Bible. Rather, an intelligent understanding of reincarnation could help to fill in certain gaps in understanding spiritual truth for Biblical Christians, especially concerning God's Justice.

The Apostle John heard and saw many truths, but he was not permitted to record all of them for others to know.[382] This illustrates that, although the Holy Bible contains everything that human beings really need to know about their salvation and sanctification, the Holy Bible does not contain every single spiritual truth. (I am not trying to suggest here that the construct of reincarnation was revealed by God to the Apostle John.)

Certainly, belief in reincarnation was never, is not now, and will never be required for the salvation and sanctification of one's

---

381   Matthew 11:13-14, 17:10-13; & Mark 9:11-13: King James Version
382   Revelation 10:4, King James Version

soul. Unfortunately, in most instances, a superficial understanding of reincarnation distracts souls from their real purpose. That is one reason that the construct was not introduced in the Holy Bible. Another reason is that the primary focus of the Holy Bible is the deliverance and salvation of God's chosen people through their faith in God and God alone and not waiting for some future lifetime to honor God.

Heaping their grief (that is, widening their separation from God), some reincarnation cultists also espouse the transmigration of souls from one species to another. Although human beings are animals *(Homo sapiens),* they also have souls, possess consciousness (a higher order awareness of who they are), and are free-will agents that make moral decisions — unlike any other creatures on Earth.

Souls are not appointed by God to inhabit any earthly creature other than the human creature. To be sure, Christ Jesus cast out unclean spirits from a possessed man and gave them permission to enter the bodies of nearby swine;[383] however, the transmigration of human souls to other creatures does not occur as part of God's plan for spiritual development. Reincarnation is meant for the purpose of spiritual development and is not meant for the purpose of retrogression and/or devolvement.

If the ember of God's Life is not rekindled in a soul during its sojourn on Earth, then the soul simply turns into another human creature and *not just any other creature.* (This, of course, does not happen if the soul refuses to re-enter corporeality. Then, as indicated previously, the soul becomes an unclean spirit.)

Reincarnation plays a major role in the pattern of God's Justice. It provides opportunities for fallen souls to progress in spiritual awareness so that they can eventually make an informed decision concerning accepting or rejecting Jesus Christ as Lord, Personal

---

383   Matthew 8:28-33; Mark 5:1-13; Luke 8:27-33

Savior, and Sovereign King.

Without understanding (1) salvation only through Christ Jesus and (2) sanctification only by the Holy Spirit, reincarnation cultists have both romanticized reincarnation and inflated it to the position of an "end-in-itself" rather than the "means to an end." Indeed, the most important moment in every soul's existence is the one in which a soul either accepts or rejects Jesus Christ as Personal Savior. After that moment, the most important moment is the one that is occurring right now and not in some distant past or imagined future incarnation. ("Now" is meant to transcend physical time.)

Disclaimer

The incarnation of God as Jesus Christ is not to be confused with reincarnation. Likewise, referring to the pre-incarnate Christ and the post-incarnate Christ is not to be confused with reincarnation. The only-begotten Son of God existed before "the Word (or Logos) was made flesh,"[384] just as he continues to exist today as the Risen Christ in his post-incarnate state. Jesus Christ did not need to progress spiritually to become the Christ (the promised Messiah of Israel and Savior of the world). Why? Jesus Christ is not only "the Son of God," Jesus Christ is God.[385]

Communications from the Here-Beyond

Communications between heavenly realms and a human being can take place in visions, dreams, audible voices, inaudible voices, insights, impressions, or automatic writing (this is not an exhaustive list); they may take place during out-of-the-body

---

384   John 1:14, King James Version
385   Colossians 2:9, King James Version

experiences or in visitations from heavenly angels or discarnate saints. (Biblically speaking, though they may not always act like it, every saved person is a "saint.")

Communication between souls in heavenly realms and a human being never takes place because a human being initiates it, causes it, enables it, consciously channels it, or controls it; because it would be unseemly or improper, such communication is impossible. Anytime you encounter someone who says that he or she can initiate, cause, enable, channel, or control discourse with angels or discarnates from heavenly realms, you have confronted a hoax. Perpetrators of such hoaxes are (1) misguided susceptible channels, (2) talented mentalists, (3) highly intuitive persons, and/or (4) outright evil charlatans greedy for recognition, money, and power.

Susceptible Channels

"Susceptible channels" are often called "sensitives" because they are more capable than others of receiving thoughts, emotions, and feelings impinged upon their consciousness from invisible realms. Susceptible channels have the capacity to receive (that is, become aware of) other-worldly thoughts, emotions, feelings, and/or images. Whether such channels are more susceptible to impressions from heavenly realms or from hellish areas depends on their purity (confirmed commitment to Jesus Christ). Simply stated, the purity of a susceptible channel depends on its purity. Or, in other words, the accuracy, clarity, and authenticity of a susceptible channel hinges on the type of relationship it has with the Creator. Susceptible channels who have an intimate relationship with the Lord — by, first, genuinely accepting Jesus Christ as their Personal Savior and, then, by living (thinking, feeling, and acting) accordingly — are open to communication from heavenly realms. On the other hand, susceptible channels who harbor unclean thoughts and feelings *(for example,* unforgiveness and hatred of others) are opened to communication from unclean spirits and possible possession by them.

If you are not a "susceptible channel" does not mean that God cannot or will not communicate with you either directly or indirectly. Nothing prohibits God from expressing Himself at any time to anyone concerning anything. (Nothing ties or unties God's hand.) If you are not a "susceptible channel" does not mean that you cannot or will not be possessed if you open yourselves up to hellish desires and permit their enactment in crimes against God and humanity.

Heavenly Bodies, Substance, and Form

When saints in Heaven visit human beings, they usually do so in forms that are recognizable to those being visited. In other words, the saints in Heaven often travel in vehicles that resemble the ones they had while they were on Earth. Although saved discarnate souls are already in Paradise,[386] and may even appear as diaphanous images in translucent white, they will not receive their new heavenly bodies (i.e., glorified somatic identities) until the time of the Rapture.[387]

How to Become a Pure Channel of God

1. Love the LORD your God with all your might, mind, heart, and soul.[388]

2. Desire purity. Desire to think the pure thoughts of God and feel the pure feelings of God as well as to see and

---

386 Luke 23:43, King James Version
387 1 Corinthians 15:49-54 & 1 Thessalonians 4:13-18
388 Deuteronomy 6:5

hear the pure things of God.

3. Tell the Lord why you desire purity. (You should desire purity in order to please Him. Seeking to live your life in purity pleases Him.)

4. Endeavor to place all aspects of your life (the good, the bad, and the ugly) under the feet of Jesus Christ.[389]

5. Understand that we overcome the world only by the blood of the Lamb, by the faith that we place in that blood, and by "the word of our testimony" about what that blood has done for us.[390]

6. Daily focus on Christian ideals (ideals that are promoted in God's Holy Bible). Recognize that indulging impure thoughts, feelings, and fantasies betrays Christian ideals.

7. Daily confess your emotional weaknesses, vulnerabilities, infirmities, lustful desires, and vulgarities to God and ask Him to forgive you[391] and to help you overcome them through daily self-sacrifice.[392] ("Self-sacrifice" includes doing what you might not want to do and not doing what you might want to do.)

8. Ask the Lord to counsel you, coach you, and comfort you through His Holy Spirit in order to resist thinking impure thoughts, feeling impure feelings, and fantasizing and committing impure acts. (God's Holy Spirit resides within each authentic Christian and is, therefore, always available to teach us God's truth.[393])

---

389 Romans 16:20; 1 Corinthians 15:25-27; Ephesians 1:22; Hebrews 2:8
390 Revelation 12:11; 1 John 5:4; Hebrews 12:2
391 1 John 1:9
392 Matthew 10:38, 16:24; Mark 8:34, 10:21; Luke 9:23, 14:27; Romans 12:1; 1 Peter 2:5
393 John 14:16-17, 14:26, 15:26, 16:13; 1 Corinthians 6:19

9. Do not use what someone else has done (or failed to do) as an excuse to think, feel, speak, fantasize, or act in impure ways.

10. Forgive all who have trespassed against you and ask God to forgive them, too.[394]

11. Recognize that, although God can change others, you personally cannot change anyone, and that, for God to change people, they must want God to change them.

12. Do not judge or condemn others even if you personally know many horrible things about them.[395] Unforgiveness, judgment, and condemnation open us up to demonic attack.

13. Recognize the source of your thoughts, feelings, fantasies, words, motives, and actions. *(For example:* Because Satan is a murderer, liar, and thief, he and his minions seek to implant in us thoughts of assassinating and cursing others, lying about others, and stealing from others. Because God loves graciously and mercifully, thoughts of forgiving others and sharing what God has given us with others have a divine origin.)

14. If you begin to think, feel, or fantasize something impure, immediately bring it to God's attention. (Although God already knows what you are thinking, feeling, and fantasizing, doing this demonstrates to Him that you no longer wish to indulge impure thoughts, feelings, or fantasies.)

15. Get off the train of impurity before it leaves the train station. Once it takes off, the train accelerates rapidly and becomes increasingly difficult to jump from without injuring yourself and others. (There is a toll to

---

394 Matthew 6:12, 6:14-15, 18:21-22, 34-35; Mark 11:25-26; Luke 6:37, 11:4, 23:34; Acts 7:60
395 Matthew 7:1-5; Luke 6:37, 23:34; Acts 7:60

pay when you continue to indulge impure thoughts, feelings, and fantasies.)

16. Recognize that you cannot predetermine a limit to what you indulge. Understand that if you indulge impure thoughts, feelings, and fantasies (images), they will quickly take hold of you and control your heart, mind, soul, and body. All impurity is dangerous to you (not just *potentially* dangerous to you).

17. Recognize that, although the Lord is patient, no impurity (no matter how small you think it is) is acceptable to Him.

18. Do not indulge religious legalism. How do you know if you are indulging religious legalism? (a) If you try to impose your own religious belief system on others. ("Imposing" is completely different from "sharing.") (b) If you try to convince others that, for them to have a right relationship with God, they must follow a specific format or special liturgy in Christian worship.

19. Don't try to minimize your sins by comparing them to the sins of others. Never accuse your brothers and sisters of iniquity and sin, neither to God nor to them. Why? Satan is "the Accuser of the brothers and the sisters."[396] At best, you can share your concerns with them while you are praying to God for them to be delivered from their iniquity and sin.

20. If you hear and see the things of God or dream the dreams of God, then offer a word of testimony to others without proclaiming your own goodness. (Never boast about yourself[397] because "God alone is good."[398])

---

396 Paraphrased from the King James Version of Revelation 12:10
397 Matthew 23:12
398 Paraphrased from the King James Version of Matthew 19:17, Mark 10:18, & Luke 18:19

21. If you have a day of victory over temptation, then do not assume that you will not be painfully tempted the next day. When you have victory over temptation, recognize that your victory is in and of the Lord and not yourself. Always have confidence in the Lord but not in yourself. (Don't set yourself up as God.)

22. If you are overcome by temptation, then remember that tomorrow is another day. (This is not meant to give you permission to sin.)

23. Feed the hungry, provide soap and clean water to the poor, clothe the naked, nurse the sick, be patient with the impatient, and love people who are unlikeable.[399]

24. Share the gospel of Jesus Christ in thought, in feeling, in attitude, in gesture, in action, and in word *(for example,* by reading and explaining the Holy Bible to them or in acts of kindness).

25. Know that purity is something that is first developed internally and, only then, demonstrated externally.[400]

26. Value simplicity.

Exorcism

Exorcism can only be facilitated by mature, authentic Christian believers. Immature, authentic Christian believers are not able to facilitate exorcism since they depend more on themselves than they depend on God. (To be sure, nonbelievers cannot facilitate exorcism.) The power of God through the blood of Jesus Christ is the only power that is capable of rebuking and binding unclean spirits as well as casting them out and away from a possessed human being.

---

399   Matthew 25:33-46
400   Matthew 23:5, 12, & 27

To exorcise unclean spirits from a possessed human being, the exorcist(s) must be willing to: (1) wait upon the Lord in patient and humble servitude; (2) read the Holy Bible silently and out loud; (3) pray without ceasing (inaudibly and audibly); 4) fast in preparation; and (5) specifically request God to deliver the possessed person by praying aloud, including the words "for Thy Name's sake."

When Christ Jesus commissioned seventy disciples in groups of two to visit various cities with the gospel message, they returned to him with great joy, "saying: 'Lord, even the devils are subject unto us through Thy Name.'"[401] In response to them, Christ Jesus said:

> {18} I beheld Satan as lightning fall from Heaven [in other words, Jesus saw Satan lose power]. {19} Behold, I give unto you power to tread on serpents and scorpions, and over all the power of the Enemy: and nothing shall by any means hurt you. {20} However, do not rejoice that the [unclean] spirits are subject to you; but rather rejoice because your names are written in Heaven.[402]

During exorcism, it is best for the exorcist not to carry on conversations with unclean spirits. Given the opportunity, unclean spirits will try to gain the upper hand by: (1) flattering the exorcist (playing to the vanity of the exorcist), (2) threatening the exorcist, (3) sharing embarrassing private matters of the exorcist with others present, (4) claiming that the exorcist has not been forgiven of certain past sins, and/or (5) justifying that the possessed person deserves to go to Hell. The only reason an exorcist might speak with unclean spirits is to verify that they are present while the exorcist is calling upon the Lord to deliver the

---

401   Paraphrased from the King James Version of Luke 10:17
402   Paraphrased from the King James Version of Luke 10:18-20 [Brackets mine]

possessed person. Because unclean spirits often do not permanently displace the soul of the possessed person, they are not always present. They must be present at the time of the exorcism.

An exorcist must discern whether a person is: (1) genuinely possessed; (2) mentally or emotionally unbalanced *(for example, in having multiple personalities)*; (3) suffering from a brain disorder *(for example, by having Tourette's Syndrome)*; or (4) just pretending to be possessed. You might ask: "Why would anyone pretend to be possessed?" Strong peer pressure in a local church or from a group of pseudo-religious people might cause an impressionable person (especially one with an unhealthy desire to be accepted) to play-act the role of a possessed person in order to be "delivered by God" from some real or imagined malady in order to "fit in," have a big group hug, and then shout "Hurrah!" (Similarly, although "speaking in tongues" is a genuine gift of the Holy Spirit, some Christian believers pretend to speak in tongues because of strong peer pressure in a local church or from a group of pseudo-religious people who impart childish guidelines and trumped-up formulas for speaking nonsense syllables in infantile babble.)

The Power of Good (God) [403]

Submit *every thought, feeling, idea, fantasy, mental image, dream, hope, and desire* to the authority of Jesus Christ. (Hereafter in this section I will be referring to the preceding italicized list by the two words "every thought.")

Controlling every thought is different from *submitting* every thought. You might think that you have the power to control every thought, but you have no power to control anything. Christ Jesus alone has all power. Without Christ Jesus you cannot

---

403   Matthew 19:17 & Mark 10:18: King James Version

overcome. You might think that you can overcome every thought through positive thinking, a good attitude, altruism, or a daily regimen that includes affirmations of life, love, health, and happiness; but it is only through Christ Jesus that we overcome. And, though evident to some Christians (yet not so evident to many others), we cannot have *the power of Christ Jesus* without having *the power of the blood of Christ Jesus*.

As we individually learn through God's Holy Spirit to subdue every thought that comes to us, there is danger in our own self-righteousness to want to personally subdue the thoughts of others or force others to subdue their own thoughts. Although we might be able to teach others to subdue their every thought, to remind them to subdue, and/or to help them to subdue (by praying with and for them), we must not try to subdue, control, or manipulate others in any way, even if we think it is for their own good. When we seek to subdue, control, and/or manipulate the thoughts of others, we are on a demonic track and not a divine track. And it is a waste of time, effort, and energy to try to cajole, threaten, shame, or penalize others to get them to submit their every thought to Christ or bring their every thought into line with what we think is right for them. (Even brick and mortar penitentiaries cannot force human beings to subdue their thoughts.) Human beings will not submit their every thought to Christ Jesus until they themselves individually desire to do so.

Taking captive every thought by submitting it to the Word of God *is* the manifest power of God.[404] *This* is the power that causes Satan to tremble and like "lightning fall."[405] Employing this truth enables us to overcome the world by faith in Christ

---

404 For the sake of clarity, "the Word of God" here refers to the "Logos," or Jesus Christ himself, as used in John 1:1 & 14, Hebrews 11:3, 1 Peter 1:23, 2 Peter 3:5, 1 John 2:14 and Revelation 19:13. The phrase "word of God," used elsewhere within the New Testament, refers to the gospel message of salvation through Jesus Christ and Jesus Christ alone.

405 Luke 10:18, King James Version

Jesus.[406]

The Source of All Well-Being

The reason that our well-being is not dependent on any other person, any economic situation, any political environment, any geographical location, or any material possession is because the source of our well-being is the Lord God Almighty. Because the Lord God Almighty is the source of our well-being, we can have both health and happiness regardless of all internal and external circumstances and conditions, and regardless of all other people.

The more we recognize that God is the source of our well-being, the more we become content, satisfied, at peace and peaceable, comforted and comforting, encouraged and encouraging. The more we recognize that God is the only source of our well-being, the more we are braced for change in our personal circumstances and conditions. Knowledge of the true source of our well-being is our stabilizer in this world.

When we assume responsibility for the actions and reactions of other mentally-able adult persons (usually loved ones and friends), we exhibit a desire to be in control. When we assume responsibility for the character defects of others and the consequences of those defects, we also exhibit a desire to be in control. When we give up our God-given sense of well-being because of the trouble someone else is in, we, in fact, showcase our own character defects. When we assume responsibility for the actions and reactions of other mentally-able adult persons, we demonstrate an inner core sickness that can be healed only by God.

For example, if we assume responsibility for someone else's sinful addictions, general malaise, or inability to perform well in

---

406   1 John 5:4, King James Version

a social setting, then we spotlight our own weaknesses, not the weaknesses of the other person. Furthermore, trying to protect others from consequences of their own unhealthy behaviors, trying to get people to become "self-starters," forcing others to demonstrate social skills beyond their capabilities or years, and expecting others to understand ideas that are significantly relevant to our own experience, education, training, and interests, and not theirs, all demonstrate our unhealthy need to be in control. Sharing with others and seeking to influence others positively are vastly different from trying to control others. Trying to control others is *a* (and sometimes *the*) major disruption to our own sense of well-being.

Our Fantasy World

What we fantasize is very important to our spiritual state of mind. If we permit worldly lusts to drive our individual fantasy worlds, then we end up sinning in thought, in attitude (that is, in expectation), and, eventually, in deed. That is why we must stand guard at the portal of thought, denying entrance to any and all unclean thoughts, feelings, and images. The only way that we can deny entrance to them is to subdue them by immediately submitting them to the purifying blood of Jesus Christ ("immediately" means as soon as the unclean thoughts, feelings, and images come to us). The blood of Jesus Christ washes us clean of all lusts, including lusts of the mind as well as of the flesh.

Satan, who is described in the Holy Bible as the "most subtle"[407] of all creatures (or, depending on the translation, "most cunning"), tries to infiltrate our consciousness and invade our lives through feeding our individual fantasy worlds with unclean thoughts, feelings, and images. Then, Satan impinges upon our own desires to permit the unclean thoughts, feelings, and images

407   Genesis 3:1, King James Version

to grow and, thereby, separate us from God by causing us to become entangled in them and in actions based on them. Eve said to the Lord: "The Serpent beguiled me."[408] In other words, Satan tempted Eve by deluding and deceiving her. Like Eve, we are beguiled when we act on Satan's delusions and deceptions as if they were real and true.

Unclean thinking and feeling are so subtle that, at times, we feel justified in indulging them, especially since most other people cannot detect them in us. Consequently, we often end up deciding that unclean thoughts and feelings are "okay" as long as we don't act on them because we think "No one else can see them." We forget that God and everyone in Heaven can.

Christ Jesus cautioned us about our fantasies when he said: "whoever looks at a woman to lust after her has already committed adultery with her in his heart."[409] In his Epistle, James explains that "every man is tempted, when he is drawn away of his own lust, and enticed. Then, when lust has conceived, it brings forth sin; and sin, when it is finished, brings forth death [or separation from God]."[410]

The Last Enemy

Scripture teaches us that "the last enemy that shall be destroyed is *death*."[411] Thus, *death* is the "last enemy" with which Christians must contend. *Death*, of course, is not just human mortality. *Death* is the mortal state (or realm) of being where incarnates are in one stratum and unsaved discarnates are in another.

---

408   Genesis 3:13, King James Version
409   Paraphrased from the King James Version of Matthew 5:28
410   Paraphrased from the King James Version of James 1:14-15 [Brackets mine]
411   1 Corinthians 15:26, King James Version

Spiritual mortality (spiritual death) is the separation of a soul from its Creator because of its transgressions against the Creator. That souls in dust wear a "*shadow of death*"[412] in the corporeal image they possess while on Earth is not death-in-itself. Transgression against the Creator results in death-in-itself, which is separation of the created from the Creator. The corporeal image of human beings is just an outward sign of their original *spiritual death* due to iniquity and sin. The Apostle Paul said: "O wretched man that I am! Who shall deliver me from the body of this *death?*"[413]

Although the human body is God-ordained, God-appointed, and God-made, it is a "stepped-down" version of the original body that God made for us before the Adamic Fall. Although the human body is cumbersome, and a result of God's curse, the human body is also part of God's plan: If we accept God's Plan of Salvation while we are in the flesh, our souls are instantaneously "saved," and God's Holy Spirit is immediately deposited within us as a guarantee (surety) of that salvation as well as the future redemption (or glorification) of our bodies.

Although living in human form alone can bring no joy, the Good News for Christians does bring joy, and it includes this understanding of our mortality *(death)* and immortality *(eternal life in God)*:

> {50} Now this I say, brothers and sisters, that flesh and blood cannot inherit the Kingdom of God; neither does corruption inherit incorruption. {53} For this corruptible must put on incorruption, and this mortal must put on immortality. {54} So when this corruptible shall have put on incorruption, and this mortal shall have put on immortality, then shall be brought to pass this saying that is written:

---

412   Psalm 44:19; Psalm 107:10, 14; Isaiah 9:2; Jeremiah 2:6; Matthew 4:16; & Luke 1:79: King James Version

413   Romans 7:24, King James Version

"*Death* is swallowed up in victory."[414]

Through the Savior, Christians are "more than conquerors"[415] of both spiritual death and physical death. This does not mean that we are not going to die physically; it means that physical death can have no sting (that is, *victory*) over us:[416]

> For we which live are always delivered unto *death* for Jesus' sake, that the life also of Jesus might be made manifest in our mortal flesh.[417]

To be sure, Jesus Christ has already "abolished death"[418] in that neither *death* nor the Interloper on God's territory (Satan, the Devil, the Enemy, and Adversary of God) have any real, long-lasting power over Christians:

> {14} Forasmuch then as the children [of God] are partakers of flesh and blood, Christ Jesus also himself likewise took part of the same; that through *death* he might destroy him that had the power of *death,* that is, the Devil; {15} And deliver them who through fear of *death* were all their lifetime subject to [its] bondage.[419]

Jesus Christ has also "abolished death" in that death-in-itself, including all strata of its mortal state of being, will one day forever be expunged from the Universe:

> [Christ Jesus said:] "I am he that lives and was dead; and, behold, I am alive for evermore, Amen; and I

---

414 Paraphrased from the King James Version of 1 Corinthians 15:50 & 53-54 (which quotes Isaiah 25:8)
415 Romans 8:37, King James Version
416 1 Corinthians 15:55
417 2 Corinthians 4:11
418 2 Timothy 1:10, King James Version
419 Paraphrased from the King James Version of Hebrews 2:14-15 [Brackets mine]

have the keys of Hell *[Hades]* and of *Death.*"[420]

{13} ... and Death and Hell *[Hades]* delivered up the dead which were in them: and they were judged every person according to their works. {14} And *Death* and Hell *[Hades]* were cast into the Lake of Fire. This is the second *death.* {15} And whoever was not found written in the [Lamb's] Book of Life was cast into the Lake of Fire.[421]

And God shall wipe away all tears from their eyes; and there shall be no more *death,* neither sorrow, nor crying, neither shall there be any more pain: for the former things are passed away.[422]

Although there is now no real death for those who belong to Christ Jesus, Christians must yet be aware of the various forms of *superficial death,* which includes: (1) corporeality itself, (2) spiritual malaise, (3) physical mortality, and (4) "deceptive death" (from which there is a false miraculous recovery[423]).

In other words, Christians: (1) must not confuse corporeality with God's Absolute Reality; (2) should not acquiesce to spiritual malaise or inactivity (unfruitful living); (3) are not to trust in the seeming permanency of "separations" at the "passing" of their loved ones; and (4) are to be suspicious of the so-called miracles of "the man of sin" (the Antichrist), who will one day emerge out of the end-time beast of Islam.[424]

---

420 Paraphrased from the King James Version of Revelation 1:18 [Brackets mine]

421 Paraphrased from the King James Version of Revelation 20:13-15 [Brackets mine]. See also Revelation 21:27.

422 Revelation 21:4, King James Version

423 Revelation 13:3, 12

424 Revelation, Chapter 13. In addition, read the present author's work entitled *The Koran (al-Qur'an): Testimony of Antichrist* or *Revelation of Antichrist* (see details at the end of this book).

Satan is a God-damned Liar!

Although the title of this section might offend the sensitivities and sensibilities of some Christians, the title makes sense when you stop to think about it objectively. Satan *is* a God-damned liar as well as thief and murderer.[425] Similarly, all demons *are* God-damned liars, thieves, and murderers. They are all God-damned because they are already damned by God to eternal torment in the Lake of Fire even though that punishment has not yet been meted out to them.[426] So, when I write that "Satan is a God-damned liar," I am not personally cursing Satan but only stating the truth.

Only God can curse and damn, we cannot. Vengeance is not ours; it is God's.[427] We are not the Judge. He is.[428]

Christians should not curse other human beings by saying that they are God-damned because, first, they have no right to judge others (that is, condemn them), and, second, they simply do not know if someone is really God-damned or not unless God tells them personally (not through their own touchy-feely human cognition or intellectual erudition). With that said, it is highly unlikely that God will share this confidence with us concerning another human being. Although we should always view other human beings as potentially salvageable by God, we need to recognize that not everyone will accept salvation, deliverance, and/or healing.

---

425   John 8:44, 10:1 & 10, King James Version
426   Revelation 20:10 & 15, King James Version
427   Deuteronomy 32:35, 41-43; Romans 12:19; & Hebrews 10:30: King James Version
428   Matthew 7:1-2; Luke 6:37; John 5:22 & 30, 12:47-48; Acts 10:42, 17:30-31; Romans 2:16, 14:4, 10, & 13; 1 Corinthians 4:4-5; 2 Timothy 4:1, 8; Hebrews 10:30, 12:23; & Revelation 20:11: King James Version

If you are tempted to say about another human being "God damn him!" or "God damn her!" then please know that you are being used as a tool of Satan and his demonic forces. Even if a person has trespassed against you, abused you, lied to you, or victimized you repeatedly, you still have no right to "pay back" and/or verbally condemn them to eternal torment. (I used the word "verbally" here because we, in fact, cannot condemn anyone.) Why do we not have that right? We are not the Judge. Vengeance (that is, "payback") is not ours; it belongs to God. And we are taught by Jesus Christ himself to bless all others, pray for them, and forgive them. If we curse others, we end up cursing ourselves.[429] How? God tells us that He uses the same standard on us that we use to measure others.[430]

Human beings are the intended victims of Satan and his demons. We are always victimized by Satan and his demons if we are not washed clean by the blood of Jesus Christ.[431] We are sometimes still victimized by them, even if we have been washed clean by the blood of Jesus Christ, when we indulge sinful thoughts, feelings, ideas, images, and fantasies and act on them as if they are our own. (Regardless of their origin, they become our own when we act on them.)

All sin first originates in our imagination (imagination is not bad, but sinful desires are bad). Satan and his demons try to seed our imagination with the sinful thoughts, feelings, ideas, images, and fantasies that are the most alluring to us individually and personally. They choose areas of our greatest weakness *(for example,* areas concerning power, arrogance, control, greed, and lust) — which areas are visible to demonic forces in the world of spirit. (These areas are invisible to our eyesight but visible to everyone in the spirit world.)

---

429   Romans 2:1-3, King James Version
430   Matthew 7:1-2, King James Version
431   1 John 1:7 & Revelation 1:5, 5:9, 7:14, 12:11, 19:13: King James Version

Even though they can see our areas of weakness through their spiritual sight, Satan and his demons are still God-damned idiots. Yes, they can be cunning and crafty, plotting and strategic, alluring and charming, but they are, nevertheless, God-damned idiots. I have already explained why they are God-damned. So, why are they idiots? They are enamored of themselves instead of the wondrous magnificence and loving splendor of the Lord God Almighty, the one true and only real Creator. You can't get more stupid than that! (Let us not follow in their footsteps by becoming impressed with our own individual appearance, characteristics, or abilities.)

As thieves, murderers, and liars, Satan and his demons seek to overturn God's power (they can't) and seek to make God miserable (they can). How can they make God miserable? Our Creator loves us so much that He laments for His people when we mess up. He sorrows for us. He misses us when we separate ourselves from Him (when we sin and then try to hide ourselves from Him).

I know that there will be those who think that I am trying to anthropomorphize God by claiming that He can be miserable. Well, God has emotions like we have emotions. (Since He is our Creator, it is more accurate to state that we have emotions like He has emotions.) Divine misery is reflected by God's lamentations for us. God laments for us since we are the objects of His selfless love. Make no mistake, divine misery is as different from human misery as divine hatred is from human hatred. Divine misery also involves divine wrath, which is different from human anger. Divine misery, divine hatred,[432] and divine wrath are separated from lower, human emotions by divine love, which includes divine justice and divine judgment. (Although the saints and angels in Heaven are divine, they are not, nor can they ever be, Deity. They are "divine" because they are "of God" — which is to say, "created by Him.")

---

432   Psalm 139:22, King James Version

Are you following Satan by being a manipulator? You are a manipulator if everyone else is a bit player in your own action-packed life adventure. When it suits you, you may let others think that they are stars *(for example,* by flattering them for an occasion or interval of time) even though you really consider them inconsequential and irrelevant to the overall scheme of things. You might be a manipulator with your fists, it is more likely that you are a manipulator with cunning, subtlety, prowess, craftiness, charm, and allure. You have decided that you can lie and that you are pretty good at it, even though people with spiritual insight can see right through you. It might take someone with spiritual insight a while to see right through you (because, *for example,* they might like to give others the benefit of the doubt), but, make no mistake, people with spiritual insight will eventually see right through you (there will come a time when they no longer can give you the benefit of the doubt but only can give you *the doubt).*

If you are a manipulator, then you are exhibiting qualities and characteristics of the God-damned even though you yourself are not yet God-damned. I asked if you are a manipulator and gave some of the criteria for being a manipulator to help you do a self-assessment, ask for God to bring you to repentance, and, thereby, avoid permanently joining forces with Evil and becoming God-damned.

For the sake of clarification, God no longer laments for those who become God-damned. To Him, they become *personae non gratae.* Although difficult for us to imagine, it is as if He never knew them.[433]

In order for you to witness Satan fall "like lightning"[434] in your own circle of activities and personal experience, you must wait upon the Lord (that is, continue to serve Him at the same time

---

433   Matthew 7:22-23, King James Version
434   Luke 10:18

that you remain patient with His timing for interaction, intervention, and change).

Epilogue

My Just Cause by God

Dear Created Ones:

I knew you before time began. How? I AM your Creator! Before the beginning of time, you were part of MY Original Creation, which was unblemished, spotless, and pure. You lived and moved and had your being in a glorious form of existence that you now can barely imagine. In fact, if you were to see how breathtaking your original state really was, you would exclaim: "How could I have left that for this!" Actually, you had no idea what would happen to you during and after your Fall until it happened because, in the world of the invisible, "knowing" necessitates "experiencing." Indeed, you are still coming to grips with the outcome of your Fall.

I created all souls at once. I created all of you collectively to be MY Companion. I made all of you as parts of a magnificent composite, which composite I indwelt. It is strange for you to hear about MY Original Creation because it is so far removed from your present existence that you are unable to comprehend its beauty. In MY Original Creation, I made some parts to be grander than others, but it did not matter to the less grand parts because they could see the grander parts and be utterly awestruck by them and overwhelmed by Who and What I AM as well as the overall magnificence and immensity of MY Creation.

A long time ago (by your standard of time), I told Moshe [Moses] to tell the children of Israel that "I AM THAT I AM." Fundamentally embedded in the original language of that statement are the concepts that "I WILL BE WHAT I WAS" and "I AM WHAT I WILL BE." In other words, I have an unfathomable nature, unless, of course, you are moving *towards*

ME — in which case your knowledge of ME continually evolves and unfolds to the degree that you are progressively experiencing ME. (Again, in the world of the invisible *knowing* necessitates *experiencing*.)

Originally, you had diaphanous bodies that were made of a substance that you cannot now see or feel. Their material was luminescent, iridescent, translucent, and brilliant. You were so beautiful! And I was so proud of you. I gave you the gift of life, self-awareness, and unstructured consciousness (as well as structured consciousness), so you could be aware of ME and appreciate who you are in ME. It is unstructured consciousness that permits you to have free will and emotions as well as make choices. Structured consciousness alone would not have permitted such freedom. By "structured consciousness," I AM referring to abilities in logic and analytical thinking, the progressive steps of which are entirely predictable. I gave you the gift of free will in order that you might serve ME by choice. The highest level of MY Creation is found in created beings with their own self-awareness, unstructured consciousness, and free will. When you think of it, what genuine satisfaction could there be for the Creator of the Universe to receive love, honor, glory, and praise from automatons, robotic creatures, or captives?

Even before it was created, I knew that MY Original Creation would fall after I created it. That did not deter ME from creating it because I had something in mind that would eventually refine what would fall and permanently restore it to ME. Many of you might ask ME: "Why bother seeking us out and restoring us?" Let ME answer by asking you: "Why should I give MY Glory to another? Why should I let what is MINE be stolen by another?" It is *MY Just Cause* to search for you, to find you, and to redeem you because, simply stated, I created you. I AM not only *just* to you, I AM also *just* to ME as well. To let you simply slip through MY fingers would be unjust to ME. MY Righteousness endures forever. I AM righteous to you, and I AM also righteous to ME, too. That does not mean that I AM so loving that I would allow unrighteousness to continue throughout eternity or allow it to enter MY Presence. *MY Just Cause* necessitates MY seeking you out and restoring you as the apple of MY eye.

MY pursuit of you has not been without great emotional pain, lamentation, and anguish — as well as restraint — on MY part. I know that you might think it strange that your Creator could have emotional pain, but I do. (I created you with emotions because I have them.) Naturally, MY emotions are not tossed about by the wind as yours are. MY emotions include perfect love, perfect hatred (to despise what is unjust, immoral, and evil), compassion, anger, fury, jealousy, mercy, and grace. MY emotions are on a much grander and more spiritual plane than human emotions. I have had to exercise great restraint because of MY emotional nature. I AM so holy that I could not ever be in the presence of unholy things without their complete destruction and utter annihilation. For that reason, I withdrew from you at the precise moment that you fell from MY Original Creation.

Had I not withdrawn from you, you would have been immediately cast into eternal torment, which is complete and permanent separation from ME, as well as into utter darkness, which is the total absence of MY Spiritual Light. If you had entered that state and condition of being, knowledge of your former state and MY Righteousness would have continually tormented you with shame and guilt, burning you in self-condemnation throughout all eternity. That is why I held MYSELF back. I withdrew MYSELF from you. I separated MYSELF from what could not hold up to being seen by ME or having ME present. I altered MY OWN state of Being so that I would no longer be a visible part of MY Creation, which is to say, I would no longer infuse it. (You see, in MY Original Creation, as well as in what you today call "Heaven," I WAS — and AM — *the* integral part of everything. Though I AM not found in physical objects, I AM found in heavenly objects, which are made of their own special substance. *(For example,* every spiritual object in MY Kingdom is opalescent and casts a glow.

And everything in MY Creation "sings" a song through its own vibratory harmonics.) At the time of your Fall, I retreated to MY highest level of Being, where I cannot be seen or heard by fallen beings. That is why I speak to you through spiritual messengers (MY angels) and through MY Holy Spirit. This is where I remain today, and will remain, until the time of the end, when all of MY redeemed are presented to ME by MY Son, at which time MY All will then enter his all (the Body of Christ) and I WILL BE, once again, *All-in-all*.

In what I have described so far, please know that I did not change MYSELF, for I cannot change. I simply retreated to a place and state where you cannot *be* until you are, once again, made pure and holy. Instead of having the totality of ME present with you, I have used MY angels and MY Holy Spirit to interact with you on MY behalf. Naturally, I knew that I would fully recover those of you who would again fit into MY Creation, which is to say, MY *renewed* creation (which will not be revealed until the end of the millennial rule of Christ Jesus on Earth). For this reason, I devised MY Plan of Salvation for your individual and collective restoration (although not everyone will be saved).

Now I would like to talk to you about the role that envy played in the Fall of MY Original Creation. Perhaps you have heard, or read, that pride was the most important element relative to the Fall of Lucifer. Pride really is just the half of it. Envy played an equally important role. As I mentioned previously, I had originally created some parts to be grander than others. Thus, some beings in MY Original Universe were (and still are) grander than others. There was one spirit being I created who was unbelievably beautiful and awe-inspiring. Because I created him to bear MY Glory in a unique way, he was called Lucifer, or "Light-bearer." Although I knew Lucifer would fall and, in so doing, precipitate the fall of others, I created him to allow all of MY Creation to eventually experience firsthand that no one — not even one of the highest in MY Creation — can usurp MY honor, glory, and power. It is a lesson that you are still learning.

The Glory that I originally bestowed upon Lucifer was so great that he himself resided in clouds of Glory, all of which enveloped certain spheres of activities for which he was responsible in MY Original Creation. Though I make a distinction between the physical and the spiritual, I use the word "substance" for either realm since there are spiritual objects as well as physical objects. Substance unique to the spiritual realm is the so-called "material" of spiritual objects. Likewise, substance unique to the physical realm is the material of physical objects. Needless to say, spiritual substance is not the same as physical substance. Physical substance, or matter, is one form of energy — a "bound" form, so to speak. Spiritual substance, or what you might call "Glory," is a different form of energy — to be sure, an "unbound" form. *For example,* because I only inhabit Glory, I do not inhabit physical objects (regardless of what aestheticians or pantheists might say). I do not inhabit wood, stone, earth, air, or water because MY Being would not permit it. It would be unseemly.

Material objects cannot contain ME. It would be unseemly for ME to inhabit matter unless it could be made holy. I would have to divest MYSELF of MY Glory to inhabit matter. To be sure, MY Son divested himself of his Glory when he was born of the virgin Miriam ["Mary" or "Maria"]. MY Son was able to inhabit a physical body because that physical body was conceived by MY Holy Spirit in consort with Miriam, which conception is a singularly unique event in the history of humankind (it had never happened before, and it will never happen again). (Whenever MY angels enter your dimensionality, they too immediately shed MY Glory and take on human form.)

Before the beginning (as detailed in the Genesis account of creation), Lucifer was well aware that he was created with tremendous power and great responsibility. Because Lucifer was created with free will, and because he permitted it, there developed within him an envy of ME and MY rightful place within Creation as both Supreme Being and Creator. Lucifer's envy of ME was so overwhelming that the instant it developed, it began to absorb part of MY Glory, much like a black hole absorbs light and "swallows" energy in the physical universe. Everything under Lucifer's jurisdiction was pulled into a newly-established place from which point you can only see an alteration, or distortion, of MY Spiritual Universe. Because I AM WHO I AM, I immediately put a stop to it going any further, and I implemented MY Plan of Salvation for those who, because they were under Lucifer's jurisdiction, would fall prey to his temptation. It was at the precise moment of Lucifer's Fall that something came to exist that had not existed previously: matter (physicality).

When Lucifer fell, he stood condemned immediately. Unfortunately, Lucifer misused his power and position to influence others to rebel. The angels who fell with him also stood condemned immediately because they, like Lucifer, clearly knew what they were doing. However, those who were originally created to be the least grand parts in MY Creation (which is to say, *you*) were deceived into giving up their inheritance and reflected glory. In other words, *you* gave up *your* original state by falling to the temptation of the Tempter. Lucifer was not deceived, but *you* were deceived. The angels who fell with Lucifer were not deceived; they were Lucifer's co-conspirators. But *you* were deceived!

Like Lucifer, the fallen angels also sought to overturn ME in an attempt to obtain a more elevated position in the Spiritual Universe. Because the beings who collectively were the "least grand" of MY Creation were deceived, I devised MY Plan of Salvation to redeem them and return them to ME and, eventually, elevate them to the status of "most grand," as members of the Body of Christ, in order to bring more honor and glory and praise to MY Holy Name. I have demonstrated through MY Plan of Salvation that I AM full of grace and mercy and, therefore, most worthy to be honored and worshiped and praised. Perhaps you have heard or read that I can turn any curse into a blessing. Yes, if it pleases ME. To be sure, I can even take things that are base and despised and exalt them. But always remember, I will never allow unrighteousness, unholiness, or depravity (including a spirit of unforgiveness) to become a part of MY Spiritual Universe.

Did you ever notice the role that envy has played in Biblical history? To cite a few examples: Cain killed Abel because of envy. King Saul hated and tried to kill David, son of Jesse, because of envy. The Pharisees sought to kill Christ Jesus because they envied him. Did you also read in MY Holy Bible how strongly I came out against envy? I even incorporated MY stand against envy into MY original commandments for the people of Israel by ordering them not to covet anything that belonged to someone else. That principle certainly extends to you today and includes not coveting the natural talents and spiritual gifts of others. Do not envy what anyone else has except, perhaps, their humility and gratitude. (I wrote "perhaps" because not everyone has humility or gratitude.)

Here, I will note the difference between the terms *envy* and *jealousy* as used in this communication. Envy is the feeling of desire for what *does not* belong to you. Jealousy is the feeling of desire for what someone else has that *does* belong to you. *For example,* I AM jealous *for* you. (I AM certainly not jealous *of* you.) I AM jealous for what I created that has been stolen from ME by deception. That is why I still search for you, and why I still look for those of you who are part of MY remnant. If you are one of the lambs that belong to ME, you will eventually hear MY voice, you will eventually understand MY saving nature and the nature of MY Salvation, and you will eventually allow ME to deliver you into MY land of heavenly promise. Of such is the compelling nature of *MY Just Cause* for those who will hear.

What happened to MY Original Creation? After Lucifer's Fall, it changed. It was altered. I permitted its change to occur at the same time that I gave direction to its change. Why? This newly-altered universe fit into MY Plan of Salvation. I turned its turning in the direction that MY Word desired it to go. Who and what is "MY Word?" MY Word, or *Logos,* is the creative part of ME. Some of you have come to know MY Word, or *Logos*, as Jesus Christ.

I AM tri-une! MY three parts are indivisible yet distinct from one another. Why did I choose the appellation *Father?* To be sure, I AM not a gendered male. However, I needed to portray MYSELF to you in ways that you can best understand, not only through the languages that you use, but in the natural hierarchies observed in the most primitive of human cultures and societies. Why did I choose to have an "only-begotten Son" rather than an "only-begotten Daughter"? In ancient times, everyone understood that the first-born male was the heir to all that his father had. Yes, Christ Jesus was a gendered male and, for that reason, he was MY "Son." To be sure, Christ Jesus was, and is, MY only Heir.

Although your contemporary linguists have rendered "sons of God" in modern versions of the Bible as "sons and daughters of God," it would have been more accurate if they had rendered "sons of God" as "heirs of God." Why? Those of you who accept MY Plan of Salvation are made co-heirs with Christ Jesus. Gender has nothing to do with being made a co-heir. If you translate the Hebrew or Greek to show only gender equality, you miss the point that through Christ Jesus you are all heirs to all that I have.

MY Plan of Salvation is the work of *MY Just Cause.* During the earliest parts of Biblical history, I tried to convey to you that MY Justified Anger toward you must be appeased. Thus, I devised the blood sacrifice of animals as a symbolic rite to help you understand that whenever someone strays from MY Will, the error needs to be atoned for before you and I can again have an intimate relationship. In what you call the "Old Testament," I spoke to you in symbols and principles that you could understand and, in fact, are still able to comprehend. To be sure, if you read Scripture, you will come to understand that the one referred to as MY "only-begotten" Son is also referred to as the "Word of Life." The concept in the expression "Word of Life" is more difficult to understand than the concept in the expression "Son." Again, I AM not a gendered male. I have attributes that are both fatherly and motherly. I have no problem with what you call ME, provided that you understand WHO I AM and what your true relationship is to ME. However, if anyone is offended by the usage of the terms "God the Father," "God the Son," and "God the Holy Spirit," then I AM offended by you. You should not be offended by MY tri-une nature. This is certainly the way in which I have presented MYSELF to humanity. In the final analysis, I choose to present MYSELF to you in ways that you can understand or, at least, eventually can come to understand.

Why were you created? You were created to worship ME and to be MY Companion. Is that conceptually alien to you? Were you created to please yourselves? Were you created to please anyone other than ME? No, and no. You were created to please ME. That is your sole eternal purpose. That is why you were created. Part of pleasing ME includes worshiping ME. For those of you who question your specific purpose on Earth, here is your answer: Whatever you do, do it to please ME, to bring honor to MY Holy Name, and to exalt ME. Even if you are doing what others consider lowly, do it for ME. That is your specific purpose. When you do this, you are pleasing ME. You don't have to be great in the world (that is, "high and lifted up") to please ME, just be devoted to ME. That is all I have ever asked of you. Seek MY Will and yield your will to MINE. Commune with ME. Seek ME. Lean on ME. Trust ME. Believe on ME. Put your hope in ME. And love ME. Just like you desire to be loved, I desire to be loved. We are so similar because I AM your Creator and you are MY Created. I created you in MY image and likeness. Your reflectance of ME even includes reflecting MY needs and desires. I even desire that you include ME in your daily mundane activities. Such inclusion makes ME feel valued and a part of you!

In the previous paragraph, I have indicated what your specific purpose is. What is your general purpose for being on Earth? To learn to accept that Jesus Christ is the *only-begotten* Son of God, the Savior of the world, and your personal Savior and the *only* Way for you to be restored to ME. In short, this constitutes MY Plan of Salvation.

I have watched you collectively develop from primitive people who could conceptually understand only a few different aspects of ME to thinkers who made ME so big that I eventually became impersonal to you. Yes, I AM a force to be reckoned with, but I AM also a sentient being. "Sentient being" here means that I, too, AM a free-will being with self-awareness and unstructured (as well as structured) consciousness. Because I have unstructured consciousness, I AM able to make choices and exercise MY Free Will. As Supreme Being, I AM also aware of everything all at once. I transcend space-time as you understand it because I am trans-dimensional.

And, of course, I possess all power. (Please don't get anthropomorphic on me and think that as a sentient being I AM only a big version of you!) And it is because I AM a sentient being that I AM able to have a relationship with you. You must seek ME by communing with ME and I, in turn, will commune with you. It delights ME to commune with you for you are MY Created. Collectively, all of you are both MY lover and MY beloved (for those of you whose mind is obsessed with the mundane, sex has nothing to do with this).

Earlier, I mentioned that I knew that MY Original Creation would fall even before I had created it. Let ME try to help you understand something. I AM omniscient. I know everything. That is part of MY very nature. I do not inhabit the space-time continuum that you inhabit, but I can see it — all of it — all at once. Picture a long glass rod with one end representing the beginning of relative time (that is, the beginning of creation) and the other end representing the ending of relative time. It actually is more convoluted and complex than that, but this image serves its purpose. Figuratively speaking, it would be as if I inhabited all space-time outside of the glass rod and could see everything throughout it all at once. To be sure, I can see all events that have occurred, that are occurring, and that will occur. MY Nature permits that. I see all of history — past, present, and future — all at the same time. I see all activities that have gone on, that are going on, and that will go on.

To you, there is a beginning and ending to everything. To ME, there is only a beginning and ending to the relative space-time that you experience. Everything else to ME is ongoing. That is how I know which of you would choose to again be infused by ME in MY renewed creation. To be sure, I don't control you. You are not MY puppets. That I can see everything you will do in your future does not mean that I AM controlling what you do. I AM just aware of the choices you will make. And, because I knew that there would be those of you who would repent of their falling to temptation, I devised MY Plan of Salvation that would both appease MY Wrath (My Justified Anger) and provide a pathway of return for the fallen through the salvation of their souls and the resurrection of their bodies from the vast wasteland most people mistakenly think of as the only reality that there is.

The physically-observable universe is *not* the only universe that there is — but more about that shortly. First, let me address the issue of MY Justified Anger. Because I AM completely *just,* I have righteous indignation whenever something is done outside of MY Will. Having free will does not mean that you can do anything that you want or that I will be pleased with whatever you do. No, with free will comes responsibility to work within the parameters of MY loving nature. When someone chooses to work outside of that nature, such a choice is an insult (that is, a "blasphemy") to ME and, consequently, stirs up MY Wrath. However, because I AM full of mercy and compassion (in addition to holiness and righteousness), I restrain MYSELF from unleashing MY Justified Anger. Instead, I hold MY Wrath in abeyance until it no longer can be suppressed. Then, at a time that I appoint, I unleash MY Justified Anger until it is spent and, then, I AM appeased.

Most of you have a difficult time understanding MY Nature because you are not pure and holy. Contrary to what you sometimes think, MY Nature is not cold and cruel. Indeed, those characteristics are correctly associated with the Evil One, Satan (the fallen Lucifer). No, MY Nature is pure and perfect and holy and righteous. For that reason, an offense to MY Nature requires punishment but not necessarily immediate punishment. Why not *immediate?* I am immensely patient. Patience includes the capacity to be wronged and not retaliate. As you progress spiritually, you will understand that when you are patient you are exhibiting one of MY characteristics. (By the way, patience really does develop your character and helps to develop your spiritual gifts. Patience is different from "not caring" in that patience requires commitment and trust and "not caring" involves acceptance concerning things you cannot change or control.)

By one definition, *the Universe* is "everything." It is the *All-that-is*. However, what you call the *universe* is really not *the All*. Why? It has a beginning and an ending. There was a time when it was formed and a time when it will end. Also, it fills a vacuum. (I don't fill a vacuum.) In MY Spiritual Universe, there is not a spot where I AM not because I fill everything in it. The physically-observable universe has a central point and outer limits. I am both the center and circumference of the spiritually-observable universe, which is invisible to your eyesight. There is neither beginning nor end to MY Spiritual Universe.

I don't inhabit the physical universe. (I do not infuse it with MY Being.) That does not mean that I cannot see everything that is going on in it. That does not mean that I cannot work through it or make things in it. Indeed, I AM your Maker in addition to your Creator! (I *create* something from nothing, and I *make* something out of what exists.) What I inhabit is *the All*. I live and move and have MY Supreme Being there. When all of you (all of those who will be saved) are presented to ME at the end of the millennial rule of Christ Jesus on Earth, MY Glory (which I have held back along with MY Justified Anger) will re-flood even the space that you currently inhabit and, in this way, I will again be *All-in-all*. In this communication, I refer to the real Universe (also known to you as "Heaven") as the Spiritual Universe. To be sure, there are objects in MY Spiritual Universe — which is to say, there is both form to it and substance in it (just not the form and substance with which you are familiar). I don't want you to get the idea that what is "etheric" to you might be composed only of "ethers" and ghostly images. MY one true and only real eternal Universe is spiritual in nature, not physical in nature.

What do I look like? That is a difficult question to answer using images with which you are familiar. Because I AM a Being, I have a form. (We'll start there.) MY form is enveloped in Glory. Did you ever read in MY Holy Bible what happened when Moshe asked ME to show MYSELF to him? I responded and said: "NO ONE CAN SEE ME AND LIVE. STAND THERE IN THE CLEFT OF THE ROCK. AND I WILL PASS BY AND PERMIT YOU TO SEE MY HINTER PARTS." Moshe was permitted to see the train of MY Glory as I passed by. He marveled! You, too, will marvel when you finally see ME and experience ME by having MY Glory actually pass through you. When you get to Heaven (the place and state of MY Supreme Being), MY Love will billow through you like one hundred million surging locomotives, and then another one hundred million, and so on, without ever stopping. Here, in Heaven, you will both see and feel what I have held in store for you. You will also hear the music of the spheres, which is the song of MY Everlasting Creation. This song is like one hundred million pipe organs playing resonating chords of complementary notes that each retain their own individual identities and yet blend together harmoniously in ever-increasing crescendos, all of which will actually convey profound meaning to you when you "hear" it (which is to say, feel it). You will find that creation's lay is like continuing explosions of joy. (You can't begin to understand this unless you have experienced joy in and through Christ Jesus.)

What, and where, is Heaven? (Remember, "Heaven" is also called "MY Spiritual Universe.") Heaven is both a state and a place. However, though Heaven may be a state without the place, it is never a place without the state. In the state in which you are currently, Heaven actually surrounds you and is, therefore, right next to you. However, though it is *about* you, you are currently not *in* Heaven. Actually, you are in Heaven to the degree that you choose to accept MY Grace and experience its resulting joy. (This last statement may sound contradictory to the previous statement, but it is not.)

MY Grace affords you a place in Heaven if you choose to accept it. I do not force you to receive MY Grace because that is not part of MY Nature. Besides, forcing MY Grace on you would negate MY having given the gift of free will to you. There are lower states of grace and higher states of grace. This truth does not take away from the grace that is imparted through MY Plan of Salvation. Rather, it simply means that there are different levels of experiencing MY Grace. Lower levels of experiencing MY Grace permit you to catch a glimpse of ME here and there, to receive simple impressions of MY Love for you, and to understand fundamental elements of truth about ME. Higher states of experiencing MY Grace occur when your conscious functioning self steps aside and permits you to unite with your higher self (supraself). Such a union permits you to experience the rest of yourself, so to speak. This really is not empty jargon. In truth, although you are not ME, I AM your one true and only real identity when you are completely yielded to ME.

There is a collective selfhood. ME! That does not mean that you do not retain your individuality when you live and move and have your individual being in ME. Quite to the contrary, no! It means that you do not really experience your one true identity and only real self unless you are living completely in ME. Living in the fullness of MY Grace permits you access to the entire Spiritual Universe. Of course, you cannot fill the entire Spiritual Universe. I fill it. You just have access to its various realms, states, planes, and levels. Remember, don't ever expect to take MY place or be ME. Such an approach to life will lead you to much frustration because it can't be done. Who made ME? No one, for I AM *the* Creator. I AM the only Self-Existent One. I have no beginning. I have no ending. I dwell in a surrounding reality of which you rarely catch a glimpse — unless you are living in humility, posturing yourself in an attitude of gratitude, and experiencing MY Grace in your penitence.

What you now know as time is just a sequence of related events. In Heaven, curvilinear space-time does not exist. All things are interrelated, and everything happens all at once (that is, "NOW"). Consciousness, being, and action are all unified in MY Spiritual Universe. Thus, whatever happens in the various corners of MY Spiritual Universe is immediately known everywhere, all at once.

This should give you some insights regarding MY ability to see you and know where you are, what you have done, and what you will do. Because I know what you will choose, I have predestined some of you to receive eternal salvation and some of you to receive eternal damnation.

You might ask: "Why not just end it all right now?" "Why not just pluck out those of us who are going to be saved and send the rest to damnation?" Let ME repeat, I AM Righteous and Just. *MY Just Cause* requires that there be a beginning and an ending, and that there be an allotted time for everyone to have ample opportunity to choose to return to ME. It is in this way, then, that MY Justice is served. And, regarding predestination, it is because I saw which souls would eventually accept MY Plan of Salvation and, as a result, return to ME that I predestined them to eventually receive the end of their salvation — eternal life in ME. In other words, the hope of eternal salvation (eternal redemption into Heaven) shall not go unfulfilled for those who choose to return to ME. Souls who are beneficiaries of MY Grace shall see ME and be with ME and in ME (and I in them) throughout all eternity. I shall not rest (neither shall you) until this expectation, which many eagerly await, is fulfilled.

Although all metaphors and analogies are flawed (some to a lesser extent and some to a greater extent), I would like to help you understand how I know the future when future possibilities change every second of your existence. If it were possible for you to know the future in your current state, then you would need to deduce all possible outcomes in every possible logical sequence for every possible situation, and you would have to be able to do that all at the same time for every variance. Then, as you were doing all of that, you would also have to factor in the heart and the intent of everyone involved in what you were sequencing to predict what they would be doing every step of the way for all possible sequences of action. You see how complicated and time-consuming that would be? To be sure, it would be impossible for any of you. Unlike you, however, because I am not constrained by structured consciousness in logic or analytic thinking or reasoning skills, I do not need to use deduction or induction (analytical thinking) to know the future. Sounds impossible? What is impossible for you is possible for ME.

Even though your future changes every second, I know all things because they are instantly evident to ME. *For example,* there are some people on Earth with uncanny abilities whom you call *savants.* Some savants can identify the number of objects that have just spilled out on the ground without using computational skills. They just simply *know* the number because the number is instantly evident to them without counting the objects one by one. Similarly, I do not need to go through a series of rapid calculations based on probability to predict the future. In fact, I do not *predict* the future because I simply *know* the future. The future is instantly evident to ME. It is also instantly evident to ME what choices you will make even though I do not determine the choices for you and even though you yourself may not know the choices you are going to make. Just because I know what choices you are going to make does not mean that your choices are predestined — because you exercise free will in making your choices. See? I know your future even though your future changes with each choice that you make. If you are gifted with intuition and foresight, then you might begin to understand what I have just written about MY knowing the future. However, even your intuition and foresight are flawed because you can only know in part and because your knowing in part cannot factor in that the future changes every second, especially in MY responses to your prayers. (One of the reasons that you should pray is that your prayer to ME can, and does, change your future.)

How do you reconcile that the future changes every second with fulfilling your destiny and predestination? I predestine your ultimate future relative to your acceptance of MY Plan of Salvation or your rejection of it. Those who accept MY Plan of Salvation are predestined to receive eternal salvation. Those who reject MY Plan of Salvation are predestined to receive eternal damnation. Fulfilling your destiny depends on your yielding to MY Will (just as your receiving eternal salvation depends on your yielding to MY Will). If you act according to MY Will for your daily lives, then you will fulfill your life's destiny — which is to say, you will fulfill the relative purpose that I have for you on Earth. In other words, I will enable you to complete what I have asked you to do if you daily seek MY Will. Your absolute purpose is to please ME by yielding to MY Will, which yielding is a form of worship. Your relative purpose (the purpose I have for you on Earth) is also dependent on pleasing ME by yielding to MY Will (and is, therefore, a form of worship, too).

If you accept MY Plan of Salvation, I have established a place for you within the Body of MY Christ. I have predestined a dynamic place within that Body and not a static place for you. In corporeality, blood is a "member" of the physical body. Its place is dynamic because it moves and changes location. In the same way are the members of Christ's Body also dynamic. They move in accordance with MY Will. To be sure, they are interdependent on one another while they are all dependent on ME.

Although I guide you, I do not control you. You fulfill your own destiny by yielding to MY Will. I do not force you to yield to MY Will. In summary, then, the only thing that is predestined for you is what you receive because of your acceptance or rejection of MY Plan of Salvation. Although I have predetermined the ultimate outcomes for your world of appearances, I have not predetermined your acceptance or rejection of ME. You determine that for yourselves. You also determine whether you fulfill your relative purpose on Earth. I determine what your relative purpose is, but you determine whether you fulfill it or not. Based on your yielding to ME, and the degree to which you yield, your relative purpose can change from day to day.

Now let ME communicate more to you about MY Grace. A long time ago, I told Moshe: "I WILL BE GRACIOUS TO WHOM I WILL BE GRACIOUS, AND I WILL SHOW MERCY TO WHOM I WILL SHOW MERCY." Perhaps you have heard or read that MY "unmerited favor" is demonstrated to you through MY Grace. You see, although I search for you because I AM *just,* MY Grace is still a gift. You cannot do, think, feel, or say anything to receive it. You need only accept it. And it is by accepting it that you demonstrate the necessary contrition and humility you need to return to ME. A primary lesson that you are to learn in your present state is that you must lean on and trust in ME (which is to say, believe *on* ME) to receive MY Grace. It is through MY Grace, and MY Grace alone, that you can experience sufficiency and contentment in your current state regardless of your present life's difficult circumstances. I desire that you believe in and rely on ME. Strength is inherent in, and to, MY Grace. When you admit that you are weak and that you must rely on ME, it is then that you experience MY Strength and

Power. It is then that MY Strength is perfected in you. Indeed, MY Strength is made perfect in weakness. To be sure, your sufficiency is not *of,* or *in,* yourselves but *of,* and *in,* ME. And, yes, it is through MY abounding Grace that you have sufficiency, in turn, to abound to every good work! In MY Grace is a state of being that knows no bounds.

Dear ones, I put you in difficult situations and circumstances to refine you. I know it is not easy for you. Please understand MY heart. I only want what is best for you. As your Creator, and as your Father, I chasten you. ("Father" is a title you may only use legitimately if you have accepted MY only-begotten Son as your personal Savior and, therefore, have become co-heirs or "sons of God" with him.) I permit you to pass through the furnace of affliction to test your love and resolve and try your faith to make you stronger so that you will never again yield to a temptation to leave the reality of MY Being.

Many of you have misconcluded that I want you to have all of the riches of the world in which you currently live, when, in fact, what I want you to have are all the riches of the next world! To be sure, I AM able to bless and reward you in your present state as well as meet your daily needs. However, I will withhold specific blessings and rewards from you if I know that they will somehow keep you from yielding your *all* to ME. I know that the greatest blessing and reward that you can ever receive is the relationship you are able to have with ME through MY Grace and your acceptance of it. If you accept MY Plan of Salvation, you will not only live in MY Glory, you will again become an integral part of MY Spiritual Universe and I WILL again become an integral part of you. Consider this before you continue in your rejection of ME. I want the best for you. You were MY Created, and I desire for you to become MY re-created through Christ Jesus!

Your faith, honor, and commitment are extremely important to ME. Why faith? Unless you believe that I AM, and that I AM a rewarder of those who diligently seek ME, it is impossible to please ME or receive MY blessings in your current state. *MY Just Cause* requires faith. In actuality, faith provides you with a link to ME. Without faith, there can be no link. The power of MY Divinity operates through your faith. That does not mean that MY action is dependent on your faith in ME. No, it means that I respond to the faith that you have in ME. Just as an airplane requires a runway to land, so do I require a connection for MY power to operate on your behalf. Figuratively speaking, your faith is a landing strip for MY power. Your faith helps establish a connection, or bridge, to ME in your current state. MY Grace completes that connection. That is why prayer is so important. Not only does prayer attest to your faith in ME, prayer helps to activate MY response. It "steps up" the connection, so to speak. Your faith does not control ME, but your faith motivates ME.

I always respond to genuine prayer, which is not to say that I always do what you want ME to do, but I always do what is best for you. I respond to your prayers for others as well as to others' prayers for you, which is why it is important to pray for one another. While on Earth, Jesus did not forget to pray for you (even for those of you on Earth two thousand years after he lived). Doesn't that say something to you about the necessity of prayer and its power? Later, I will talk to you about your attitude during prayer, levels of expectancy, and how to frame your prayers (yes, I will even give you tips on how to say your prayers to ME).

Faithfulness through honoring your commitments both to ME as well as to others is also very important to ME. *For example,* I hate divorce. Why? It is a sign of lack of commitment on your part, a failing to follow through with what you have promised, and, thus, grievous to ME. Does that mean that I won't forgive you if you break your vows of holy union to one another? No, all "sins of the world" are forgivable (provided that you not eternally refuse to confess them to ME or eternally refuse to ask for forgiveness for them). Simply stated, if you break your covenant vows to one another, it means that you won't receive all the rewards and blessings that I have in store for you. You will understand this better when you get to Heaven, but I hold both rewards and blessings in store for you as you make your way through your earthly journey. If you remain true to yourself — that is, your higher self (the supraself that you have in ME) — then you will receive each reward and blessing in due time and at the proper season. However, if you permit yourself to continually fall prey to selfishness and sin, then MY rewards and blessings are withheld from you. In effect, you keep MY rewards and blessings from you through your improper actions and inactions. This is complementary to the idea that spiritual error, or iniquity, carries its own punishment. In this case, the punishment comes in your failure to receive particular rewards and blessings.

I will now return to the topic of prayer. There is a difference between prayer and meditation. Prayer is when you communicate something to ME, and meditation is when you wait for ME to communicate something to you. The way you approach ME is most significant for it determines whether I hear you and answer you. First and foremost, your heart must be in the right spot to "connect" with ME. The intent of your heart must be good. If your heart is in the right spot, then you are *almost* there (for, then, I AM reachable even if you are not articulating things accurately). Second, your rudimental understanding of ME must be correct. *For example,* if you think that I can be found in rough stone, hewn marble, or painted picture, then your prayers will fall flat. Or, if you think that I AM some mindless higher power, then, generally speaking, I AM not going to respond to your prayer (UNLESS I KNOW THAT IT WILL HELP YOU GRADUALLY ACCEPT WHO I REALLY AM AND COME TO BETTER UNDERSTAND WHO YOU ARE IN ME). If you have unknowingly adopted something blasphemous to ME in your own belief system, then I will refrain from acting on your requests. As I said, your approach to ME is very important. Would you expect to approach an important person on Earth in a cavalier or less than respectful manner? No, you would mind your manners. So, too, you are expected to be respectful when you approach the Sole Sovereign of the Universe! I must be approached in an attitude of reverence and honor. If you adamantly refuse, then you don't belong to ME, and you cast your lot with the Devil. If you genuinely seek to know from ME whether Jesus Christ is really the Son of God, then I will grant you the knowledge of salvation and repentance through him. If you profess that God cannot have an only-begotten Son, I will not respond to any of your prayer requests. If you disbelieve that Jesus Christ is the only-begotten Son of God, your prayers are earthbound and of null effect.

One prayer that Christ Jesus prayed provides an excellent example of how to pray to ME. It starts with "Our Father." Again, the title "Father" affirms recognition of your personal relationship to ME through Christ Jesus. "Who art in Heaven." This acknowledges where MY throne is (where I reside and have MY Supreme Being) or, in other words, that MY Habitation is set apart from you. "Holy is Your Name." This acknowledges MY Nature and the Mystery of MY Name. Though I revealed MYSELF to Moshe as "I AM THAT I AM," MY REAL NAME could never be pronounced by a human being because it indwells MY entire Creation and is a *supersonic* intonation. "Your Kingdom come. Your Will be done on Earth as it is in Heaven." This contrasts where you currently are with where I AM and invites ME into your current experience and current plane of consciousness. "Give us this day, our daily bread." This request acknowledges your ongoing dependency on ME both as Provider and Protector. "Forgive us our trespasses (sins or debts) as we forgive those who trespass against us." In other words, "forgive us *to the degree* that we forgive others." This request acknowledges implicitly that I WILL NOT forgive your sins unless you forgive others of their trespasses against you. MY forgiveness of your sins is nullified by your not forgiving others. (Such nullification is either temporary or permanent, depending on the degree of hardness of your heart.) Your unforgiveness demonstrates that you have absolutely little or no clue as to the real nature of MY Kingdom and that you are willfully disobeying MY commandment to forgive others. (A little more about forgiveness will come later in this communication.) "Lead us not into temptation but deliver us from evil." This asks that I direct your footsteps, which includes giving MY angels charge over you so that you do not stumble and fall. In praying, you must remember to wait *upon* ME, which is to say, you must serve ME while you are waiting *for* ME. How do you serve ME? By seeking to do MY Will. How do you know what MY Will is for you? By studying MY Holy Bible and listening for the still, small voice within you. And, above all, pray "for Thy Name's sake." In other words, remind ME of *MY Just Cause*. Remember that MY Grace and Mercy are dependent on ME and not on you, who you are, or what you do. Unless you pray, you will not see evidence of MY power in your lives.

Of course, I understand that some of your acceptance and understanding of ME is time-dependent and development-dependent as well as situational. Consequently, I make allowances for your spiritual immaturity and stubbornness. However, if you continually refuse to yield to ME, your heart becomes increasingly hardened, and your conscience becomes increasingly seared. Then, it becomes increasingly difficult for MY Holy Spirit to minister to you (you are not able to hear His voice and His truths do not resonate within you). Then, I cannot soften and prepare your hearts to receive thoughts, feelings, and ideas that are of MY divine nature.

Your stubbornness disgusts ME. Really, all arrogance disgusts ME. It reminds ME of the willfulness and selfishness of MY eternal enemy, Lucifer. For that reason, I permit some of you to experience almost a "Hell on Earth" to help bring you to the point where you yield to ME and come to depend on ME during good times as well as difficult times. I have every right to do this. I AM your Creator. *MY Just Cause* requires that you yield to ME and come to depend on ME. If you continually refuse, then ultimately you don't belong to ME and you cast your lot with

Satan. If you are a stubborn person and are experiencing "Hell on Earth" because of that stubbornness, better that you suffer here and now rather than throughout all eternity.

Speaking about suffering, some of you have it all wrong. I can use suffering to achieve MY ends. For some of you, suffering is the only thing that will catch your attention and cause you to lean on ME as *the Sustaining Infinite.* Moreover, some of you have wondered why I have withheld certain rewards or blessings from you. It is either because I know your receiving them would drive a wedge between us or I know that your receiving them would prevent you from getting closer to ME. Indeed, try to remember (especially through difficult times) that MY Grace is sufficient for you and that MY Strength is made perfect in your weakness. Embrace difficulty as an opportunity for you to turn to ME and, then, remain facing ME.

Before we return to MY Plan of Salvation and how I have used it to implement *MY Just Cause,* let ME take a moment to reiterate that I created all souls at once and that, after Lucifer's Fall, when curvilinear space-time as you know it really began, all immortal souls fell at the same time (because, at that time, all souls in your sphere were under the jurisdiction of the one who was known as Lucifer). I immediately put all fallen souls in a "holding tank" while I *made* the physical universe. In other words, I brought order out of the chaos that ensued because of Lucifer's Fall. Matter, or physical material (the "bound" energy that I spoke of earlier), was formed as a result of Lucifer's Fall, but there was no real order to it. Many of your physical scientists have so struggled with the idea of creation versus evolution that they have failed to recognize that the order existing today, including life as you know it, proves MY existence as Creator. How? Mechanisms of chance and the law of entropy dictate that in order to get order out of chaos in the physical universe, a Prime Mover must have been necessary. That Prime Mover is ME! Without MY intervention, the nothing that was the physical universe would have remained nothing. I *made* something from what came into existence due to Lucifer's Fall. The intricacies of the order that is evident in the physical universe today cannot be attributed to mere chance for, as you may know, in a closed system such as the physically-observable universe there is a growing increase in disorder and randomness. Left to its own devices — which devices are the laws of physics — physicality proceeds toward increased chaos and not toward increased order. Simply stated, without ME there is no order. Not a whit.

That there is an interchangeability between matter and energy is true. Matter first appeared when energy became bound at the time of Lucifer's Fall (some, not all, energy that exists became bound). Nevertheless, though it became bound, I chose to make something from it that would further *MY Just Cause*. I restyled MY Original Creation in an allegorical, physical miniature, so to speak. It was then that I reduced major meanings of Life to symbolic forms. *For example,* the planets, solar systems, stars, and galaxies serve as metaphors for aspects of MY Supreme Being and MY Original Creation. Though I am not to be found indwelling the physical referents just mentioned, they all point to ME. They give evidence of MY existence, and they represent aspects of MY true nature and the reality of MY Supreme Being. In other words, they point to MY Intelligent Design of all physical creation.

For the sake of clarity, it is important for ME to remind you that there were two distinctly different Falls. The first Fall was Lucifer's Fall from Me, which instantly altered, or distorted, the Universe. It was because of this Fall that angelic immortal beings first became encumbered, or enmeshed, in a warped universe. The second Fall was *your* Fall from ME (also known as the Adamic Fall). In some ways, they constitute two steps of the same Fall, but, because they are dependent on the free will decisions of two different kinds of beings (that is, the Angelic race and the Adamic race) and are sequenced events, they are, in effect, distinctly different. The second Fall would not have happened without the first Fall because you would not have been tempted to disobey ME. The second Fall was dependent on the first Fall, but the first Fall was not dependent on the second Fall. Hence, they are distinctly different. I permitted the first Fall to test MY entire creation's devotion to ME. If you are sincerely devoted to ME, you have nothing to worry about. If you are not sincerely devoted to ME, you have everything to worry about.

That the human form has evolved over thousands of years should be evident to you through anthropology. I gave direction to primate physical change so that the evolved human form might optimally be made habitable for each soul that resides therein. Whence comes each soul that is born into your physical plane of consciousness? From the "holding tank" that I mentioned earlier. That is the place where all fallen souls dwell while they await an earthly corporeal experience — which is to say, while they wait for their individual souls to be born in human flesh. If, during their earthly experience, they humble themselves to ME, acknowledge ME in all that they do, and accept MY Plan of Salvation, they are then fully restored to ME after they die. After the saved die, they serve as ministering spirits, working on behalf of *MY Just Cause*. If, during their earthly experience, souls consciously and unwaveringly reject MY Plan of Salvation, they condemn themselves to eternal separation from ME. They are then excluded from MY Presence forever. In Heaven, it is known by everyone that the Family of God includes by excluding, increases by decreasing, and often varies yet never changes. (Take time to examine the truths within the previous statement.)

It is recorded in Scripture that I said: "MY SPIRIT SHALL NOT ALWAYS STRIVE [ABIDE] WITH MAN, BECAUSE HE ALSO IS FLESH." It is also recorded in Scripture that "FLESH AND BLOOD CANNOT INHERIT THE KINGDOM OF GOD," and "IT DOES NOT YET APPEAR WHAT WE [HUMAN BEINGS] SHALL BE, BUT WE KNOW THAT, WHEN HE [CHRIST JESUS] SHALL APPEAR, WE SHALL BE LIKE HIM." In other words, what you were originally created to look like before the Adamic Fall, and what you will eventually be re-created to look like in your glorified and translated form (that is, your resurrected body) is not now seen nor will it be seen until the reappearance ("Second Coming") of Christ Jesus. In the final analysis, what is most important to ME is your spiritual being and not your physical form.

What happens to those souls who have not made a conscious decision or clear choice to serve either ME or Satan? They are returned to the "holding tank" to await their rebirth in flesh. Unfortunately, most Christians have not been taught correctly concerning reincarnation. And, even more unfortunately, most people who believe in reincarnation do not know the only-begotten Son of God as their personal Savior and Lord. The Scripture that is erroneously used to refute reincarnation is: "It has been appointed to men once to die, and then after this the judgment." (Hebrews 9:27) Just as "men" is used in that passage in the generic sense, so, too, is the death spoken of generic (that is, death as an all-encompassing, spiritual separation from ME). In other words, all souls in existence at the time of the Adamic Fall were separated from ME in spiritual death [the "first death"]. And, at the appointed time of the Final Judgment, there then will be a "second death," when separation is made permanent and eternal for those who have confirmed their rejection of ME by remaining steadfast in their rejection of MY only-begotten Son as their personal Savior. Such souls will then be "twice dead" — "dead once" in their separation from ME at the time of the Adamic Fall and "dead twice" from their rejection of MY Plan of Salvation.

Yes, there was a "first death," and there will be a "second death." The "first death," or initial separation from ME, came about as an immediate result of the Adamic Fall. The "second death," or final and permanent separation from ME, will come at the time of the Final Judgment, specifically for those souls who consciously reject ME by deliberately rejecting MY Plan of Salvation (in other words, although they are able to comprehend MY Plan, they still reject it). Remember, I AM a perfectly *just*

God: perfectly *just* to you and perfectly *just* to ME. That I have allotted a specific interval of time for souls who fell from ME to return to ME comes from MY Grace and MY Mercy, which are integral components of the perfect love I have for MY Creation. To permit chaos to continue *ad infinitum* in MY Universe, even if it were only in one corner of it, would be unfair to ME and unfair to those who belong to ME. To be sure, the whole creation groans as it waits for its release from the current limitations and constraints that I have imposed on it (for good reason).

Here is what MY Holy Spirit wrote on this subject through MY Apostle Paul (recorded in Romans 8:18-23):

> {18} I [the Apostle Paul] consider that what we suffer at this present time cannot be compared at all with the Glory that is going to be revealed to us. {19} All of creation waits with eager longing for God to reveal His heirs. {20} For creation was condemned to lose its purpose, not of its own will, but because God willed it to be so. Yet there was the hope {21} that creation would one day be set free from its slavery to decay and would share the glorious freedom of the children of God, {22} For we know that up to the present time all of creation groans with pain, like the pain of childbirth. {23} But it is not just creation alone which groans; we who have the Holy Spirit as the first of God's gifts also groan within ourselves as we wait for God to make us His heirs and set our whole being free.[435]

Even the saved already in Heaven eagerly await the time when order is restored throughout the whole universe (the Universe), when spiritual warfare is over and all are at peace, in harmony,

---

435 Paraphrased from *Good News for Modern Man: The New Testament in Today's English Version,* Diglot Edition, Deutsche Bibelgesellschaft Stuttgart, Second Edition, 1984, page 463. (Originally published by the American Bible Society, 1976, New York.)

and at rest. "At rest" does not mean that activity will cease. It simply means that souls will no longer need to toil in physicality or labor spiritually, mentally, and emotionally to keep themselves pure and unspotted from the world by resisting temptation and fighting evil. In other words, they will only be resting from their work on Earth.

How does the Evil One operate? As I mentioned earlier, Satan's primary motivation is envy. (That is why he tries to induce you to envy others and covet what they have.) But he also operates through the spirit of fear, which is antithetical to MY Holy Spirit, and through the spirit of hatred, which is antithetical to MY perfect love (that is, MY forgiving love). Yes, I hate with a perfect hatred because I AM perfectly *just,* but Satan's hatred for, and fear of, all who are good is borne of injustice, specifically envy. Satan is still envious. But now he is not just envious of ME, he is also envious of you. Satan is envious of you because you have what he can never have. You not only possess the capacity for salvation, you also receive salvation. Salvation is something Satan can never have. And he knows it. That is why he hates you. And that is why he fears you. (Did you not know that fallen created beings fear what they hate and hate what they fear?)

Satan operates through envy, hatred, and fear. Unforgiveness results in bitterness, which, in turn (when left unchecked), develops into hatred. Satan tries to precipitate that emotion to negatively influence souls in dust. Gradually, he harnesses the hatred that indwells a soul and uses it to control its spirit as well as to try and thwart others from receiving salvation. Hatred in a soul permits Satan (as well as discarnate entities who have given themselves over to him) an opportunity to influence the souls of corporeal beings and, sometimes, even possess and control them.

Earlier, when discussing prayer, I indicated that I made a law reciprocal to your forgiveness that is often neglected, ignored, or refuted. MY law is that if you do not forgive those who trespass against you, I WILL NOT FORGIVE YOU! Evidently, many of you think that this is an idle threat. Please be assured that it is not. This law is in effect and is the only law that cancels MY forgiveness of your sins and withholds from you the eternal salvation that I extend to you through the sacrifice of MY only-begotten Son. By not forgiving others after you have come to the saving knowledge of Jesus Christ (having already received forgiveness yourself), you demonstrate that you want no part of ME. You demonstrate that, even after knowing MY Will concerning this area of your life, you still desire that your own will be done and not MY WILL. Souls who refuse to do MY Will by not forgiving those who have harmed them, damaged them, or hurt them in any way put themselves in a precarious position by jeopardizing their own salvation. No, you cannot "lose" your salvation and Satan cannot steal your salvation, but you can throw your salvation away.

If you do not do what I have commanded regarding the forgiveness of others, you are in great danger of becoming unclean spirits (also known in MY Holy Bible as "demons," "evil spirits," or "devils"). This does not mean that I do not understand that your forgiveness of others is often a process, or that I am not considering that your forgiveness of others depends on MY help and support. I give you sufficient opportunity and time to forgive those who have trespassed against you, and I help you to forgive. But you need to ask ME to help you and be willing to undergo the process of excising unforgiveness from your heart, the core of your being. Pray that MY Love so indwells your heart that you will be able to find the love necessary to forgive others who have wronged you. I know that this is an extremely high standard. But it was established by MY Son on the cross at Calvary. You must conform to this standard if you wish to become and remain a part of ME and a member of the Body of MY Christ. I can't "know" you if you do not forgive others. I won't permit it. I won't allow it. It would be unseemly. (Created beings are not permitted to tell the Creator what to do.)

What about the spirit of fear? The spirit of fear is an actual force. It moves across the land looking to overshadow susceptible channels, endeavoring to shackle them with the fears of their own worst nightmares. It hangs as a dark cloud in a dimensionless space, looking for areas of vulnerability, weakness, and infirmity in its prey. It penetrates a soul through these areas and, then, gets the soul to use its own imagination to conjure up images, feelings, and ideas that are potentially incapacitating. The spirit of fear seeks to make things that are unreal appear real, hoping to fool souls into believing what is false is true. The spirit of fear tells you that there is a 99.99 per cent chance that something harmful or negative is going to happen. It terrorizes you in this way. Even if such odds were true (and, in most cases, they are not), you should remember that I have control over all things, that I AM able to intervene (and often do when you ask ME), and that I can cause 180-degree reversals in the final nanoseconds before a "disaster" occurs or even immediately after a "disaster" happens.

What about when you do all of the right things and disasters still happen? Remember, I have the bigger and clearer picture, not you. *For example,* I can easily attend to more than seven billion souls on Earth simultaneously while I am aware of their individual thoughts, feelings, and behaviors. Such cognizance is just a drop in the ocean of MY Omniscience. This is not a cop-out. I permit certain disastrous things to happen in order that certain good things can occur. What good things? (1) Lessons and warnings for you. (2) Greater intimacy between you and ME. (3) Appeasing MY Justified Anger. (4) Exacting MY Justice. (5) Rewards and blessings for you. And (6) positive impacts on others. I have long been criticized by you for allowing negative things to happen to you, but you don't have the big picture, do you? No. But I do. Really, I could have eradicated all evil and negativity the instant that it initially appeared, but I would have lost you in the process. It is part of *MY Just Cause* to allow the good and the bad to develop side by side and not to uproot the bad before the good is fully developed so as not to destroy the good in the process of destroying the bad. See? (If you had been studying your Bibles, you would have known that already, and I would not have had to reiterate it here.)

Now I would like to address MY Holy Bible in relationship to MY Plan of Salvation, which plan I designed to effect *MY Just Cause*. MY Holy Bible is an inspired and inspirational work. It has brought, and still brings, the message of salvation to many. It consists of the record of MY covenant with the people of Israel through Abraham (the "Old Covenant," or "Old Testament") as well as the record of MY covenant with all nations through Jesus Christ (the "New Covenant," or "New Testament").

A covenant is an agreement that is ratified by a seal. During ancient times, the seal of ratification was signified by the "cutting of a deal" through the "letting of blood." Why blood? Blood was understood by the ancients to represent life. Even primitives knew that without blood one could not live. Sometimes, a covenant was sealed through the comingling of blood between covenant partners. Sometimes, it was sealed through the sacrifice of an animal whose blood was shed as a substitutionary offering (that is, as a substitute for the blood-letting of the covenant partners). Regardless, blood-letting represented the formation of a permanent bond between the participants. Through blood sacrifice, I chose to use a symbol that the ancients could understand. And I chose to establish this requirement to appease MY Wrath. The ancients were primitive and barbarous people, stiff-necked, stubborn, and rebellious from the first day that I sought to establish an intimate relationship with them. (So, you see, humanity has not really changed!)

Next for you to understand is the necessity of a "covering" (or *atonement)* to hide your iniquity and sin from ME in order that I might have an intimate relationship with you. First, you need to understand that there is a difference between iniquity and sin. In this communication, *iniquity* is defined as "the act of turning away from the Creator," and *sin* is defined as "any action based on that turning." To be sure, both are forms of error and both need to be "covered" if you are to have any part in ME. Second, because I AM perfectly pure, holy, and righteous, I cannot establish and maintain a relationship with MY fallen created beings without expiation for their iniquity and sin. That would neither be *just* to you nor *just* to ME. Consequently, I decided — such decision within the parameters of MY jurisdiction — to require animal sacrifice during Old Covenant times: (1) for MY Anger to be appeased, (2) for MY Justice to be served, (3) for your iniquity and sin to be "covered," and (4) for the establishment of an agreement, or understanding, between us. Additionally, I established rules, regulations, ordinances, and commandments for the children of Israel to help teach them, as well as others through their basic principles, that people must be set apart from the mundane and worldly if they are to become and remain MY chosen people. Obviously, Levitical Law and the blood sacrifice of designated animals were imperfect ways to deal with your iniquity and sin. If they had been perfect, I would not have had to establish a New Covenant through the sacrifice of MY only-begotten Son.

To be sure, the ancient measures I established during Old Covenant times were perfectly fitted to MY Plan of Salvation. They were only imperfect to the degree that they were temporary and not permanent. For this reason, before the beginning of creation, I provided for a perfect sacrifice through a personal Savior. A true Savior is someone who would be unblemished and unspotted from the world and, in this way, be able to offer up a perfect sacrifice for the complete and permanent remission (that is, cancellation) of iniquity and sin through the shedding of his own innocent blood. Here, I need to make a distinction between "atonement" and "remission." *Atonement* means "covering" and "hiding." Atonement through the sacrifice of animals did not remove your iniquity and sin. Your iniquity and sin were still there, but they were temporarily and periodically "covered" and "hidden" from ME by the shed blood of these imperfect sacrifices. *Remission* means "cancellation through complete payment." In other words, the blood sacrifice of Jesus Christ makes you pure and virginal as if you had never fallen from MY Original Creation. This restoration only occurs for you personally if you accept the means of escape. You must agree to it in order to be included in MY New Covenant.

For various reasons, many of you do not understand MY Plan for your eternal salvation. For what reasons? Either you are too proud or too lazy. Some of you fancy yourselves as too intelligent to accept such a simple plan. (MY Plan was meant to be simple so that even the simple could understand it.) Some of you think that it is good to be self-reliant, individualistic, and independent. You don't understand that you cannot really live without ME! Why? I designed you to be dependent on ME. You are not really complete without ME indwelling you. Some of you seek to control situations and dominate others. In effect, you want to be little lords of the universe like your father, the Devil. Some of you lack inquiring minds and, thus, choose to remain in ignorance. And some of you assume that believers in Christ Jesus, and followers of his Way, are stupid. All of this is off-putting to ME. But I will be patient with you for a while longer because I AM jealous *for* you. The desired end of *MY Just Cause* comes in your complete restoration to ME as members of the Body of MY Christ. Eventually, you will end up either with ME or against ME (a part of ME or apart from ME). It is as simple as that.

In order for you to be fully restored to ME, I required a sacrifice for your iniquity and sin that was pure, perfect, and holy. Since such a sacrifice does not exist in your state of being, I provided it through MY only-begotten Son, the Logos of MY Life, Jesus Christ. His was the only sacrifice that is acceptable to ME. Consequently, you must accept him as your Savior if you are to be returned to ME. Such an acceptance demonstrates the necessary humility that I require from you to re-enter MY shores. Also, such an acceptance demonstrates the necessary faith that I require for you to appease MY Justified Anger as well as please

ME. As I mentioned earlier, it is impossible for you to please ME unless you believe that I AM! Paradoxically, faith is MY supernatural gift to you through MY Son, who is the originator and perfecter of all faith. Why do I reiterate this? I continue to communicate this to you in the hope that you will be able to free yourselves from the bondage of iniquity and sin through the only sacrifice acceptable for your iniquity and sin in the person of Jesus the Christ, Y'shua H'Moshiach. It is most unfortunate, but, for many of you, the mere mention of MY Son's Name turns you off, shuts you down, and closes you up. That you don't like MY Intelligent Design for your deliverance speaks of your continued arrogance, willfulness, and stubbornness, which are not only grievous to ME but grievous to you as well. (In this communication, grief *is* separation.)

I will now end this communication *(MY Just Cause by God)* by answering a question that is difficult for many of you to ask as well as difficult for most of you to answer: "Why does God kill some people and permit others to be murdered?"

Of all the biological worlds that I peopled, the planet Earth has been the most problematic for ME. Why? People of Earth have always been barbaric, idolatrous, cunning, thieving, murderous, and ungrateful. As a result, there were many times that I repented of creating *Homo sapiens* and teetered on deciding to force the entire species into extinction. However, during the worst of such times, there was always at least one person whose existence made the difference and kept ME from extinguishing the entire species' flame of biological life.

For example, consider the case of Noah and the flood: I removed (killed) all the people living at that time because of their immoral lifestyles and pagan practices. I saved only Noah and his wife and their three sons and their wives. Basically, I saved the sons and their wives for the sake of Noah, who was righteous in MY sight and, for that reason, deserved to be spared. (To be sure, I saved Noah's offspring not only for Noah's sake but for the purpose of repopulating the Earth after the flood.)

There has always been at least one person who would stand out by standing up for ME and, for that reason, I either spared humanity from complete extinction or spared one of its populations from total annihilation. As already presented, Noah was such a person. Abram/Abraham was also such a person. So was Lot, Moshe/Moses, and Jonah. And, of course, MY only-begotten Son, Jesus Christ, was such a person. One person in each case made the difference between the survival or annihilation of the entire human population or of an entire segment of its population. (Let this be a lesson that one person, even you, can make a huge difference in some very important matters.)

The words that best describe the human race include *recalcitrance, recidivism,* and *feral.* The spirits of unsaved human beings are recalcitrant in that they are obdurate and unwilling to be disciplined or discipline themselves. The spirits of unsaved human beings are recidivistic because, even though they may pay a civil penalty for the crimes they commit, they refuse to learn from their mistakes and routinely return to their criminal thinking and behaviors. The spirits of unsaved human beings are feral because, without my Holy Spirit residing within them, their minds default to animalistic, criminal thinking and actions.

Many well-intentioned human beings do not like reading the Old Testament because they think it portrays ME in a negative light. They think that the Old Testament shows ME to be a vengeful God. They refuse to acknowledge (1) that I AM a vengeful God and (2) that I have not stopped being a vengeful God during these New Testament times. They do not understand that I'M vengeful because I AM jealous for the love and worship that I deserve from MY created beings: I am the sole Sovereign, only Creator, and single Savior of the entire Universe.

Just because I sent MY only-begotten Son to pay for the personal iniquity and sin of individually-saved souls does not mean that I have refrained from being who I AM: The God of the Old Testament is the same God as the God of the New Testament even though there exists a great dispensation of grace and mercy from ME during New Testament times in response to MY Son's sacrifice for your personal iniquity and sin. As a compelling example that I have not changed, during New Testament times MY Vengeance is unleashed through MY angels in the apocalyptic woes that are recorded in the Book of Revelation and meted out in response to your world's festering iniquity and sin. Indeed, during the Great Tribulation (the second three-and-one-half-year period of the seven-year Tribulation), a significant number of people are killed by ME.

In MY Holy Bible, and in this communication, a distinction is made between *murdering* and *killing*. *Murdering* is always the intentional spilling of innocent blood. *Killing* includes: (1) the unintentional (accidental) spilling of anyone's blood, (2) the intentional spilling of a perpetrator's blood (a) in retribution for their attacking innocent people or (b) in protection of the innocent people being attacked, and (3) the intentional spilling of blood from any one of MY committed and proven enemies. For the sake of clarification, a committed and proven enemy of MINE is one who is eternally reprobate (as determined by ME) because he (or she) has consciously and permanently joined his (or her) soul to Satan. (Only I can determine without error who is eternally reprobate. Except for a few instances of extreme evil in some human beings, you are unable to assess MY eternal condemnation of others.)

I, the Lord God Almighty, do not murder. I do not shed innocent blood. Satan is a murderer, but I AM not a murderer. I have never murdered, and I will never murder. It is against MY Nature to murder. However, I do *permit* the murder of some of MY sheep for the following joint reasons: (1) as a testimony and witness to unsaved people of the victims' unalterable commitment and complete devotion to ME and (2) as a testimony and witness of the perpetrators' guilt that deserves punishment from ME. To be sure, perpetrators who deserve punishment from ME may not receive that punishment if they repent of their sins, ask for forgiveness for those sins, and accept the Lord Jesus Christ as their personal Savior. However, if they never ask for forgiveness and, in fact, revel in their spilling of innocent blood, especially if that blood has been sacrificed to a false god (either Satan or his proxy), then I will mete out MY punishment on them through MY Wrath (MY Justified Anger) in the form of earthly woes and eternal damnation. Earthly woes include plagues, pestilences, natural disasters, famines, and human warfare. Eternal damnation is the ongoing supernatural woe specifically referred to in the Holy Bible as "the second death" in "the Lake of Fire," which condition of being is restricted to all blasphemous people whose names are not inscribed in MY Book of Life.

Although one of MY commandments is often translated in the Holy Bible as "Thou shalt not kill" (Exodus 20:13 and Deuteronomy 5:17), this imperative is more accurately translated as "Thou shalt not murder." If I did not permit killing, I would not have instructed the children of Israel to kill all the inhabitants of the land of Canaan because they were adherents of pagan religions. Killing them was intended to prevent eventual domination by the Canaanite pagans over the children of Israel through Canaanite physical aggression as well as intermarriage. As recorded in Deuteronomy 7:16 (KJV Paraphrase), I said to them: "YOU MUST KILL ALL PEOPLE THAT THE LORD YOUR GOD DELIVERS TO YOU. YOU MUST NOT HAVE PITY ON THEM: NEITHER SHALL YOU SERVE THEIR GODS BECAUSE THAT WILL BE A SNARE TO YOU."

Although Christians are not permitted by ME to murder anyone, they may do what is necessary to protect themselves and their families and communities when they are attacked physically.

Books by the Author

As I See It: The Nature of Reality by God by Rev. Joseph Adam Pearson, Ph.D., Christ Evangelical Bible Institute, Copyright 2022. ISBN 978-0615590615.

Classroom Version of As I See It: The Nature of Reality by God by Rev. Joseph Adam Pearson, Ph.D., Christ Evangelical Bible Institute, Copyright 2022. ISBN-13: 978-1734294705.

God, Our Universal Self: A Primer for Future Christian Metaphysics by Rev. Joseph Adam Pearson, Ph.D., Christ Evangelical Bible Institute, Copyright 2020. ISBN 978-0985772857.

Divine Metaphysics of Human Anatomy by Rev. Joseph Adam Pearson, Ph.D., Christ Evangelical Bible Institute, Copyright 2022. ISBN 978-0985772819.

Hello from 3050 AD! by Rev. Joseph Adam Pearson, Ph.D., Christ Evangelical Bible Institute, Copyright 2021. ISBN 978-0996222402.

Christianity and Homosexuality Reconciled: New Thinking for a New Millennium! by Rev. Joseph Adam Pearson, Ph.D., Christ Evangelical Bible Institute, Copyright 2021. ISBN 978-0985772888.

The Koran (al-Qur'an): Testimony of Antichrist by Rev. Joseph Adam Pearson, Ph.D., Christ Evangelical Bible Institute, Copyright 2020. ISBN 978-0985772833.

Telugu Version of Quran: Testimony of Antichrist by Rev. Joseph Adam Pearson, Ph.D., Christ Evangelical Bible Institute, Copyright 2020. ISBN 978-0996222457.

Urdu Version of Quran: Testimony of Antichrist by Rev. Joseph Adam Pearson, Ph.D., Christ Evangelical Bible Institute, Copyright 2021. ISBN 978-0996222440.

Revelation of Antichrist by Rev. Joseph Adam Pearson, Ph.D., Christ Evangelical Bible Institute, Copyright 2021. ISBN 9780996222488.

Intelligent Evolution by Rev. Joseph Adam Pearson, Ph.D., Christ Evangelical Bible Institute, Copyright 2021. ISBN 978-0996222426.

The Biology of Psychism from a Christian Perspective by Rev. Joseph Adam Pearson, Ph.D., Christ Evangelical Bible Institute, Copyright 2020. ISBN 978-0996222464.

The Threeness of God by Rev. Joseph Adam Pearson, Ph.D., Christ Evangelical Bible Institute, Copyright 2021. ISBN 978-1734294729.

About the Author

Dr. Joseph Adam Pearson is a college and university educator with more than fifty years of classroom and administrative experience. Dr. Pearson has been the International President and Chief Executive Officer of Christ Evangelical Bible Institute (CEBI) for over twenty-five years. At the time of the publication of the latest edition of this book, he still oversees thriving branch campuses of CEBI in India, Pakistan, and Tanzania.

Currently, Dr. Pearson spends most of his time developing, designing, and deploying curriculum for Christian education nationally and internationally. And he preaches, teaches, and leads international crusades as well as provides group pastoral training in global mission settings.

During his professional life, Dr. Pearson has also served in the role of Senior Pastor of Healing Waters Ministries in Tempe, Arizona and as Dean of Instruction for Mesa Community College in Mesa, Arizona — where he was founding instructional dean for its Red Mountain Campus as well as Director of its Extended Campus.

Dr. Pearson believes that after we are saved, and at the same time we are being sanctified, our individual actions are part of an "application" for the jobs that we will each hold during Christ Jesus' Millennial reign on earth. Dr. Pearson's greatest goal is to be one of the many committed Christian educators who will be teaching during that time.

Contact the author at

drjpearson@aol.com

or

drjosephadampearson@gmail.com

Visit the author's website

at

www.dr-joseph-adam-pearson.com

or

www.christevangelicalbibleinstitute.com

www.ingramcontent.com/pod-product-compliance
Lightning Source LLC
LaVergne TN
LVHW061222060426

835509LV00012B/1382